M000235198

THE SCIENCE AGENDA

TO EXTERMINATE BLACKS ...

Bombshell Health Ranger
Lecture Documents
Race-Based Crimes
Against Humanity
By Mike Adams - 2017

(Natural News) As promised, I've now released a one-hour science lecture video that documents the multiple vectors through which people of African descent are being targeted for depopulation, covert infertility, and extermination by "science" and "medicine." Watch the full video lecture at: www.NaturalNews.com.

 This video lecture documents the pattern of heavy metals poisoning, medical experimentation, organ harvesting, covert fertility task forces and other tactics that seek to eliminate blacks from our planet. It uses, with credit, video footage from the shocking documentary film Maafa21, available at www.Maafa21.com. (not affiliated with this site, but it's filled with shocking information on many fronts).

You can hear more news from watching, Counter Think with Mike Adams on www.InfoWars.com.

And, to view NaturalNews's Videos, go to: <u>https://vimeo.com/healthranger/videos</u>.

These genocidal tactics are carried out in the name of science and medicine via the following vectors:

- Food supply (laced with infertility chemicals, confirmed by the New York Times quoting a U.S. President's science advisor).
- Water supply (heavy metals poisoning, as we recently witnessed in Flint, Michigan).
- Medical experimentation (Tuskegee, Guatemalan prisoner experiments funded by the U.S. Government, etc.).
- Immunization campaign (covert sterilization of young women in Africa).
- **Cancer (disproportionately affects people of darker skin color due to vitamin D deficiency).**
- Abortion activities that target blacks in order to harvest baby organ tissue for use in vaccines – medical cannibalism.

EXTERMINATE BLACKS IN THE NAME OF "SCIENCE" AND "MEDICINE"

By Mike Adams - 2017

I am the only predominantly Caucasian scientist in the world who dares to tell the truth about the science agenda to exterminate blacks. The reason I can do this is because my science laboratory receives no funding from any government or university. I have zero financial ties to the medical establishment that's systematically exterminating blacks; thus they cannot threaten me by attempting to withhold funds from my scientific research.

The real America is not simply carried out by a small number of people in white pointy hats. The real, deep racism is carried out by men in lab coats who are systematically pursuing an agenda to exterminate blacks through food, water, medicine, biological weapons and more.

Today, Maafa 21 is exposing the hidden and bitter realities of Black Genocide in modern America. But the mainstream media – and the multi-national corporations who control our nation's film distribution system – will not help us deliver this message to the people. And the simple fact is, this holocaust won't end as long as the public doesn't even know it exists.

MY QUESTION TO THE FIVE-FOLD MINISTRY (THE SHEP-HERDS) IN THE BODY OF CHRIST: WHAT NOW? WHAT SAY YOU ABOUT THIS CRISIS? WHAT IS GOD'S CHURCH GOING TO DO ABOUT THE WOLVES IN **(WHITE LAB COATS)** SHEEP'S CLOTHING. AND, ESPECIALLY YOU MEGA CHURCHES. MEGA PEOPLE HAVE MEGA POWER! WHY DO YOU THINK GOD CREATED MEGA CHURCHES? FOR SUCH A TIME AS THIS! TO PROTECT GOD'S PRECIOUS LAMBS FROM EXTERMINATION! AND IF WE PERISH – WE PERISH! WE HAVE BEEN CALLED TO FIGHT THE GOOD FIGHT OF FAITH FOR THE KINGDOM OF GOD!

MY QUESTION TO GOD'S PEOPLE: ARE YOU NOT YOUR BROTHER'S KEEPER? AND, IS THERE NOT A CAUSE? IT LOOKS LIKE HISTORY IS TRYING TO REPEAT ITSELF. REMEMBER, HITLER TRYING TO EXTERMINATE JEWISH PEOPLE FROM PLANET EARTH? SO, THIS LOOKS LIKE A GOOD TIME FOR THE CHURCH **(DAVID)** TO PICK-UP A ROCK & YOUR SWORD! GOLIATH **(SATAN)** IS APPROACHING! I HOPE EVERY BORN AGAIN CHRISTIAN ON PLANET EARTH IS FEELING **RIGHTEOUS INDIGNATION** IN YOUR SPIRIT ABOUT THIS HORRIFIC SATANIC ATTACK AGAINST BLACK PEOPLE AND ESPECIALLY **GOD'S BLACK PEOPLE** ON PLANET EARTH!

THE NATIONAL CLERGY NETWORK

Scripture tells us that a good man leaves an inheritance to his children's children.

(Proverbs 13:22a)

We have a plan. **CURE's National Clergy Network** seeks to educate our pastors to understand the damage of current policy related to poverty, family, and religious freedom issues. If clergy are concerned, knowledgeable, and engaged in these topics, then they can more easily help the real congregations and communities who are struggling every day. **CURE** seeks to equip pastors and their congregations with principles of faith, freedom and personal responsibility so that all can give input and voice to the critical issues we face together.

The **National Clergy Network** will have collaborative power and influence as we grow with like-minded team members. Too often we have seen examples of clergy engaged on important issues and then disengaged when they pass. Our times demand more consistency, as these issues are not going away. The sustaining leadership of the **NCN** will allow for **CURE** to remain in this space and build up for future generations. Cohesion is a challenge in this day and age, but yet we know that more than 1/3 of the population thinks similarly. It is time for a united organization to arise and make an impact.

Indeed, there is currently no organization like **CURE** whose direct mission is to be in our nation's Capital and advocate for the issues and people we hold dear. From our book club program, our policy summit, and our regular clergy briefings, **CURE** travels the country every year counseling, listening and educating pastors on solutions to the issues facing their communities.

The Voice of Clergy is crucial as we seek to renew the forgotten conscience within our culture. Your participation in the growth of our network will advance **CURE's** voice in the halls of government and provide a practical way for pastors to actively engage in this movement from a broken society to a stronger world. Knowing that you are making a difference will build pride not only in self but in our cooperation with others to accomplish real change." (**Taken From CURE's Website**).

I highly recommend, to **All Black Pastors in America**; please contact Star Parker, President, and Founder of **CURE**, which is located in Washington, D.C. The Center for Urban Renewal and Education is a 501 (c) 3 non-profit think-and-do tank. www.urbancure.org.

CURE has a solid track record; and would make an excellent, resource to **HELP** deal with this **CRISIS TOWARD BLACK HUMANITY!**

Also, please **HELP** by getting the word out that, Scientist Mike Adams, has revealed on NaturalNews.com; by causing the information to go **VIRAL ON SOCIAL MEDIA!** Thank you!

Don Lemon —

KWANZAA
IS SATAN!
JOHN 10:10

The Greatest Deception Of
The 20th & 21st Century!
Karenga — Kwanzaa — Kawaida

(The Black KKK)

BY
BARBARA A. DE LOACH
A.K.A. – TIKISA

*Mother of Matthew Rushing, Rehearsal Director,
Alvin Ailey American Dance Theater*

*John 8:32 = "You will know the truth,
and that truth will give you freedom."
(VOICE)*

Published By: Barbara Ann De Loach Ministries, Inc.
P.O. Box 2641
Victorville, CA 92393

Printed In: The United States of America
Cover Design: Barbara Ann De Loach
ISBN – 0692852603
De Loach, Barbara Ann – First Edition

1. African American History – USA
2. Black Americans – Family & Politics
3. Black Cultural Nationalism
4. Black Cultural Revolution
5. Black History – USA
6. Black Power Movement
7. Christianity
8. Cultural Studies
9. Karenga, Ron
10. Kawaida
11. Kwanzaa
12. Maulana Ron Karenga
13. Religion
14. Spiritual
15. The Freedom Movement
16. US Organization History
17. USA History

US Copyright © 2018 By Barbara Ann De Loach

All rights reserved. No part of this book may be reproduced, stored in a retrieval system or transmitted in any form or by any means, electronic, mechanical, photocopying, recording, or by any information storage without permission in writing from the publisher. Scripture references from, The Amplified Bible, The King James Version Bible, The Living Bible, The Message Bible, The New International Version Bible, The New King James Version Bible, and The New American Standard Bible, all by permission.

ALL POWER TO THE PEOPLE!

Based on: Deuteronomy 8:18
"Always remember that it is the Lord your
God who gives you power to become rich,
and He does it to fulfill His promise to your ancestors."

All Power To The People!
This Is Not - **The SIXTIES** - You Say
This Is **The NEW MILLENNIUM** - Okay
<u>But - We Still - Show Rage</u>
<u>Violence And Protest</u>
Trying To - Drive The Enemy
Far From - Our Nest
With - Not Much - Success

All Power To The People!
Yes - Angry Protests - And Violence
Is Still Shown - On Prime Time
Trying To - Hold Us Down
By Promoting
<u>Black On Black Crime</u>
You Know - A Lot Of People
Got Thrown - When
Dr. Martin Luther King, Jr.

Went To His - Heavenly Home
To Be With - "The King" - Of Kings
But People - Take Courage
Knowing - That - God
Is Still - On The - Throne
And God - Has A - Dream
That's BIGGER - Than Dr. King's
For ALL - The People - In The World

All Power To The People!
Can Only - Come From God
Through Spiritual Recovery
And Self-Discovery
By Realizing And Utilizing
Our God - Given Gifts
And - Boldly - Daring
To - Take - Some
Calculated - Risks

All Power To The People!
Is Lining-Up - With God's Word
To Truly Value
And Define - Our Place
In This World
Yes – By Truly Knowing
Our Purpose – For Living
And To Make – Our Quest
For Good – Better – And Best
And Never – Let It Rest
Until – The Good – Gets Better
And – The Better – Gets Best
And Side Stepping – All The Rest

All Power To The People!
Is Coming Out
From Behind - Our Masks
And Taking Courage
To Stand-Up
<u>To Our – God Given - Tasks</u>
<u>Of Being – Faithful - Christians</u>
<u>Like We - Were In - The Past</u>

All Power To The People!
Is Thinking - Focusing
And Learning - All The Time
How To Expand
And Cultivate - Our Minds
<u>By Releasing - Powerful Ideas</u>
<u>That - Will - Change</u>
<u>The Course - Of Time</u>

All Power To The People!
It's A - Liberating - Thing
Enabling Us - To Explore
Things That - Have Never - Been
Exposed - To Us - Before
<u>And To - Make Things - Happen</u>
<u>That - Will - Change</u>
<u>The World's Decor</u>

All Power To The People!
<u>Will Reach Our - Young And Old</u>
To Give - Them Hope
For Their - Future - And Salvation
For Their Souls

All Power To The People!
<u>Will Reposition Us - In The Land</u>
To Create - And - Articulate
To Own - Our Own
And To – Be Able – To Relate
To The Fact – That – We Need To
Change Our – Present – Financial State
So That – Our People
<u>Will Have – Power – To Negotiate</u>!
(The Bottom Line)

DEDICATION

A CLARION CALL TO:

ALL FIVE-FOLD MINISTRY

AND ESPECIALLY

ALL BORN AGAIN CHRISTIANS

AND ESPECIALLY

ALL BLACK AMERICANS

AND ESPECIALLY

EVERYBODY – YOUNG & OLD

WORLDWIDE!

Hosea 4:6 (KJV)

"My people are destroyed, for lack of knowledge: because thou hast rejected knowledge, I will reject thee, that thou shalt be no priest to me: seeing thou hast forgotten the law of thy God, I will also forget thy children."

ACKNOWLEDGEMENTS

I Thank My Father, for His Love and Divine Supernatural Guidance; So That I Can Finish My Assignment on Planet Earth. I Love You Papa.

I Thank My Sons, for Their Love, Prayers, and Support, Throughout This Long Journey. I Love You.

CAPITALIZATION

Barbara has taken Author's Prerogative in capitalizing certain words which are not usually capitalized according to the standard grammatical practice. This is done for the purpose of clarity and emphasis.

CONTENTS

INTRODUCTION

I will be addressing {Four Questions} that you might be interested in knowing the {Four Answers}.

1) Why Did I Write This Book?
2) Why Am I Just Now Writing This Book?
3) Why By This Author When Other Authors Have Already Written Articles, Books/E-Books, Essays, Interviews, Open Letters, and Website Blogs?
4) What Are My Plans After This Book Is Published?

I was born on, February 10, 1946, in Los Angeles, California. I was reared by my Mother, and I had two older Sisters. We lived together with my Grandmother and my Aunt. My Father became a paraplegic at the early age of 21; from a terrible car accident. His car turned over three times and severed his spinal cord. The Doctors said, "He would never walk again." But God! He did walk again! My Father also lived in Los Angeles, with his Mother. (Big Mama lived to be 100 years old!) Both of my parents and family were from Louisiana. My Father, and his Father and Mother, by way of New Orleans. My Mother, and her Father and Mother, by way of Shreveport. My two Sisters and Aunt, by way of Shreveport. And, myself, by way of Los Angeles. I was the only one born in California.

At the age of five, I attended Russell Avenue Elementary School. I started in Kindergarten and stayed to the 5th Grade. Every Sunday at the tender age of eight, I walked to Sunday School at Miracle Baptist Church, on 85th Street and Central Avenue. I was the only one in my family that attended Church. I served as the Superintendent's Assistant. I would arrive at Sunday school, early before Church started so that I could place a Bible, a piece of paper and a pencil on each seat in our classroom. I loved my job! My Late Grandmother, nicknamed me, 'the little preacher.' We then moved to 120th Street off Avalon in L.A., and I attended 116th Street Elementary School.

I went on to attend Gompers Junior High School, where I became active in Student Council. I ran for School Secretary and won! After graduating, I attended, John C. Fremont High School, in Los Angeles. In my senior year, I ran for a Class Cheerleader, and I won, for the Adelphians, Summer Class of 1963!

In my senior year, I decided to take a part-time job after school. I went to work after third-period; because I had more credits than I needed to graduate. The reason, I had so many credits, was due to attending Summer School every year. My part-time job was at a Pediatrician's office, as a Medical Stenographer. My starting salary was fifty cents per hour. I soon, after that, received a one-dollar per hour raise. I worked five days per week, and four hours per day. I walked to work from school, and the Nurse took me home after work. I was fifteen years old at that time.

After high school, I had my first son; and I married my middle school sweetheart. We lived in a duplex on 91st Street in Los Angeles. During this time, I was eight months pregnant, with my second son. Then, suddenly the Watts Riots broke out on, August 11, 1965! I will never forget seeing the military jeeps, traveling up and down the streets. The soldiers were holding rifles; and if looks could kill, all of us would have, been dead for sure! They were searching for people that were participating in the riots. They were, also looking for looters, of the stores in the neighborhood.

I watched everything from my front porch. I felt like I was on the inside of a horror movie! I thought to myself; this couldn't be happening in my neighborhood; it was frightening. The smell of burning wood, cement, and iron permeated the air; quite an undesirable stench. The sky was lit up by all the burning fires.

The fires burned a lot of properties, stores, and houses. Watts wasn't the only place that was up in flames; it was happening all around the nation. This riot changed things so much that, at the time of this writing, Watts\South Central Los Angeles still hasn't fully recovered.

There are still stores boarded-up, vacant lots, and most of the buildings that were burned down, have never been rebuilt. I believe that South Central Los Angeles, can still be restored; God willing. There were boys, and men running down the streets, and some of them were bleeding, and crying out loud. Some boys were ducking behind bushes when they saw police cars coming.

The police were out in full force. It was announced on television and the radio, that there was a curfew at 10:00 p.m. Everyone had to be off the streets, or they would be arrested. The days were long, and the nights were longer. The weather was so hot; that you could fry eggs on the sidewalk; which assisted the fires to burn more out of control.

I'll never forget the loud sirens of the ambulances, fire trucks, police cars, non-stop for hours and hours all day and all night long; it was hard to go to sleep or even rest. I didn't quite know how to process all this violence, and I was pregnant!

The next day was a shocking sight to see. People were pushing sofas, chairs, and televisions down the street! Some were even carrying lamps, clothes, dishes, blankets, and all kinds of stuff to their homes! People were stealing until they dropped! It was so sad to see people disrespect their neighbors. They were breaking into stores and businesses, which had been serving our community for years. It was heartbreaking.

The Watts Riots will be etched into my brain forever. The five-day riots resulted in 34 deaths, 1,032 injuries, 3,438 arrests and over $40 million in property damage. It was the most severe riot in the city's history, until the Los Angeles Riots of 1992. The entire incident was devastating. Then, from the 1965 Watts Riots; The Watts Summer Festival was birth! It seems like the Lord always sends me, where there is a crisis. I became a Community Activist, after the Watts Riots. I just knew that I had to do, something to help my community.

So, I got involved with The Watts Summer Festival. I presented to the Chairman of The Board of Directors, the Late Tommy Jacquette, that we needed to have an Afro-American Fashion Show included in The Watts Summer Festival. The Board of Directors approved The Fashion Show. And, I volunteered to be the Coordinator.

I gave The Afro-American Fashion Show the theme name: "The Versatility of Blackness." The Fashion Show was at Markham Junior High School's Auditorium in Watts. I went to a local business in our community and asked for a donation to help sponsor the Fashion Show.

The business was very generous and excited to give back to the community at a time of need. I listed the sponsor of the Fashion Show in the Program. We bought beautiful, 'Original African Garb,' with the donated money. The models were from sizes 3 to 18. I had these full-body women, and men as models because God, didn't make us all the same size and height; therefore, whatever your size and height; you are good-looking. God's Word Says It Best: "I will give thanks and praise to You, for I am fearfully and wonderfully made; Wonderful are Your works, and my soul knows it very well." (Psalm 139:14) AMP.

I also used the donated money, to have stage props built; for the different skits in the Fashion Show. I had the models acting out skits, as they modeled their outfits. For example, one of the skits was a 'party scene.' The models were dancing with a partner on stage; some were standing and talking, and some were sitting at a table (like at a nightclub).

The music was playing loud, and when it stopped, the models would pause. A model couple, would leave the group and walk down the runway to display their outfits, and strut their stuff! The Master of Ceremony would introduce the model couple to the audience. The model couple would walk down the runway, one person at a time, and their outfit described to the audience.

The model couple would return to their position on stage; continue to do whatever they were doing, and the music would start playing again. The models would continue to take turns; until all the models had modeled their outfits on the runway. The models on stage would show off their dance moves, acting crazy, laughing, and making the audience laugh! All the models, walked the runway, as our Grand Finale; as the audience gave them a standing ovation!

It was fun. It was a 'revolutionary' type of fashion show for that period. "The Versatility of Blackness" Afro-American Fashion Show" was covered by local TV News Stations, in Los Angeles. It was an incredible experience! After the Fashion Show ended, I told the models they could keep the outfits they modeled, as a thank you gift.

Other activities were at Will Rogers Park in Watts. There were so many musicians, and singers like Roberta Flack, and speakers that came out to show their support; in helping things get back to normal. We had all kinds of food, refreshments, and vendors, throughout the park; selling their products, and we also had fun rides for the children.

People were coming from miles around, with their families, and friends to celebrate peace, coming back into our community. Everything just flowed, and there were no incidents. Some people were an opportunist and had a hidden agenda for participating in the Watts Summer Festival. I believe Karenga, was an opportunist; with a hidden agenda.

A lot of organizations were started, because of the Watts Riots. The Sons of Watts, Own Recognizance (O.R.) and Rehabilitation Project, was one of those new organizations. I worked there as an Executive Secretary to the Vice-President. After a few years, unfortunately, the funding for 'new' organizations disappeared.

Why Did I Write This Book?

I was a former member of US Organization for one year. I ended my membership in 1969. After leaving US Organization, I wandered in the wilderness, if you would, for years trying to rebuild my life. Then in 1976, I became a Born Again Christian, and attended Crenshaw Christian Center in Inglewood; where Apostle Fredrick K.C. Price was the Founder and Senior Pastor.

I went back to school, to practice my shorthand skills. During that time, I worked at The Department of Public Social Services, on Adams and Grand, in L.A., as an Intermediate Clerk Typist. After completing the shorthand class, I took the Stenographer's exam; passed, and promoted to an Intermediate Stenographer. I went to work at The Administration Division of The Department of Public Social Services, downtown, L.A.

In 1977, the Holy Spirit gave me instructions to invent a Christian Family Board Game called, The Game of Revelations! (Not the book of Revelation). The Game sold nationally. Thus, making me the 'First Black American Woman,' to invent a Christian Family Board Game, in The United States of America.

Then a year later, I took another exam and was promoted to a Legal Stenographer with The District Attorney's Office, Downtown, L.A. This was also during, the time that the Late Johnny L. Cochran, Jr., Esquire, won the election, for Assistant District Attorney. I along with, so many others, had the honor and pleasure of his friendship.

Years later in 1986, I remarried and started working at The California State University, Los Angeles in 1988. I was the Office Manager, for the Special Services Project, in the Learning Resource Center Office, and supervised fourteen student workers. A few years later, my husband and I were ordained and licensed into the Ministry of Jesus Christ.

In November 1989, The Holy Spirit gave me instructions to invent another board game called, Build Me Up! The Self-Esteem Board Game, for children, youth, and their families; which also sold nationally. Thus, making me the 'First Black American Woman' to invent/design a Self-Esteem Board Game in The United States of America. In 1992, 'The Famous Rodney King Beating' took place in Los Angeles. The 'Civil Unrest' was sparked on April 29, 1992, when a jury acquitted three White Officers, and one Hispanic Officer accused in the, videotaped beating, of a Black motorist, Rodney King; following a high-speed pursuit. Thousands of people in the Los Angeles area, rioted six days, following the verdict!

According to The Los Angeles Times, widespread looting, assault, arson, and murder occurred; 63 lives were lost in the riots, with an estimated total economic cost pegged at $1 billion, with $735 million in property damage and 1,550 buildings destroyed or damaged. Again, the Lord sent me out as a Community Activist, in a time of CRISES. The Lord gave me Favor with Principals, and Teachers, from Middle and High Schools. I volunteered to facilitate Self-Esteem Empowerment (SEE) Seminars, with the students in their classrooms.

I visited with fifteen different classes, which had forty students per class; for one hour each; over a period of five months. The (SEE) Seminar, gave the students a platform to discuss their concerns and fears about the 'Civil Unrest.' That tragic incident changed my entire life! It was the beginning of my ministry, as a Life Coach. The 'Civil Unrest,' in 1992 caused me to have such an 'intense thirst' for more knowledge regarding facilitating self-esteem seminars and workshops. Moreover, I decided to seek professional training from, America's #1 Success Coach, Jack Canfield, Cocreator of the Chicken Soup For The Soul Series. The excellent training, I received changed my entire life! After completing my training with Jack Canfield, I volunteered for one year, as a Chaplain, and Life Coach, with The San Bernardino County Sheriff's Department; at the West Valley Detention Center, in The Inland Empire. Along with my duties as a Chaplain; I also facilitated, The Build Me Up! Self-Esteem Program; once a week, for male and females, together as a class; in an assigned classroom at the facility. The Build Me Up! Self-Esteem Program; was a powerful, transforming experience; for the inmates, and for myself, as well.

I was the Chief Executive Officer, of my company named, Way-Kool Toys, Inc. I would be remiss, if I didn't pause, to share one of the greatest blessings, of my life. My Pastors and dear friends, the Late Rev. Jerry P. Louder, PhDs., and his wife, Philia; were Co-Pastors, of the New Jerusalem Church in Riverside, California. Pastor Louder, was the President of The United States Pastor's Association, African American Clergy. I believe that Rev. Jerry P. Louder, PhDs.; was a quintessential Priest in the Kingdom of God.

Moreover, Dr. Jerry P. Louder started an Investment Group at New Jerusalem Church; so that members of New Jerusalem, could buy stock in Way-Kool Toys, Inc. He also wrote a letter to the Honorable, Mayor of San Francisco, Willie L. Brown, Jr., asking for an appointment to discuss the possibility of getting "Build Me Up!" into schools and prisons; to help build the children, youth, and prisoner's self-esteem. Mayor Willie L. Brown, Jr., is known as, The Education Mayor.

Thus, Build Me Up! The Self-Esteem Board Game was submitted, evaluated and approved by The Curriculum Frameworks and Instructional Resources Office, of The California Department of Education, for its Social Content, that can be used, in all the schools in California. The Late Rev. Jerry P. Louder, Ph. Ds. was a great man of God. The City of Riverside, named a street after him; to honor him; and his outstanding work that New Jerusalem Church, accomplished in the Riverside communities; for The Kingdom of God. For instance, The Lord's Kitchen, feeding dinner daily to the Community needy; Life Bible College, and CCU College, "Providing

Seminary Classes for Ministry." I will forever be humbled, and grateful to the Late Reverend Jerry P. Louder, Ph.D. for his assistance in the development of my business.

Fast forwarding, to a beautiful cold day in December; I was at home, opening my mail. I opened a card, from a dear friend, and outcomes a greeting card that said, "Happy Kwanzaa!" I said, is Ron Karenga, still deceiving people, with that phony celebration. I went to the Internet and typed the word, Kwanzaa. I saw pages, after pages about Kwanzaa. I immediately went into shock!

Later that evening, I started wondering, why in the world did my friend, send me a Kwanzaa card; instead of a Christmas card? It was about one week before Christmas. After I calmed myself down, with a cup of warm chamomile tea, stevia, and a little lemon juice, I started to reflect on my long-forgotten past; of being a member of US Organization. I remember thinking; it seemed like a lifetime ago, on another planet, in a horror movie! After I ended, my membership in 1969; I never looked back. I moved on with my life.

Then, my thoughts came back, to the present. It dawned on me that my friend didn't know, about my testimony, of being a former member of US Organization. She didn't know; that I had once celebrated Kwanzaa. She didn't know because I never told anyone. I was too embarrassed, by the unwise decision, I made to join US Organization; although, I was not involved, in any of the violence, between US Organization and the Black Panthers. My friend never talked to me about any violence between the two groups; while I was a member.

Also, I never had any conversations about the Black Panthers, with any of the members during my entire membership. In retrospect, I can understand, why no one talked to me about the Black Panthers; because they all knew, that the FBI, did not hire me; and they didn't want me to find out, about their evil assignment against the Black Panther Party. In other words, I am innocent from any violence; that Karenga committed in US Organization.

I had to care for my two young Sons, and I worked forty hours per week, at The 53rd Street Elementary School. Therefore, my participation was limited to my Karate Class, for one hour, on Wednesdays, along with my Sons. I taught at the Afro-American School of Culture, for one hour on Saturdays, along with my Sons. And, I attended Soul Sessions for one hour on Sunday, along with my Sons. To make a long story short; my experience, as a member of US Organization, was one of the worst decisions, that I have ever made in my entire life!

At this moment, I feel like, I am writing about another person's life, instead of my own. The Lord made it clear that He had me as a 'Watchman on The Wall' if you would; as a former member of US Organization. God sent me to spy out the land, if you would, to bring back a Report. This **Book is the Report** that I am bringing back to **YOU.** However, the Lord told me, that the Primary Purpose, of writing this book, is to tell: <u>The Five-Fold Ministry</u>: **TO GET THE SIN (KWANZAA) OUT OF HIS FATHER'S HOUSE OF PRAYER!** The other Purpose of writing this book is for our Children and Youth. The Lord stressed the point that the Children and Youth need to learn, the Truth about Black History, not Lies!

Why Am I Just Now Writing This Book?

I am just now writing the book, because it was not yet, God's appointed time. I knew the Lord would tell me when the time was right. So, I started writing down notes, about some of my experiences, and kept them in my filing cabinet. In May 1993, I was on my way home from work, at California State University, L.A.; and I was riding the RTD Bus. I did not want to drive all the way to work, so I parked my car at the County Fair Ground's parking lot in Pomona and rode the bus the rest of the way to work.

On the day I sat in the front facing the bus driver, in the seat next to the aisle; suddenly, I was up in the air! Everything seemed to be in slow motion, for a quick minute. I remember thinking, "Jesus, I'm in the air!" Then everything went back to real-time! I came down and hit my head on the hand-rail! Then I fell between the row of seats; twisting my back and spine. The RTD Bus and a big truck had collided on the freeway!

The Doctors didn't know why I was not healing, and why I was in so much pain. They begin sending me to a lot of Specialists, and I was diagnosed, as having Fibromyalgia and Chronic Fatigue Syndrome. Well, long story short, that was the beginning of a long 21 years journey, to becoming permanently disabled. After the RTD Bus accident, I could no longer drive into Los Angeles. So, I started working part-time jobs through Kelly Girl Services, and Remedy Temporary Agency for a while; until the pain wouldn't allow me to continue to work. Therefore, included in the back of the book are a few letters, photographs, and information about myself, so that you can get to know me and my work; before I became disabled.

Why By This Author, When Other Authors Have Written Articles, Books, E-Books, Essays, Interviews, Open Letters & Website Blogs?

One of the reasons being, that God told me to "tell the truth," about Karenga's diabolical, evil mindset, and plans for Black Americans. I also have, personal eye-witness experiences that I want to share with you so that when you finish reading the book, you will have more knowledge, and understanding, about Karenga, Kwanzaa, and Kawaida. Moreover, what you do with the Truth is your decision to make. God's Word Says It Best: "And ye shall know the truth, and the truth shall make you free." (John 8:32) KJV.

What Are My Plans After This Book Is Published?

I first started working with the Los Angeles Unified School District, at the age of eighteen, as a Substitute Clerk Typist. I later became a full-time employee. I have worked in an Elementary School, Middle School, High School, Elementary School for the Disabled, Adult Night School, Elementary Summer School, (I worked as the School Secretary in the office by myself and also as the Acting Nurse).

I took an exam and was promoted to work at the L.A. Southwest Community College, as a Maintenance Office Clerk. Much later, I worked at the San Bernardino Valley College and was also a student during the day. I have worked at Riverside Community College, Loyola Marymount University, L.A., California State University, L.A., California State University, San Bernardino, The University of California, Riverside, and The L. A. Unified School District, Administration Office.

That said, I am familiar with some of the inner- workings, of the Educational System. To be honest; I find it to be quite alarming! If you haven't seen the "Waiting for Superman" Documentary by Geoffrey Canada, please check it out. It is an eye-opening documentary, about America's Failing Educational System! You can watch it at the following address: www.documentarylovers.com. It is also on YouTube.

I plan to have the celebration, study, rituals and practice of Kwanzaa, taken out of all The Public Schools in The United States of America. All races of children deserve to know the Truth about their history, not Lies! Therefore, I am also requesting The United States Postal Service, to have the Kwanzaa Stamp recalled, due to Kwanzaa being a Lie, told by a Convicted Felon, with a Violent Background of committing heinous crimes against members in his organization. Dr. Ron Karenga, is not a good Role Model for our children and youth to follow, because of his lifestyle of violence, and criminal activities. Last, but not least, I plan to have Kwanzaa removed from all Calendars and Museums in The United States of America.

I plan to take the Kwanzaa Holiday Case to The Supreme Court in Washington, D.C., if necessary. All profits from the sale of the book, and all donations, are tax-deductible; and will be used toward the financial support of The Kwanzaa Holiday Supreme Court Case. And this book, will be a part of the Kwanzaa Court Case as **'The Book of Evidence.'** And, Barbara Ann De Loach Ministries, is a 501 (c) 3 non-profit organization.

In conclusion, I am sharing my Personal Testimony for the 'First Time,' with the Purpose of Exposing the Evil Works of Satan. God's Word Says It Best: "And this I pray, that your love may abound more and more [displaying itself greater depth] in real knowledge and in practical insight, so that you may learn to recognize and treasure what is excellent [identifying the best, and distinguishing moral differences,] and that you may be blameless until the day of [actually living lives that lead others away from sin] ..." (Philippians 1:9-10) AMP. Also, I am no longer afraid of Ron Karenga! God's Word Says It Best: "For God hath not given us the spirit of fear; but of power, and of love, and of a sound mind. (2 Timothy 1:7) KJV.

SO

WALK WITH

ME AS I TAKE

YOU

ON THE JOURNEY

OF

MEMORY LANE

IN

THE BLACK POWER MOVEMENT
1960s – 1970s

CHAPTER 1

WHY I QUALIFY TO WRITE THIS BOOK

Los Angeles Southwest College - 1967

In 1967 after my job ended, at The Sons of Watts, O.R. & Rehabilitation Project; I started working at Los Angeles Southwest Community College during the day as a Maintenance Office Clerk; and in the evening, I was a student. The College had not been completed. My office was located, inside of a trailer on campus. While I was an evening student, I entered the contest for Campus Sweetheart and I won First Runner-up. The Winner beat me by only 17 votes.

That said, I honestly believe they should have, never allowed me to enter the contest, as an evening student, if the evening students could not vote for me. They turned away all the evening students at the voting pole; although, they had their student identification cards, proving that they had the right, to participate in all school activities. In other words, I could have won the contest; if the evening students were allowed to vote. (Whew! I had to get that off my chest). The contest was fun, challenging; and I learned a lot. Then, the next year, I ran for, Miss Young, Gifted & Black; and won!

In retrospect, so much was going on in the '60's. The Civil Rights Movement and The Black Power Movement; were happening at the same time. It was also an exciting time to be on a college campus. Students were protesting and rallying for different causes by walking out of the schools, and some were having sit-ins, and I would walk out with them, and sit-in with them; if I agreed with them.

One of my classes was Sociology. The Instructor gave the assignment to survey any local organization. We were to find out how many African American people, within the organization, had a college degree; and how many didn't have a college degree? Also, to find out how many were, the first in their families to attend college?

A friend of mine suggested that I go to US Organization in L.A., to conduct my survey. I had never heard of Ron Karenga. So, I phoned my Late Aunt, to ask her if she ever heard of Ron Karenga? My Late Aunt, owned a Public Relations Firm, in Los Angeles, and everyone knew her. She told me that, she had heard some of his lectures. She ended by saying, "I might be surprised, to find that a lot of US Organization's members held college degrees." That was my green light, as it were, to visit US Organization; to conduct my survey.

I went to US Organization's Headquarters in Los Angeles that same week. Upon entering the building, I ran into a friend from John C. Fremont High School. I shared with him my purpose for coming to US Organization; and he said, that he could help me. He took me, on a tour of the building. He also, told me that his new name was Msemaji.

Then Msemaji introduced me, to a lot of the members, which held Associate and Bachelor degrees. After interviewing the members; he invited me to return on Sunday to attend a Soul Session. I asked him, what was a Soul Session? He told me that it was a lecture, given by Maulana Ron Karenga, to the members of US Organization, and to the public. I said, that I would love to attend a Soul Session.

My First Soul Session - 1967

I returned on Sunday to attend the Soul Session. The room was large and had a small kitchenette to prepare food for different events and meetings.

The chairs were set-up like a Church setting; chairs on each side, and the isle down the middle. There was a platform, in the front of the room. The building had a few offices. I remember, seeing posters on the walls with 'black power,' messages on them. The door had a long black cloth, and you had to push it to the side to go through the door.

I remember, walking through the door, and being overtaken, with the electrifying crowd, rocking from side to side, and clapping to the song, "I Heard It Through The Grapevine," by Marvin Gaye. The music was playing loud, thereby causing one to feel the beat.

Then Ron Karenga, entered the room. He was walking and shaking his head-up and down to the music. He was wearing, a long black shirt called, a Buba and a black talisman, around his neck; with two Simba Wachunga, (Young Men) walking behind him. He went up onto the podium, and stood there, shaking his head-up and down to the music. The people in the crowd were saying things like, alright Maulana! Go ahead Maulana! As if he, were Michael Jackson, doing the Moonwalk Dance.

The crowd continued to cheer him on, and he continued to shake his head; for a few more minutes. He reminded me of one of those, little 'Bobble-Head Figures' that people put in the back window of their cars. I must say, he was amusing. Then, at the end of the song, I heard someone hollering real loud; sounding like an African bush woman! I remember thinking, that the atmosphere made me wonder what was going to happen next? I had never attended a lecture like this before. Karenga's lecture was about, Black people and Christianity; which I found to be interesting on some levels; at that particular time, in my young life.

My First Kwanzaa Celebration - 1968

My first Kwanzaa was memorable. The concept was simple to understand. However, I was intrigued, because it was something new and different. The table setting was beautiful and festive. Members told me that, everyone used their own creativity to set-up the table at their home. The lighting, of the candles, and saying the Seven Principles, for each day of Kwanzaa, never impressed me that much.

I enjoyed, the part where you bought gifts after Christmas; because of all the sales, that were taking place. Still, celebrating Kwanzaa, was a huge change for my family; and it never fulfilled our hearts like Christmas. It could not fulfill the needs of our hearts because, it had no life in it nor no anointing on it!

Joining US Organization - 1968

After attending several Soul Sessions, I ran into another friend from John C. Fremont High School, Hekima. My friends kept encouraging me to join the Movement.

Then I was introduced, to Karenga. He had a strange sounding voice; with a good sence of humor. He asked me, did I enjoy his lecture? I told him, it was informative.

I also shared that I had never heard about the information that he shared in the Soul Session about Christianity. He said, "The White man brainwashed you, and they didn't tell you everything." He further stated, "That is why I created Kwanzaa so that our people could have our own African Religion, Black God, and make ourselves Eternal.

We all sat down in his office, and Karenga continued to tell me the difference, in the White man's religion, Christianity and compared it to Kwanzaa, or The Nguzo Saba.

He also warned me, that my family wouldn't approve of my Blackness; because they still have a Slave Mentality. He said, "Our families are still Negroes." We talked for a while longer; and I told Karenga, that I wanted to join the Movement. He responded, "Welcome to the Movement."

Later on, I came to realize, that Karenga liked to divide the members from their families so that he could have greater access and control over their lives. He was teaching the members to look at their families, as enemies to our Black mindsets. In retrospect, I had to admit that I did not do my homework, as far as, researching and asking a lot of questions, before joining US Organization. I thought that, I was joining the **Movement**, not the **Mafia!**

My Traditional Swahili Name: Tikisa - 1968

After welcoming me into the Movement; someone said, "Maulana, Barbara, will need a traditional name." Karenga said, "I want to do some research, to give her the right name." I remember, looking forward to receiving my new Black name; based on a positive quality, in your personality or character.

Karenga said, "I found, the perfect name for you. Your new name is, Tikisa." There were several of us, in his office at the time. He went on to say, "Tikisa means - The one who excites others and causes them to tremble." And, from that day forward, every one called me, Tikisa. I liked the name when I first heard it. It's pronounced like: Tea - Key – Sa. And, also like the Tiki Torches.

After that, I started educating my family, that I had changed my name to Tikisa. I told them, the meaning, how to pronounce it, how to spell it, that it was Swahili, and gave them a little history, about traditional names. However, they didn't go for it! My Grandmother, said, "Those, bald-headed Negroes don't have the right, to change your name! Your Father and Mother named you, Barbara Ann De Loach; and we are not going to call you Tikisa!" A few weeks later, I changed my Son's names; and my family didn't accept their names either.

> After becoming a Born Again Christian, the Holy Spirit changed the meaning of the name Tikisa. It now means, the one who excites others to come to Christ and Receive Eternal Life; and causes demons to tremble!

CHAPTER 2

RON KARENGA:
THE BLACK POWER MOVEMENT

Happy Kwanzaa! The Holiday
Brought To You By The FBI

By Ann Coulter - 2012

I found an interesting and humorous article, written by Ann Coulter, New York Times Bestselling Author. She stated, "I will not be shooting any Black Panthers, this week because I am Kwanzaa-reformed; and we are not, that observant. Kwanzaa celebrated exclusively by White liberals, is a fake holiday, invented in 1966, by Black radical\FBI stooge, Ron Everett – aka Dr. Maulana Karenga, founder of United Slaves, the violent nationalist rival to the Black Panthers.

In the annals of the American '60s, Karenga was the Father Gapon, a stooge of the czarist police. In what was ultimately a foolish gambit, during the madness of the '60s, the FBI encouraged the most extreme Black nationalist organizations, to discredit and split the left. The more preposterous the group, the better. By that criterion, Karenga's United Slaves was perfect.

Despite modern perceptions that blend all the Black activists of the '60s, the Black Panthers, did not hate Whites. Although some of their most high-profile leaders, were drug dealers and murderers; they did not seek armed revolution.

Those were the precepts, of Karenga's United Slaves. The United Slaves were proto-fascists, walking around in dashikis, gunning down Black Panthers; and adopting invented "African" names. And, hasn't that been; a huge help to the Black community?"

Karenga: FBI Agent With An Anti-Panther Mission? Maulana Karenga's Haunting Ghosts

By Mukasa Afrika Ma'at - 2012

I remember the time like it was yesterday when Karenga shared with a few members, information that I didn't quite understand; and didn't give it much thought. He said, "If the police stopped them, for any reason; let them know who you are, and they would let them go; because, the FBI had a Dossier on them." He was bragging. At that time, I did not know what a Dossier was. I thought he meant, something similar to, Professional Courtesy. I admit I was gullible. I truly didn't know about the violence, that took place in US Organization.

I did not know how Karenga was supporting himself and his family. US Organization never had fundraisers, never passed a basket, for donations from members or the public. Haiba, his first wife, always had money to go shopping. They lived in a home that was nicely furnished. Karenga leased US Headquarters in L.A., and in San Diego. Their children were well taken care of; they were doing fine.

During my research, I found this eye-opening Essay, by Mukasa

Afrika Ma'at, a Writer. He stated, "According to confessed agent provocateurs and infiltrators, Earl Anthony and Louis Tackwood, and suspected former agent provocateur and infiltrator, Elaine Brown, says that Karenga was an agent in 'Taste of Power.'

Colton Westbrook, working with the LAPD's CCS (Criminal Conspiracy Section) and Division Five of the FBI, used certain newly "Africanized" and modified recruits to set-up two primary synthetic terror groups, known as the US Organization, with police agent, Ron N. Everett, a.k.a. Ron Karenga; and SLA, or Symbionese Liberation Army with police informer and provocateur, Donald DeFreeze.

According to CCS, police snitch and provocateur, Louis Tackwood, Ron Karenga and his US (later known as the United Slaves) organization, were funded by the Ford Foundation, the LAPD and his good friend, Mayor Sam Yorty, through municipal funds.

Financing to the tune of over $50,000 per year, plus two offices and five apartments, as indicated in the September 6, 1969, edition of the Black Panther Newspaper. The Wall Street Journal revealed that Karenga, "maintained close ties to the eastern Rockefeller family;" and that, a few weeks, after the assassination, of Martin Luther King, Jr., Mr. Karenga, slipped into Sacramento, for a private chat, with Governor Ronald Reagan, at the Governor's request. The Black Nationalist, also met clandestinely with Los Angeles Police Chief, Thomas Reddin after King had been killed.

Through Tackwood, Ron Karenga, and his United Slaves were given their, large numbers of Blacks. Karenga, was directly ordered, to curtail the Panther Party's growth, no matter, what the cost, and that no rang-a-tang (CCS slang for US members) — that's what we called his people — would never be convicted of murder. Tackwood also stated that he provided Karenga with assassination orders, from the FBI to kill Panther leaders, Elmore Geronimo Pratt, and Alprentice "Bunchy" Carter. You be the judge; what do you think?"

Why I Don't Celebrate Kwanzaa

By WeBeNews

Interview With Judge Joe Brown - 2015

During my research, I found an enlightening, Radio Interview with Judge Joe Brown, by WeBeNews:

Interviewer: Do you celebrate Kwanzaa?

Judge Joe Brown: I don't celebrate Kwanzaa because Ron Karenga murdered two of my good friends.

Interviewer: Did you know Bunchy Carter at all?

Judge Joe Brown: Yes, I knew him. Bunchy Carter had been a Slauson gang member, and he got out of the penitentiary, but he wrote poetry, and he was very smart. He taught himself how to read and write; so, he got recruited to UCLA under a Special Program.

He was doing alright, as a student, he and John Huggins, who came in from out of town, who was also a good student; who got recruited to UCLA under a Special Program.

They were good students, who got gunned down in front of 43 witnesses, in a cafeteria in broad daylight; by four people who were members, of the US Organization.

The interesting thing to me was that they only caught two of them; who were accessories. And, I remember seeing them, after they got prosecuted; hell, I testified as a witness. They got prosecuted, locked up in the penitentiary; and two years later, I ran into them, at a concert at the Palladium in Hollywood.

They were sitting at the table, and I said, what are you two doing out? They had escaped, and they had an all-points bulletin out for two days, and then they canceled it. And, to make a long story short, about 5 to 6 years ago, they showed up to surrender; and they were told nobody was interested.

The two people who did the shooting, their names were known, addresses were given, and I think one of their Mothers, identified the place where they were staying; and the police didn't even go by there to get them. And, within forty days of Ron Karenga's release from prison, he became a tenured Professor at California State University, Long Beach.

Why I Don't Do Kwanzaa

By Bruce A. Dixon - 1969

I found this heartfelt article, by Bruce A. Dixon, Black Agenda Report. He stated, "I don't do Kwanzaa. I just don't. I never have, and the very thought of it evokes some difficult memories and feelings for me ..."

But for many of us, who took part in, or were simply aware of the Black Panther Party in the late '60s and early '70s, the Kwanzaa holiday is inseparable, from the career and persona, of its inventor, Ron Karenga, now a tenured professor in California.

Back in the day, Karenga headed-up an organization called, US as a tool of COINTELPRO, the federal counterintelligence program directed at movement organizations. Karenga's US Organization murdered two leading members of the Black Panther Party in Los Angeles, Alprentice "Bunchy" Carter and John Huggins, and two more in San Diego, Sylvester Bell, and John Savage.

To my knowledge, Mr. Karenga has never expressed the faintest remorse or regret for these murders, or for his part in furthering the nefarious aims of federal and local police agencies in their assault upon the movement of those times.

Karenga was later convicted along with his wife, of kidnapping and torturing two women in his own organization, a crime for which he served four years in prison, and one of which he still claims to be innocent. Some of Karenga's close and credible associates, however, like former US Chair, Wesley Kabaila, maintained Karenga was not only responsible for those women's torture, but that it was part of an ongoing pattern over the years.

"I'm a feminist," Kiilu Nyasha, a former Black Panther in New Haven CT, told Black Agenda Report, "How can I honor a holiday made up by a man who tortures women, in his own organization?"

What rankles many of us, about the annual hoopla Kwanzaa, and what should disturb, those engaged in building today's movements, against injustice and oppression, is that the elderly, Mr. Karenga, much like Bill Cosby, before his fall, is enjoying an ill-deserved, and unrepentant victory lap.

To this day, he has utterly evaded, any accountability, for his part, in the murders of Carter, Huggins, Savage, and Bell. For us, what others call "Kwanzaa," has become a time to remember, and celebrate the contributions, of the freedom fighters, which Karenga's US Organization murdered.

"I worked with John Huggins, I knew John Huggins personally," continued Kiilu Nyasha. "He was a beautiful, young brother, only 21 or 22. John left an infant daughter, less than a month old. He stood in defense of our people's right to be free."

Pretty much, everybody knew, Alprentice "Bunchy" Carter. "He had a real track record," said former LA Panther, Harold Welton. "Before helping organize, the Southern California Chapter, of the Black Panther Party, he was known, to many as, 'the mayor' of Los Angeles, and as an accomplished poet and vocal stylist."

"Even now, after all these years, if Karenga would come forward, and admit what he did, and begin in his final years, to apologize, and asked for forgiveness, to somehow begin, to atone for the murder, and the torture and the other stuff," Harold Welton, told Black

Agenda Report, "We'd have to begin, figuring out how to respond, in the right spirit. People do sometimes change and come in from the cold. But he's saving us the trouble. He's arrogant and unrepentant, and even looked-up to by a generation of young folks, who know little or nothing, about the man or his history."

Forgiveness Reigns Supreme!

Interview With Jewel Carter - 2012

In 2012, a dear friend of mine, James L. Crawford, for sixty-six years, went home to be with the Lord. He was the brother, of two of my best childhood friends, which were unidentical twins; Carolyn A. Crawford and Patricia A. Crawford-Douglas. We were friends, from kindergarten until they both went home to be with the Lord, in their adult years. James L. Crawford was a good Christian man. He has a loving and large family; and he owned a Photography Studio, in Los Angeles. He was the 'Stevie Wonder' of Photography.

I attended his Homegoing Service, and I ministered a poem I wrote entitled; "Don't Cry Too Long For Me - 'Cause I'm As Happy - As I Can Be!" I arrived at the Church early. When I walked into the Church, the Holy Spirit spoke to me (in my spirit). He said, "Go sit next, to that man, right there, at the end of the row." So, I did. While we were waiting, for the Homegoing Service to begin, the man and I started sharing, some of our memories about our mutual friend.

Then, he asked me, "What do you do?" I told him that, I am writing my first book. He asked, "What is the book about?" I told him, the book was about The Black Power Movement, in the '60's & '70's. I briefly shared, about Ron Karenga, Kwanzaa, and the UCLA Murders. He looked at me, took a deep breath, and said, "Alprentice (Bunchy) Carter was my brother." I was speechless! Immediately, I knew our meeting was a 'Divine Appointment' arranged by the Holy Spirit! After the Homegoing Service ended, everyone went over to James' home. We both were sitting in the living room, along with others, talking about the '60's & the '70's.

He shared that his family members were devastated and broken, by Bunchy's death. He said, "Bunchy was loved by so many people. He also said, "Bunchy was working on getting a good education, at UCLA to help himself and his family.

I asked Jewel Carter, what were his feelings, toward Ron Karenga? He said, "I forgave the brother, a long time ago; and so, had my Mother, who is ninety-four years young." Jewel Carter further stated, "I'm still praying, and believing, that Jesus Christ, will save Ron Karenga, the two Stiner Brothers and everybody who had something to do with Bunchy and John's death.

Jewel Carter minister's the Word of God, at local hospitals in Los Angeles. He is a good Christian man. I was moved, by the compassion and forgiveness that he has toward Karenga and the two Stiner Brothers. That said, Jewel, I salute you!

Definition of Forgiveness

A definition of forgiveness could be – giving-up my right to hurt you, for hurting me. It is impossible to live on this fallen planet without getting hurt, offended, misunderstood, lied to, and rejected. Learning how to respond properly is one of the basics of the Christian life.

The word forgive means to wipe the slate clean, to pardon, and to cancel a debt. When we wrong someone, we seek his or her forgiveness in order for the relationship to be restored. It is important to remember that forgiveness is not granted because a person deserves to be forgiven. Instead, it is an act of love, mercy, and grace.

How we act toward that person may change. It doesn't mean we will put ourselves back into a harmful situation or that we suddenly accept or approve of the person's continued wrong behavior. It simply means we release them from the wrong they committed against us. We forgive them because God forgave us. (Ephesians 4:31-32 and Romans 5:8)

What Does God Say About Forgiveness?

The Bible Gives Us Much Instruction When It Comes To Forgiveness:
- We forgive because we have been forgiven by God. (Ephesians 4:32)
- We forgive in obedience to God. (Matthew 6:14-15; Romans 12:18)
- We forgive others to gain control of our lives from hurt emotions. (Genesis 4:1-8)
- We forgive so we'll not become bitter and defile those around us. (Hebrews 12:14-15)

What If I Don't Feel Like Forgiving Others?

There are times we don't feel like forgiving those who have wronged us. It is easier to act our way into feeling than to feel our way into acting. Having a nature of not forgiving others brings about bitterness, and bitterness has been linked to stress-related illnesses by some medical researchers. By forgiving others, we free ourselves spiritually and emotionally. Forgiveness is an act of our own personal will in obedience and submission to God's will, trusting God to bring emotional healing.

How Can I Help Those Struggling With Forgiveness?

People who have experienced abuse, trauma or loss need time to sort things out and let God bring them to the place of forgiveness in His time. God's timing is always the right time for each individual. The act of forgiving others is between God and us.

There are things we can do to help those struggling with the forgiveness of others. We can support them with encouraging words and by listening to them. Taking our time and being gentle with them will allow them to progress through the steps of forgiveness the way God wants them to proceed.

A Prayer For Forgiveness

Dear God, I choose as an act of my will, regardless of my feelings, to forgive the person who has wronged me. I release them, and I set myself free to Your healing. With Your help, I will no longer dwell on the situation or continue to talk about it. I thank You for forgiving me as I have forgiven them. I thank You for releasing me. I ask this in Jesus Name. Amen.

CHAPTER 3

THE US ORGANIZATION

The Quotable Karenga

I wondered, after all the years that have passed; had Karenga changed from the '60s & '70s? Moreover, I read in one of his columns, in The L.A. Sentinel Newspaper, when he stated, "US Organization, has not been defeated, dispirited or diverted, from its initial commitment to Black Liberation Cultural Revolution, constant struggle, and excellence on every level."

Therefore, that said to me, he is still, the same arrogant, and narcissistic fool, which he was in the '60s. And, he is the same person that hates my Lord Jesus Christ; and he is the same person that hates White people.

I was hoping, after all these years, and with all the education he has garnered, especially with a Ph.D. in Social Ethics; would have matured and gone to another level. I remember Karenga stating, "The bloods (Black folks) don't even know, that they need my leadership; because they have been so brainwashed by the White man."

And, on another occasion, Karenga displayed his arrogance, for lack of a better word, to several members who were at his home. We were sitting around eating Chinese food; and talking about Karate.

Karenga said, "He didn't have to show us that he could do Karate. All, I have to do is to think that I can; and I can. I can without showing you that I can. I can prove that I can by my thoughts and my words."

Then, one of the members said, "Teach Maulana." A few were shaking their heads, as if to agree with that stupid statement. A few people said, "Alright Maulana." And, Tasamisha started hollering like an African Bush Woman. Karenga said, "He wished that he didn't have to use the White man's words; to get his message out and to explain anything. I sometimes just want to spit the words back, into the White man's face!" He further stated, "That's another reason, why I want the bloods, to learn to speak Swahili; as an alternative to speaking English." It was on, occasions like this; that had me questioning my membership in US Organization.

Karenga copied Mao's strategy; of The Chinese Culture Revolution. Mao's Book of Proverbs (Quotes) for The Chinese Cultural Revolution, was also created in the '60's. Upon joining US Organization, the new member received a copy of (The Little Red Book) written by Mao, to study as an example of The Black Cultural Revolution. And, the members of US Organization were also given a copy of Karenga's, The Quotable Karenga, (The Little Green Book); so, that they would know how to respond, to questions that people might have, about the Black Cultural Revolution.

For the record, I didn't receive a Little Red Book, nor did I receive a Little Green Book. I discovered that these little books existed; after I ended my membership in the organization. Members would use The Quotable Karenga, in the same way; that Christians used quotes from the Holy Bible.

<u>Quotes From: The Quotable Karenga:</u>

1) Perhaps the teachings of US are harsh, but it's better to work with hard facts than to play with pleasant but unproductive dreams.

2) Yes, if we could get a man to see how worthless, unimportant, ignorant and weak he is by himself, then we will have, made a contribution.

3) The only real things Negroes produce are problems and babies.

4) US Organization seeks to create a superior people.

5) You must put the Nation first and yourself last.

6) US doctrine is a shield to protect you, a weapon to attack with and a pillow of peace to rest your head.

7) The Sevenfold Path of Blackness is to Think Black, Talk Black, Act Black, Create Black, Buy Black, Vote Black, and Live Black.

8) To go back to tradition is the first step forward. Self-love is invalid unless you see yourself as part of the Black World.

9) We stress culture because it gives identity, purpose, and direction. It tells you who you are, what you must do, and how you can do it.

10) Without a culture, Negroes are only a set of reactions to White people.

Para-Military Organization

US Organization was set-up like a Para-Military Organization. In other words, <u>no one did anything, without Karenga first giving the order to do it</u>. Within the ranks of US Organization, most of them knew, what was going on about the violence, and some didn't. Like I said before, I did not know US members and the Black Panthers were in a war against one another.

I didn't even have a clue, about the rule that said; 'If you ended your membership in US Organization; you would get beat-up!' Quite a few other members were just like me, <u>Clueless and Naïve</u>. <u>We were also innocent</u>; because we joined, US Organization, for the right reasons; to help our people.

During the '60's, many of the members of US Organization were still in high school; especially the Simba Wachunga (young males). Some of them were only 17 to 19 years old. These young people hoped that they could learn how to be Black. Many of them, didn't have Fathers, in their homes to provide them with, a positive role model.

Karenga: Type of Leadership

The Late Dr. Myles Monroe, Senior Pastor, of the Bahamas Faith Ministries, International Church, was teaching at a leadership conference, regarding, "<u>The Problems In Leadership</u>." I discovered that five of the qualities, fit Karenga's Leadership. They are the following:

- Charismatic Leader Without Character
- Gifted Leader Without Convictions
- Leader Without Principles That Work
- Intellectual Leader Without Morality
- Visionary Leader Without Values

<u>God's Word Says It Best</u>: "In fact, evil men and false teachers will become worse and worse, deceiving many, they themselves having been deceived by Satan!" (2 Timothy 3:13) TLB.

The Simba Wachunga (Young Men) Training

1) The Revolution being fought now is a revolution to win the minds of our people. If we fail to win this, we cannot wage the violent one.

2) When the word is given, we'll see how tough you are. When it's "burn," let's see how much you burn. When it's "kill," let's see how much you kill. When its "blow-up," let's see how much you blow-up. And when it's take that White girls "head too," we'll see how tough you are.

3) We must gear the money going from the Church to the support of the Revolution. Revolution cannot succeed without finance.

4) I remember my mother used to tell me if you are bad the devil will get you. I didn't know that until the cops came.

5) We have come to set a series of precedents, to do what the old men, of the Civil Rights Movement, didn't have the will, or ability to do!

6) Blacks, have to stop talking about, what is good or bad, but what is necessary. We live in a political society, and what is important, in this society, is power, not morality.

7) Nationalism is a collective vocation, and a perpetual movement, to realize and make oneself eternal.

Karate Training

Karate training was taught mainly by Amiri Jomo. He was a Black Belt in Karate. He taught classes, on Wednesday nights, along with Tamu's husband. I forgot his name; he was also a Black Belt in Karate. Both men were excellent Instructors. I enjoyed learning the art of karate. I was progressing quite well; if I must say so myself. Amiri Jomo was at that time, Karenga's bodyguard.

The Afro-American School of Culture

Karenga interviewed me after I joined, to see what I was interested, in doing within US Organization. I told him, that I would like to work with children. He suggested, I work at the Afro-American School of Culture.

I agreed that teaching at the school would fit me, quite well. However, to teach at the school, I had to learn how to speak Swahili fluently. Well, I was up for the challenge. I enrolled in an evening class, at Manual Arts High School, in Los Angeles. At that time, I was working at the 53rd Street, Elementary School in Los Angeles; as an Intermediate School Clerk Typist.

In the Swahili class, I learned to hold conversations with others, in US Organization. I enjoyed learning Swahili; it's a beautiful language, and I received a 'B' at the end of the semester.

Haiba was the Principal, and there were four other teachers, that worked at the school, besides me. After school ended, we would feed the children a snack; and their parents, would pick them up. It was a rewarding experience for me.

Soul Sessions
Fighting For US, Maulana Karenga The US Organization, And Black Cultural Nationalism

By Scot Brown- 2005

In my research, I came across, an interesting book, by Scot Brown, Associate Professor of History, University of California, Los Angeles. Professor Brown stated, "US's Cultural Nationalist alternative, as presented in its weekly gatherings, called "Soul Sessions" at the organization's headquarters, took on the tenor and feeling of the African American Church that Karenga once knew.

As one former US member recalled, the Sunday afternoon meetings, nourished members and sympathizers, just as "Christians going to Church on Sunday" (were) getting their message that was going to carry them, through the week.

Karenga's oratorical style captured the cadence of Baptist ministry, and beckoned the call-and-response participation, of his audience." For example, where the Soul Sessions, were held, had seats in the room, with an aisle, down the middle. There was a platform, in the front, and there was a podium, on the platform.

The Soul Session would begin, by playing soulful music. The music was rock and roll, by famous singers, like Marvin Gaye. While the music was still playing, Karenga would enter the room, with two Simba Wachunga (young men) walking behind him.

Karenga would lecture, for approximately one hour, on different subjects. For example, the topic of Christianity. After the lecture, people were welcome to stay and talk and have refreshments."

Karenga's key points in a lecture about Christianity

"Thus, if persons want to fast or pray, read numbers, stare at stars, chant spookistic slogans or anything similar, they may, but it is imperative, that they not add these, to or pretend they are a part of the 'Seven Principles' and 'Practices' of Kwanzaa."

"… It is in simplistic and often erroneous answer to existential ignorance, fear, powerlessness, and alienation. An example is the Hebrew myth of the seven-day Creation and the Tower of Babel, or Christian myths of resurrection, heaven, and hell."

"… It often denies and diminishes human worth, capacity, potential, and achievement. In Christian and Jewish methodology, humans are born in sin, cursed with mythical ancestors, who have sinned and brought the wrath of an angry God on every generation's head ... If a mythical being has done, does, and will do everything, what's our relevance and role in the world?"

"Belief in spooks, who threaten us if we don't worship them and demand we turn over our destiny and daily lives, must be categorized, as spookism and condemned."

"The Holy Ghost, Spookism on the other hand, is intense emotional commitment to non-human-center principles and practices which place humans at the mercy of invisible and omnipotent forces and thus, deny the right and capacity of humans to shape reality and their future, according to, their own needs and desires."

The Polygamy Rule

Polygamy was allowed by Karenga because; he said that, our ancestors in Egypt practiced polygamy. Karenga believed that, if it worked for them, it would work for US Organization's members. He went on to say, "If polygamy works out in your house, then don't allow others to discourage your decision. However, if it didn't work out for your house; then I wouldn't suggest that you practice it.

Furthermore, there are fewer men in the world than women, so it will help sisters out not to be alone. They will have somebody to "laugh" with." Karenga called having sex, laughing. He said, "He was looking out for the sisters. The sisters have to accept what our ancestors did; not what this White man's religion tells us to do."

Personally, it was a no-brainer; I didn't practice polygamy; however, many in US Organization did. I remember having a conversation, with Haiba about polygamy. I told her, I didn't agree with it, and she said, "Tikisa, I don't agree with it either." Then, I said, well why does it exist in the organization? She said, "I agree, with my husband. If it's not a problem between all those involved, then it's nothing wrong with it; because it worked for our African Ancestors."

I felt so sad for Haiba when I found out that Karenga was committing adultery with his secretary, Tiamoyo. One day, Hekima and I took Karenga, over to Tiamoyo's home. I thought that we were going there, to pick-up some work that she had for Karenga. When we arrived at her apartment, he invited us to come inside with him. So, we got out of the car, went up to the front door; and Karenga pulled out a key and opened the door!

We went inside with him. He called out to Tiamoyo, telling her that; it was him coming into the apartment with Hekima, and myself. Karenga had already stated, "If it wouldn't work in your house, then don't do it." Haiba had, already told me that she didn't approve of it for her marriage.

Therefore, he was either committing adultery; or she lied to me, and they were practicing polygamy, or he successfully talked her into accepting polygamy later in their marriage.

Maulana Karenga's Haunting Ghost

By Mukasa Afrika Ma'at - 2012

In this profound Essay by, Mukasa Afrika Ma'at, he stated, "Karenga was indeed a polygamist. He would have his "first" wife sit down and tell prospective wives about the great deeds of "Maulana" to convince them to join in their polygamist marriage. This I have established, directly from a woman, whom the wife, attempted to seduce her, into the arrangement.

Karenga has been seen, out and about, with his wives, over the years. Besides the fact, that polygamy is not a common practice in

America, while common in some Afrikan cultures, it is against the law. It is but further evidence of a cult leader."

A Cult of Personality And Hero Worshipping Maulana Karenga's Haunting Ghost

By Mukasa Afrika Ma'at - 2012

In this eye-opening Essay by, Mukasa Afrika Ma'at, he stated, "A cult of personality is when a person or a group develops unrealistic praise for an individual. They cease to honor the principles which someone and others might stand for, and instead, they begin to honor and worship the person. The problem is that men are flawed, and when a cult of personality develops, the mind of the follower will find it very difficult, to accept normal human faults.

Additionally, when the leader has committed heinous crimes, the cult follower will not even hear such unspeakable "ideas" against their leader. This is when the cult of personality becomes hero worship, which is even more unrealistic, even more ridiculous, and even more dangerous. Hero worship develops when a cult of a person\leader elevates them to the status of demi-god – in some cases, the leader may even become "God."

Karenga has followers of varying degrees. Firstly, some are simply respectful of his intellectual work, and they may or may not question his ghost and dirty past. Secondly, the next level up for Karenga are those who are ardent followers of one or more of the concepts associated with him such as Kwanzaa or Kawaida.

This third set of followers may or may not be partially engulfed in the next set of followers. The third group is made of the cult worshipers who not only live Karenga's principles as part of their lives but refuse to accept any questions of wrongdoing against him.

Anyone who questions their cult leader must be doing the work of the White man or defaming a great Black leader. Karenga is innocent of all charges against him. It was all a COINTELPRO conspiracy against him. He didn't do it! This group is beyond the realistic and trying to reasonably convince them or debate with them is a waste of time.

The fourth or last groups of followers are Karenga's hero worshippers who simply consider him near divine or even divine. These hero worshippers are the ones who would bow, kneel to the ground and kiss his hand. Yes, this was a practice of members of the US Organization. I am informed of this from people who witnessed his cult following hero worshippers kneeling, kissing his hand, and mumbling "Maulana, Maulana, Maulana."

Mukasa Afrika Ma'at further stated, "While in Senegal, Karenga was upset with Dr. John Henrik Clarke, because the Senegalese, had elected Dr. Clarke, head of a group of respected Afrikan Americans, due to his work, over the years with them. According to Dr. Clarke, Karenga approached him, upset and said to him, "You don't know the definition of my name, "Maulana means God!" This further establishes the cultist rituals, practices, and leadership of Karenga."

The (Real) Meaning of The Name Maulana

I discovered from my research, that the word **Maulana in Swahili** means: **The Lord, God** and Master. Therefore, to call him: **Maulana Karenga** would mean that one is calling him: **The Lord, God Karenga.** The word, **Mwalimu in Swahili** means: **Teacher.** Therefore, to call him: **Maulana Mwalimu** would mean that one is calling him: **Master Teacher Karenga.** In other words, what I **discovered**; is just another **LIE** told by: **The Master Liar Karenga!**

I also discovered from my research that the word, **Maulana**, is **not** a name, but, a **Title**; used by devout **Muslims**. They believe the title, should not be used by anyone, since it is a designation, of their God\ Allah, and therefore, the Title, 'Maulana' was such a 'Holy Title,' that it should not be spoken in everyday conversations. **"Maulana" means, "Our God" or "Our Lord" in Arabic.** Karenga was aware of this fact; because he speaks fluent Arabic. So, when one calls him, Maulana, they are in fact, calling him, **"Our God" or "Our Lord."**

You know, it could be that; Karenga was very **Angry** at Jesus Christ for taking so much of his Father's time away from him, (in a child's thinking) when he was a young kid; feeling alone; and outnumbered, between himself and his siblings; since, he was the fourteenth child in his family; that he unconscientiously became, **'an enemy of Jesus Christ.'**

In terms of, Jesus Christ came to Save People in the World from Satan. Ron Karenga, could see himself as coming into the World to Save Black People from Jesus Christ and White People. Jesus Christ is our Master Teacher. Ron Karenga named himself Maulana, and told everyone the **LIE** that it meant, Master Teacher in Swahili.

Also, Jesus Christ, is our High Priest. Ron Karenga named himself High Priest; in his own Religion called, Kwanzaa. Karenga thought that Jesus Christ, brought Bad into the World. Therefore, he states that Kwanzaa brings Good into the World. And, last but not least, Jesus Christ had a Religion named after Him called, Christianity. Ron Karenga named his Religion after himself, called, Kwanzaa. You get it? **Christ = Christianity. Karenga = Kwanzaa.**

CHAPTER 4

KWANZAA: CELEBRANTS HAVE BEEN HOODWINKED & BAMBOOZLED!

Black Minister: Say 'No' To Kwanzaa

By Rev. Jesse Lee Peterson - 2004

In my research, I discovered a profound and gripping article by, Rev. Jesse Lee Peterson, Founder and President of BOND, and Author of, The Antidote. He stated, "While public officials, schools, and the ACLU worked overtime this year to ban every vestige of Christmas from the public square, the recently, invented holiday known as Kwanzaa is gaining in popularity among Black Americans. These occurrences are not unrelated.

In an earlier time, Blacks held a strong faith in God. But, over the last 40 years, the Black community has largely let God slip away. Sure, the community has maintained the outer trappings of religion but, the solid morality; at its core is nearly gone.

Enter a God-hating Black man, named Ron Karenga. Born Ron Everett on a poultry farm in Maryland, Everett invented Kwanzaa in 1966, based on an African harvest festival (through it takes place during the Winter Solstice!) and celebrating the first Kwanzaa with his family and friends.

Calling himself "Maulana" (Swahili for "Master Teacher"), Karenga became a black nationalist at UCLA and formed his group, the United Slaves (US) for the purpose of igniting a "cultural revolution" among American Blacks. US members followed Karenga's "Path of Blackness," which is detailed in his Quotable Karenga: "The sevenfold path of blackness is think black, talk black, act black, create black, buy black, vote black, and live black."

The United Slaves had violent confrontations with the Black Panthers on campus and were actually considered more radical than the Panthers. The biggest dispute between the United Slaves and the Panthers was for the leadership of the new African Studies Department at UCLA, with each group backing a different candidate. Panthers John Jerome Huggins and Alprentice "Bunchy" Carter verbally attacked Karenga at the meeting, which infuriated Karenga's followers. After the meeting ended, two US members, George and Larry Stiner, reportedly confronted Huggins and Carter in a hallway, shooting and killing them.

Incidentally, on March 31, 1974, it was discovered that both Stiner brothers had escaped from the family visiting area in San Quentin State Prison. Larry Stiner turned himself into the FBI in Caracas, Venezuela, on December 13, 1994. He remains in custody at San Quentin. But George Stiner remains at large, and his whereabouts remain unknown. He is currently on California's 10 Most Wanted List.

The shooting at UCLA apparently caused Karenga to become extremely suspicious. On May 9, 1970, Karenga and three others tortured two women who Karenga believed had tried to poison him by placing "crystals" in his food and water.

The Los Angeles Times described the events: "Deborah Jones, who once was given the title of an African queen, said she and Gail Davis were whipped with an electric cord and beaten with a karate baton after being ordered to remove their clothes at gunpoint. She testified that a hot soldering iron was placed in Miss Davis' mouth and placed against Miss Davis' face and that one of her own big toes was tightened in a vice. Karenga, head of US, also put detergent and running hoses in their mouths, she said."

Karenga was sentenced to one-to-ten years in prison on counts of felonious assault and false imprisonment. At his trial, the question arose as to Karenga's sanity. The psychiatrist's report stated: "This man now represents a picture which can be considered both paranoid and schizophrenic with hallucinations and illusions, inappropriate affect, disorganization, and impaired contact with the environment." The psychiatrist reportedly observed that Karenga talked to his blanket and imaginary persons, and he believed he'd been attacked by dive-bombers.

Eight years later, California State University, Long Beach, named Karenga the head of its Black Studies Department. By this time, Karenga had "repented" of his black nationalism and had become just a harmless garden variety Marxist. This must be our esteemed university system's idea of repentance!

Karenga's Kwanzaa celebration consists of seven 'principles.' They are Umoja (unity), Kujichagulia (self-determination – code for "buy black"), Ujima (collective work and responsibility – groupthink), Ujamaa (cooperative economics – socialism), Nia (purpose), Kuumba (creativity), and Imani (faith – in man, not God). To provide a symbol of his seven 'principles,' Karenga used the menorah from Judaism with Kwanzaa's colors (red, black, and green), and re-named it the "kinara."

Karenga also created a Kwanzaa flag that consists of black, green, and red. The Kwanzaa Information Center states the color red represents blood: "We lost our land through blood, and we cannot gain it except through blood. We must redeem our lives through the blood. Without the shedding of blood, there can be no redemption of this race." The Kwanzaa Information Center also notes that this flag "has become a symbol of devotion for African people in America to establish an independent African nation on the North American Continent." (Emphasis added.)

Through ignorance, growing numbers of Black Christians are either, celebrating Kwanzaa or incorporating it into their Christmas celebrations. Now, many preachers are incorporating Kwanzaa, into their messages. This is a horrible mistake.

First of all, as we've seen, the whole holiday is made up! You won't find its roots in Africa or anywhere else. Second, Kwanzaa's 'principles' are straight from Hell. Third, and most importantly, Christians who celebrate or incorporate Kwanzaa are moving their attention away from Christmas, the birth of our Savior, and the simple message of salvation: love for God through His Son. To add or subtract from that message is evil.

It is now clear that Kwanzaa is a phony, wicked holiday created by an ex-con who hates God, Christians, Jews, and Blacks – yes Blacks. Why else would he try to pull them away from Christianity and indoctrinate them in socialism? Blacks, particularly Black Christians, need to stand up for Christmas and reject Kwanzaa. If they refuse, they will be helping to stamp out the true meaning of Christmas and allowing evil to have its way in America. This is a future we cannot allow.

Kwanzaa Born of Separatism, Radicalism

By Mona Charen - 2002

I found an interesting and insightful article, written by Mona Charen, BigEye. She stated, "The International Black Buyers and Manufacturers Expo and Conference, an association representing more than 1,000 black-owned businesses, has sent a blistering letter to large American firms like Hallmark Cards and Giant Food, telling them to keep their hands-off Kwanzaa-related products. The sale of Kwanzaa products by nonblack businesses, the organization contends, is "arrogantly exploitative of the culture of African people."

According to The Washington Post, Sala Damali, one of the founders of the IBBMEC, said, "Many companies look at it as a normal exercise of commerce. We find it insulting and disrespectful to the actual spirit of Kwanzaa."

Well, first, let us consider what the response would be if an association of white business owners (that very idea is anathema) were to issue a statement saying that blacks should not sell items related to, say, St. Lucia's Day, a Swedish festival. It would be called racist within a nanosecond.

The notion that only blacks should buy and sell Kwanzaa products is equally offensive. As to the "spirit of Kwanzaa," that is a more sensitive matter. Americans have clasped Kwanzaa to their bosom. Major TV stations elevate it to the same status as other winter holidays, like Christmas and Hanukkah, by broadcasting "Happy Kwanzaa" greetings between Christmas and the New Year. Products for Kwanzaa, including candelabras and greeting cards fill the stores. A quick Lexis-Nexis search of Kwanzaa stories in major newspapers turns up hundreds of feel-good features about the "spirit of sharing" (Los Angeles Times), the "feast for body and soul" (Baltimore Sun), "food fellowship and pride" (Seattle Times) and "community unity" (The Orlando Sentinel). Most Americans, eager to respect the traditions of every group, assume that Kwanzaa is what it sounds like: a traditional African celebration handed down over the generations.

A Spiritual Tragedy

Kwanzaa had been in existence, for many years before the Internet. It went Global, because of the Internet. I know you have, probably heard, the old cliché, 'If you give, the Devil an inch, he will take a mile.' And, that's what, he did. Now, Karenga is calling Kwanzaa, a Miracle!

Karenga began the celebration of Kwanzaa, on the day, after Christmas. He knew that Christians were still celebrating, our Lord's Birth; and that we would, continue to celebrate until at least, New Year's Day. And, now he is telling his celebrants, to start preparing to celebrate Kwanzaa on Thanksgiving Day! Why, Thanksgiving Day? Because he knows, that a lot of us Christians, start celebrating, Jesus Christ's, Immaculate Birth, on Thanksgiving Day. Why on Thanksgiving Day? Because, Jesus Christ, is the reason, that Christians are thankful!

Deception has gotten people, to celebrate Kwanzaa, without realizing, that it is Religious. And, even worse than that, some misinformed people, have started celebrating, Kwanzaa, in July! Some Scholars, say that according to the Hebrew calendar Jesus Christ was born sometime around September or October, and not in December. However, it doesn't matter to me. What does matter, is the fact that, He was born! So, December is good enough for me.

I remember Karenga, mocking Jesus Christ, in Soul Sessions. For example, he told everyone, "That Mary, the earthly Mother of Jesus Christ, was a whore." He said, "She had sex, with so many different men, that she didn't know, who the Father, of her unborn child, was." He went on to say, "Mary lied, to save her life, because, in those days, they would stone a woman, to death for having sex, without being married."

He further stated, "Jesus does not look like us, so, why should we bow-down to a blue-eyed White man?" He said, "Control is the reason, that the White man, wanted the Black man, to celebrate, worship, and praise their God." He said, "When our Ancestors, were taken, from Africa, they were brainwashed, by the system, to worship their God. And, taking all, those facts, and looking at, all the pictures, of Jesus Christ, and his Mother Mary, clearly shows, that Christmas, is a White man's holiday, and not meant, for Black folks to celebrate!"

Karenga didn't put Kwanzaa, in February; because it would not fit into a Black History Month. It wouldn't fit because it had nothing to do with the History of Black Americans. Karenga, wanted it to be included amongst the other Religions being celebrated, at that time of the year; the Jewish Holiday of Hanukkah, and the Christian Holiday of Christmas. My spirit was grieved when I found out, how Kwanzaa, had infiltrated God's Church! How dare Karenga try to **STEAL JESUS CHRIST'S GLORY**! And, how dare the Body of Christ let him do it! God's Church was **SILENT!**

The Kwanzaa Con: Created By A Rapist And Torturer

By Warner Todd Huston - 2013

I found a profound article, by Warner Todd Huston, with the Publius Forum. He stated, "Of course, if it weren't, for an Old Media establishment, that had given, this Karenga's criminality, a wholesale whitewashing, this faux holiday, could never, have gained the little traction, it got in the first place.

Put it this way; imagine if, famed Ku Klux Klan member, David Duke, had created a holiday. Do you think, the Old Media, would have, happily sold his creation, to a misinformed public, without mentioning, Duke's personal history? Not a chance, and rightfully so."

Should Born Again Christians
Celebrate Kwanzaa?

The Kingdom of God represents the Spiritual\Supernatural World. We as Christians, must not allow our culture to override our Faith in the Word of God. We are all surrounded by culture and the environment in this World's System. However, that doesn't mean that we should get involved, in worldly practices. Some things that our Ancestors, believed in and practiced, doesn't mean that we as Christians, should incorporate those 'unclean' things, into our daily lives.

For instance, in Africa, some tribes believed in and practiced, voodoo, witchcraft, worshiping of idol gods, and worshiping the dead. Some understood and practiced, the marrying of more than one wife, better known as polygamy. They also practiced many other, ungodly things that we as Christians, should not participate in or practice; because it doesn't line-up with God's Holy Word.

By not participating, in those ungodly things doesn't mean; that we are any less of Ancient African descent. It just says that some things are neither wise nor beneficial, for Born Again Christians, to believe in or practice. Our 'New Birth' transcends 'Culture!' Looking at things, from the right perspective, blows away, the evil strategy of Satan; to divide and conquer.

Kwanzaa's foundation and reason for existence are because of Karenga's hatred for Jesus Christ. Karenga has committed "Blasphemy Against The Holy Spirit!" He states, "The Holy Spirit, is a Spook, and should be Condemned." He rejects, that God made the World, in seven days; Karenga calls it mythical.

Kwanzaa has No Life in it! It has No Anointing! It has No Anointing because God cannot Anoint a **LIE!** Thus, you decide who you, will follow: Jesus Christ, from Nazareth, or Ron Karenga, from Los Angeles? God's Word Says It Best: "No man can serve two masters: for either he will hate the one and love the other; or else he will hold to the one and despise the other ..." (Matthew 6:24) KJV.

As Born Again Christians, we must be 'very alert,' in these End-Times. <u>God's Word Says It Best</u>: "For there shall arise false Christ and false prophets and shall shew great signs and wonders; insomuch that, if it were possible, they shall deceive the very elect." (Matthew 24:24) KJV. By mixing the Truth (God's Word) with a Lie (Karenga's word) will cause your Faith to become Lukewarm. <u>God's Word Says It Best</u>: "So then because thou art lukewarm, and neither cold nor hot, I will spue thee out of My mouth." (Revelation 3:16) KJV.

Kwanzaa Is An Absolute Fraud

By Rev. Pat Robertson - 2004

During my research, I found an article that is gripping and truthful, By Rev. Pat Robertson, founder of The Christian Broadcasting Network's, The 700 Club. Rev. Pat Robertson called Kwanzaa, "an absolute fraud" during the news segment of The Christian Broadcasting Network's, The 700 Club, on December 6, 2004.

After lamenting that, "left wing educators and left-wing judges are stripping every vestige of our Christian heritage." Robertson, host and Christian Coalition of America founder, said: "Kwanzaa is an absolute fraud. You know, there was no festival in Africa called 'Kwanzaa.' I mean, it's made up by a bunch of hippie-types on the West Coast. I mean, it's not something that goes back to Africa. No way."

Kwanzaa is an African American holiday celebrated in African communities around the world. It was founded in 1966 by Maulana Karenga, professor, and chair of the black studies department at California State University, Long Beach.

The official Kwanzaa website notes that Karenga founded Kwanzaa as "an African American and Pan-African holiday" based on ancient African history and culture. Celebrated from December 26 through January 1, Kwanzaa is rooted in "the first harvest celebrations of Africa from which it takes its name."

According to Karenga, "The name 'Kwanzaa' is derived from the phrase 'matunda ya kwanza' which means 'first fruits' in Swahili, a Pan-African language which is the most widely spoken African language." Karenga also notes that Kwanzaa "draws from the cultures of various African peoples and is celebrated by millions of Africans throughout the African world community."

Kwanzaa

By La Shawn Barber - 2006

In my research, I discovered an interesting, and genuine article, entitled: "Kwanzaa," By La Shawn Barber, Christian Research Institute. She stated, "It is understandable that descendants of a people who were stolen from their African homeland and placed in bondage in a foreign land would be attracted to a so-called African culture-based celebration. It is not immoral or unbiblical for members of racial groups to gather and talk about the history of their people and their culture.

It is wholly understandable that Blacks in America would try to connect with their heritage. It is strange, however, that Black Christians would be drawn to the amalgamation of Marxist ideology, 1960's-style radicalism, pseudo-history, and spiritualized "African" rituals that constitutes Kwanzaa.

Another religious belief Karenga claims is that Kwanzaa is a time of giving "reverence to the Creator." Christians should take note when someone who says he reveres "the Creator" rejects the Biblical account of Christ; anyone who does so denies Christ as Creator and as God and thus does not revere the true Creator.

Another Kwanzaa belief Karenga based on African religion is that ancestors are "spiritual intercessors between humans and the Creator."

The Bible teaches, however, that Christ alone and no created being - is the intercessor between God and man. (1 Timothy 2:5)

Christians who observe Kwanzaa may not realize that its inventor holds to such blatantly unbiblical beliefs. The Bible repeatedly warns Christians to beware of this kind of spiritual deception. The Apostle Paul exhorts us to put on the "whole armor of God" so that we may be able to stand against such deception. We fight against "principalities, against powers, against the rulers of the darkness of this world," and not against mere flesh. (Ephesians 6:12) NKJV.

Those who do not believe in God may fill the God-shaped vacuum in their hearts with spiritualized celebrations like Kwanzaa. For Christians, however, that vacuum has already been filled with the bountiful love of a Creator who died so that we could live with Him forever. We are to be living examples of that love and sacrifice and tell the world that empty rituals are not the cure for what ails them."

The Kwanzaa Hoax

By William J. Bennetta - 2000

In my research, I discovered an interesting article by William J. Bennetta of The Textbook League. He stated, "Anywhere we are, Us is." That looks like a line from an Amos 'N Andy show. One can easily imagine that it served as the motto of the Mystic Knights of the Sea and that it was recited by such characters as The Kingfish, Andy Brown and Algonquin J. Calhoun.

In fact, however, the line that I have quoted is the motto of a real organization – a real organization that was originally named United Slaves but now calls itself The Organization Us (or simply Us or US). It was created some 40 years ago, in Southern California, by a black racist who had begun life as Ron N. Everett but later had assumed the name Maulana Karenga.

Karenga is still working at CSULB and is still running The Organization Us, and he and Us are still promoting his proprietary holiday, Kwanzaa. Prentice Hall is promoting it too, so The American Nation displays a picture of "an American family's celebration of Kwanzaa" – but The American Nation doesn't tell anything about Karenga, about his rules for carrying out a 'celebration of Kwanzaa,' or about his make-believe Africanism. Let me supply some of the information that Prentice Hall has hidden.

In Karenga's Kwanzaa-lingo, ears of maize are called by the Swahili name "Muhindi." In fact, all the objects that Karenga has worked into Kwanzaa have names taken from Swahili, which The Official Kwanzaa Web site describes as "a Pan-African language" and "the most widely spoken African language." The labeling of Swahili as a "Pan-African" language is rubbish. Swahili – a Bantu tongue that includes many words absorbed from Arabic, from Persian, and from certain Indian languages – is spoken by some 50 million people (i.e., about 7% of Africa's population). Most of those Swahili-speakers are concentrated in eastern Africa, in a region that includes Uganda, Kenya, Tanzania and a strip of Zaire. The language which is used most widely in Africa is Arabic; and indeed, Swahili was originally written in Arabic script. Kwanzaa is a hoax – a hoax built around fake history and pseudo historical delusion. By attempting to dignify and promote Kwanzaa in The American Nation, Prentice Hall has joined in a flimflam.

The True Spirit of Kwanzaa

By William Norman Grigg - 1999

In my research, I found an interesting article by William Norman Grigg, The New American. He stated, "Among Bill Clinton's numerous despicable distinctions is the fact that he is the first occupant of the Oval Office to extend official recognition to the ersatz holiday called "Kwanzaa," a seven-day annual "African" festival that runs from December 26ᵗʰ to New Year's Day. Mr. Clinton has described Kwanzaa as, "a vibrant celebration of African culture" that "transcends international boundaries ... link{ing} diverse individuals in a unique celebration of a dynamic heritage." In fact, Kwanzaa is a product of violent black separatism, and it was designed to foment insularity and a sense of racial grievance.

Kwanzaa's seasonal colors (red, black, and green) and rechristening it the "kinara." No Kwanzaa pledge: "We pledge allegiance to the red, black, and green, our flag, the symbol of our eternal struggle, and to the land we must obtain; one nation of black people, with one God of us all, totally united in the struggle, for black love, black freedom, and black self-determination."

This is the stuff of parody; it is a photographic negative of the rites conducted by bedsheet-bedecked white supremacists who cavort around burning crosses, or neo-Nazis who offer oblations to their pagan deity Odin. Yet "Karenga" and his black nationalist holiday have been eagerly embraced by the apostles of multiculturalism and tolerance. In his presidential messages commemorating Kwanzaa, Bill Clinton has stated that" Karenga's" seven principles "ring true not only for African Americans, but also for all Americans ... bring{ing} new purpose to our daily lives." In recent years the mainstreaming of Kwanzaa has proceeded at an astonishing pace. The U.S. Postal Service issued a commemorative stamp in 1997, and the Smithsonian Institution sponsors an annual celebration.

Christian activist Carlotta Morrow, whose sister was lured into "Karenga's" United Slaves organization in the 1970s, is much less enchanted with the observance, describing its message as "anti-Christian, anti-Jewish, and black separatist" in nature. To the extent that the holiday bears the impress of its creator, it should also be seen as a celebration of depravity and violence.

On several occasions, factional quarrels between "Karenga's" US organization and the Black Panthers erupted into open gunplay, which resulted in the death of several people."

The 'Real' Truth About Kwanzaa

By Carlotta Morrow - 2010

In my research, I found, an incredible, and powerful, E-Book by, Carlotta Morrow, a Freelance Writer, Researcher, and Owner of Christocentric Press. She stated, "No other foundation than Jesus Christ: "For no other foundation can anyone lay than that which is laid, which is Jesus Christ." (I Corinthians 3:11)

Churches that bring Kwanzaa, into their buildings are teaching, their members that the Bible is not enough. Jesus Christ is not enough. To help their, congregants become, better people, many Churches are teaching, that changes, must be made, through cultural teachings, as well as Biblical teachings. This is, a very dangerous teaching, and one must choose, either follow after God or follow after man.

There is no Righteousness without Jesus Christ: "But we are like an unclean thing, and all our righteousness are like filthy rags; we all fade as a leaf, and our iniquities, like the wind, have taken us away."

(Isaiah 64:6) "Righteousness," is a theme throughout Kwanzaa as well. It is highlighted, in the last principle, of the Nguzo Saba, Imani (faith) when said of the "righteousness and victory of our struggle."

Black people are painted as a "righteous" people with righteous purposes. This contradicts what God says in our initial standing with Him – ALL people are unrighteous, and the only way to obtain the righteousness of God is through Jesus Christ.

Even if Kwanzaa is speaking a different kind of righteousness, the Christian only knows one kind – and that is the righteousness of God Himself. God created "righteousness," and only He can set its standards."

Before you wish someone "Happy Kwanzaa:" The most insulting thing, anyone can do, to a Black person, is assume that, just because they are Black, they celebrate Kwanzaa. Many other Blacks, such as myself, do not celebrate it, as well, because we consider Kwanzaa an affront to our belief in Jesus Christ. Many, do not celebrate it, because, they are clueless, to what Kwanzaa, is even about.

Kwanzaa is a Black separatist's dream come true. Most, Kwanzaa celebrations are in the office or in schools and public places are done, for the "African-American." So please, ask before, greeting someone with, "Happy Kwanzaa," if they even, celebrate it or not. And no, just because, a Black person, refuses Kwanzaa, it does, not mean, they do not, appreciate, their culture. They just don't, want to make, their heritage, their religion."

Christians, Church, And Kwanzaa
<u>The 'Real' Truth About Kwanzaa</u>

By Carlotta Morrow - 2010

Again, I refer to the incredible, and powerful, E-Book, by Carlotta Morrow. She stated, "Many will say, at this point, that it does not matter what Karenga believes about Kwanzaa. They will insist that what counts is how they celebrate Kwanzaa.

For instance, many Christian Churches substitute the Nguzo Saba with Bible verses instead of practicing it as Karenga has prescribed, with no scriptural references at all. The question Churches must ask themselves is what purpose does celebrating Kwanzaa serve?

Many will say that the purpose is to celebrate their culture. More will say that celebrating Kwanzaa is an affirmation of our togetherness as African people in America.

Nonetheless, there are several problems that present themselves when the Christian attempt to combine their "religion" of Christianity with the "religion" of Kwanzaa. This paradox:

1. Makes the assumption that the Bible is not enough to spiritually feed us as a people.

2. Requires the belief that we somehow must define ourselves in the context of culture.

3. Encourages the idea that unity is possible without Christ, by simply uniting with those that share the same color of skin.

On the one hand, it is not wrong to celebrate culture. On the other, when culture begins claiming to do for the human being the same as God claims to do; then it ceases being culture and treads onto the religious.

Clearly, Karenga intended for Kwanzaa to be more than a once-a-year event. Kwanzaa was meant to be a completely new religion that would change the lives of many and spiritually rebuild followers into better persons."

A Historical Examination: The TRUTH About Kwanzaa

By Tony Snow

Interview With Keith Richburg - 1999

In my research, I found an excellent article written by Tony Snow, with the Washington Post, interviewed, Keith Richburg. Tony Snow stated, "Keith Richburg served for three years, as the African Chief, for the Washington Post; and offers a challenge for the likes of Karenga. "Talk to me, about Africa, and my Black roots and my kinship with my African brothers, and I'll throw it back, in your face, and then, I'll rub your nose, in the images, of rotting flesh."

Keith Richburg, Author of, <u>Out of America: A Black Man Confronts Africa</u>, in which, he stated, "Blacks in America, have suffered, an endless series of insults, and degradations, and the latest, of which, goes by the name, of Kwanzaa. Ron Karenga (a.k.a. Dr. Maulana Ron Karenga) invented the seven-day feast, from (Dec. 26-Jan. 1) in 1966, branding it a Black alternative to Christmas. The idea was to celebrate the end of, what he considered, the Christmas-seasoned, exploitation, of African Americans.

Worse, Kwanzaa ceremonies have no discernible African roots. No culture, on earth, celebrates a harvesting ritual, in December; for instance, and the implicit pledges, about human dignity, don't necessarily jive, with such still-common practices, as female circumcision and polygamy.

Even the rituals, using corn, doesn't fit. Corn isn't indigenous to Africa. Mexican Indians developed it and the crop was carried, worldwide by White colonialists. The fact is there is no Ur-African culture. The continent remains, stubbornly tribal. Hutus and Tutsis, still slaughter one another for sport.

Nobody, ever ennobled a people, with a lie, or restored stolen dignity, through fraud. Kwanzaa is, the ultimate, chump holiday – Jim Crow, with a false and festive wardrobe. It praises practices – "cooperative economics, and collective work and responsibility" – that have succeeded nowhere on earth, and would mire, American Blacks, in endless backwardness.

Our treatment of Kwanzaa, provides a revealing sign, of how far, we have yet, to travel on the road, to reconciliation. The White establishment has thrown in with it, not just, to cash in on the business, but, to patronize, Black activists, and shut them up."

Kwanzaa Is Wack! There I Said It!

By Roland Martin - 2011

During my research, I found an excellent, and humorous article, written by, Roland Martin, at NewsOne. He stated, "The other day, I said this, on my Facebook page: I said, "Is it wrong of me, to say that I love, AFRICA, but I think Kwanzaa is Wack?"

He stated, "Now, when I said it, I admit it, I gave no thought, to how it might affect people. I'm kind of, bad like that. A ton, of people (some Black and some not), got on, and said, they thought, Kwanzaa was whack too. I never thought, about it again, really. Just a funny little thread.

Then, someone got upset. I felt bad, about that, truly. But, the reality is that Kwanzaa was created by an FBI informant named, Dr. Maulana Karenga. Straight up! That's a fact. Beyond that, stuff like corn, that is used, in a lot of rituals, is not even native to Africa. A friend of mine noted, "it's truly corny."

Now hold on. I did participate, in a few, Kwanzaa events, back when '89, was the number. I always tried, to observe it. But, once I did, the history of its founder, and some of the deeper elements, of a hollow cultural base, it was hard to continue on ...

Look, I love Africa and what it means to be Black. I love almost, everything African, (aside from, the tribal fighting, and the needless, murder and rape, of women, across the continent). But, Kwanzaa, is not African ...

Kwanzaa, is like, a bad weave. People might kinda like it, but, we all know, it ain't real. Dr. Maulana Karenga was an informant, who hated on Geronimo Pratt and caused, a lot of damage, to the African American community. How do we know, he didn't "found" Kwanzaa in 1966 as a social experiment on Black people for the FBI? How could, such a knowledgeable man, just forget that corn is not, from his homeland?"

The (Hidden) Mystery Of The Corn

First, let's not forget, that Karenga, was reared by a Baptist Preacher. Hence, he is very familiar with the stories, in the Holy Bible. Secondly, Karenga also grew up on a farm, thereby, making him very familiar with seasons of harvesting. For example, Karenga used the Feast of the Pentecostal, Firstfruit, of the Wheat Harvest, in the Book of Leviticus 23. Apostle Paul, let us know, that the harvest, of the Pentecostal Feast, represents the saints, from the whole, of the Gentile Dispensation. It commenced on the sixteen day of Nisan, with the waving, of the Firstfruit, of the Barley Harvest.

A sheaf of the First Ripe Grain was "waved before the Lord by the Priest." God's acceptance and blessing, of the first ripe grain, was accounted to the whole of the grain harvest, which would be gathered in, over the remaining forty-nine days.

Except a Corn of Wheat, falls to the ground and dies, it abides alone; that's the economics of farming. One grain is planted, to the intent; it will reproduce itself, many-fold. Christ was the Corn of Wheat, who fell to the ground and died for His Bride. As Daniel foretold, "He was cut off, but not for Himself," waved before the Father, and raised for our justification, to become the Firstfruit of them that slept. God will never, be alone anymore, for when Christ was accepted, all in Christ, were accepted, and those that sleep-in Jesus, will bring with Him, at the first Resurrection.

Seven Sabbaths followed the sheaf wave offering, typing the Seven Church Ages, which followed Christ's waving. The priest, then offered a new wave offering, of two loaves, made from wheat flour, from the Pentecostal Harvest, baked with leaven, to represent the Gentile Bride, who unlike Christ, was born, in the leaven of sin, shapen in iniquity, and comes into the world, speaking lies.

He is Alpha and Omega, the pure Word at the beginning, and the pure Word, at the ending, of the Gentile Dispensation, reproduced in the two loaves, of the Bride from Pentecost, who fell, and went through, the Dark Ages, revived, in the Reformation and is restored, to the same faith in Christ's End-Time Gentile Bride. Thus, His many membered, Bride, is symbolized, by these two identical loaves, prepared from the same Corn of Wheat."

Since one Corn symbolizes Christ, (Master Teacher) Karenga, added one Corn to the Kwanzaa mat, symbolizing, Maulana Karenga (Master Teacher). The second ear of Corn symbolizing, The End-Time Gentile Bride. So, he added a second ear of Corn, symbolizing Maat. The two loaves were prepared from, the same Corn of Wheat.

Karenga saw the Reformation, and the restoring, to the same faith, in Christ's Gentile Bride, and worship; the same as the Reformation, and the restoring to the same faith, as back to Ra (god). Karenga sees Ra (god) as the Alpha and Omega, not Jesus Christ.

Due to the rise, of Christianity, (The New Kingdom) in the Roman Empire; put an end, of the worship (The Old Kingdom) of Ra; by the citizens of Egypt. Karenga saw the second ear of Corn, as restoring, the laws of Maat. The Corn also represents the future, which symbolizes Children.'

Karenga is the Priest, who offers, a new wave offering, of two loaves, made from Corn of Wheat flour; from the Pentecostal Harvest. Unlike the Gentile Bride, coming into the world, speaking lies; Karenga turned it around; by saying, "Kwanzaa and Kawaida are bringing good, into the world."

Kwanzaa – A Made-Up Holiday

By Warren Beatty, Ph.D. - 2014

I found a profound article by Warren Beatty, Ph.D. (not the liberal actor) of American Thinker. He stated, "Did you know that "Kwanzaa," that made-up holiday celebrated from December 26 through January 1, was invented by Ron N. Everett, known today as Dr. Maulana (Swahili for 'master teacher") Karenga? About Kwanzaa, Karenga said: "People think it's African. But it's not. I wanted to give black people a holiday of their own. So, I came up with Kwanzaa. I said it was African because you know black people in this country wouldn't celebrate it if they know it was American. Also, I put it around Christmas because I knew that's when a lot of bloods [blacks] would be partying!"

Now, inventing a holiday is fine, as is celebrating it. But celebrating a so obviously bogus holiday invented by a criminal convicted ... on charges of torturing two women who were members of United Slaves, a black nationalist cult he had founded, is something only liberals can do.

The United Slaves evolved into "Us." From the Us web page (no mention of United Slaves or Karenga's conviction on it) an organization Karenga heads: "…the essential task of our organization Us has been and remains to provide a philosophy, a set of principles and a program which inspire a personal and social practice that not only satisfies humans; but transforms people in the process…"

What philosophy? None can be found on the Us web page, so we look to Karenga's personal philosophy, which is one that closely follows Karl Marx. In 1848, Karl Marx said: "There is only one way in which the murderous death agonies of the old society and the bloody birth throes of the new society can be shortened, simplified and concentrated, and that way is revolutionary terror."

About Marxism and violence, John Molyneux had this to say: "… in the struggle for this new society Marxists do not reject all violence." So, Karenga's philosophy is one of violence. Al Sharpton, where are you on this? You supposedly abhor violence. Are you giving Karenga a pass because both of you were FBI informants? Or is it because you said in 1971 that Kwanzaa "… would perform the valuable service of 'de-whitizing' Christmas."

So, Kwanzaa is a made-up joke of a holiday. But to hear the liberals and the MSM talk about it, you would think that it has deep-rooted meaning. Its seven principles (Nguzo Saba) are themselves quite profound and worthy of attainment, but they are lost in all the fakery of Kwanzaa. One must then ask if the seven principles are themselves fake. But that's just my opinion.

Kwanzaa: An Anachronism

Anachronism is an interesting word. It means, an act of attributing a custom, event, or object to a period, to which, it does not belong. Also, a Professor of History, the Late Arthur Marwick, has argued that "A grasp of the fact, that past societies, are very different, from our own, and … very difficult, to get to know, is an essential and fundamental skill, of the Professional Historian; and that "anachronism," is still, one of the most, obvious faults, when the unqualified, (those experts in other disciplines, perhaps) attempt to do history."

Anachronism, in academic writing, is considered at best, embarrassing, as in early – 20th Century scholarships, use of Translatio Imperii, first formulated in the 12th Century, to interpret 10th Century literature. Genuine errors, will usually, be acknowledged, in a subsequent erratum." In other words, Karenga's writings, about African history, is infected, with "naivety of analysis," or coming down simply, to patriotic polemic.

Kwanzaa Wasn't Created!
It Was Borrowed!

The Nguzo Saba: The Seven Principles were "Borrowed" from, the Symbionese Liberation Army, the pro-Marxist; terror organization that famously kidnapped the heiress, Patricia Hearst in the 1970's or Borrowed from the FBI or got them from Webster's Dictionary. It is also, an attempt by Karenga, to introduce humanistic principles, for improving life, without God.

An example is a quote from the Kwanzaa Information Center website: "The Nguzo Saba (Seven Principles) is Social and Spiritual Principles, dealing with ways for us, to relate to each other and rebuild our lives in our own images. The evidence that Kwanzaa was not Created, but Borrowed will be proven, in the following comparisons. Keep in mind, that we are dealing with symbols, metaphors, and analogies, from the Christian and Jewish perspectives, in the Holy Bible.

The following comparisons will show the Original Symbolic Meanings, in Christianity and Judaism, compared with the Symbolic (Hidden) Meanings in Kwanzaa, written in **BOLD.** I will start with the symbolic, two Ears of Corn; which I described in the previous paragraph entitled: "The (Hidden) Mystery of The Corn." You can refer to the photograph, on the front cover of this book. Let's take, a closer look, at the Corn on the Kwanzaa setting:

The First Ear of Corn, on the Kwanzaa setting, symbolizes Jesus Christ (The Master Teacher & Creator of Everything). The Second Ear of Corn symbolizes, The Holy Ghost (Comforter, Counselor, Power from on High, Third Person in the Godhead, and Teaches the Truth).

The First Ear of Mazao, on the Kwanzaa setting, symbolizes, Maulana Karenga (The Master Teacher & Creator of Kwanzaa). The Second Ear of Mazao symbolizes, Maat (The Goddess of Truth).

The Books, on the Kwanzaa setting, symbolizes, The Word of God\ The Holy Bible and the other books symbolizes Sacred Bible Writings.

The Books, on the Kwanzaa setting, symbolizes, The Sacred Holy Word of God and the other books symbolizes Sacred Writings.

The Books, on the Kwanzaa setting, symbolizes, The Sacred Writing, Kawaida and Questions of Life and Struggle, and the other books symbolizes Sacred Writing.

The Seven Candles, on the Kwanzaa setting, symbolizes, The Ten Commandments, in the Holy Bible. It also symbolizes, The Seven Days of Creation in Christianity.

The Seven Candles on the Kwanzaa setting, symbolizes, The Jewish Holiday, of Hanukkah, which has, Nine Candles in Judaism.

The Mishumaa Saba on the table symbolizes, The Nguzo Saba, The Seven Principles. The colors of the candles: The three red candles symbolize, ancestral blood, the three green ones represent the African Motherland, and the black one positioned, in the center represents, the face of the people.

The Candle Holder, on the Kwanzaa setting, symbolizes, The Ark of The Covenant\Temple of God, housing the Sacred Ten Commandments, in Christianity. It also symbolizes the foundation of the Sacred Scriptures.

The Candle Holder, on the Kwanzaa setting, symbolizes, The Menorah, in The Jewish Holiday of Hanukkah in Judaism.

The Kinara on the Kwanzaa setting, holding the Candles, symbolizes The Temple, Organization Us, housing, The Seven Principles.

The Fruit, and the Woven Basket, on the Kwanzaa setting, symbolizes, Jesus Christ became the Firstfruit of them that slept. The Firstfruit, of God's harvest, of souls, into The Kingdom of God. The Fruit also symbolizes, The Fruit of The Spirit, in the Word of God\Holy Bible.

The Fruit, and the Woven Basket, on the Kwanzaa setting, symbolizes, The Firstfruit, of Zion in Judaism. It also symbolizes, the foundation, of the Sacred Scriptures.

The Fruit, on the Kwanzaa setting, symbolizes The Firstfruit of Harvest, in Kwanzaa. It also symbolizes, the historical roots, of the holiday, as a celebration of the harvest.

The Communion Cup, on the Kwanzaa setting, symbolizes, The Supernatural, Holy Communion Ceremony. It symbolizes, The Victory of The Crucifixion\Cross. It also symbolizes Healing, and Forgiveness; according to, The New Covenant\The New Testament, of God's Grace.

The Kikombe cha Umoja, on the Kwanzaa setting, symbolizes The Communion with Ra (god), and Witchcraft Liberations, of Worshiping Dead Ancestors.

The Woven Mat on the Kwanzaa setting symbolizes, Israel\Jerusalem, The Holy Land for Judaism and Christianity.

The Mkeka, on the Kwanzaa setting, symbolizes, The Mother Land, Egypt\Africa.

The Celebration of Christmas, on the 25th Day of December, symbolizes, the Immaculate Conception\Birth of Jesus Christ. "The New Kingdom of God" symbolizes The New Testament of Forgiveness and Grace.

The Celebration of Hanukkah and The Lighting of The Candles; takes place over eight days; from the 25th Day (at sunset - 19 days) of December until January 1st (at nightfall). Each day, shortly before Sunset, they light candles, which usher in peace and blessing to their homes, and to the world. There is a ninth candle, called the "Shamash" or "Servant" candle, which is used to light the other candles.

The Celebration of Kwanzaa, on the 26th Day of December, until the 1st Day of January, symbolizes Ra (god), and "The Old Kingdom of Ra, being restored. It also symbolizes, The Seven Days of Kwanzaa. Each day, a candle is lit for each Principle.

A Jewish Man on a Cross, worn around the neck, symbolizes, what The Creator, Jesus Christ, did for All Mankind, in the Victory of the Crucifixion/Cross.

An African Man's Face\Demon, called a Talisman, worn around the neck, symbolizes what The Creator, Maulana Karenga, did for His people. It also, symbolizes, protection, from evil spirits.

The Many Falsehoods of Kwanzaa

By Steven Hutson - 2002

During my research, I discovered an excellent article by Steven Hutson of Grace Centered Online Christian Magazine. He stated, "In recent years, Kwanzaa has gained traction in the popular media as an occasion for family gatherings. It's rooted in the seven principles of unity, self-determination, collective work and responsibility, cooperative economics, purpose, creativity, and faith. Hallmark sells Kwanzaa-themed greeting cards that emphasize these principles, conveying a message of dignity and empowerment to an oppressed people.

At least, that's the popular account that most people hear. Even the reputable textbook publisher Prentice-Hall fell for the hoax when they added this sanitized version of the Kwanzaa story to their high school history text The American Nation.

Peruse the Official Kwanzaa Website, and it praised the "values of African culture." But what is that, exactly? Could it be that the nations of Africa constitute a single monolithic civilization with a shared culture and traditions? For any serious student of history, this sweeping generalization should pose major problems.

I wonder, has anyone ever dared to make such claims about the countries of Europe? Do they sing "God Save the Queen" in the opera houses of Lisbon, or can you order bratwurst at the cafes on the Champs-Elysees? I don't think so.

So exactly what aspect of Kwanzaa is distinctly African, that it should hold special significance for Americans descended from the continent? Hard to say. Everett calls it a "pan-African" holiday. Not quite. Large-scale observances there are rare. In many isolated tribal areas, the people don't even know or care who their national leaders are. I have a friend, who served as a missionary in Nigeria for many years, and by her account, every Nigerian only laughs at the notion; will they really set aside their centuries-old traditions and embrace a new holiday brought by a foreigner?

He's misinformed: The Christian faith thrived in Africa long before it became a major force in Europe. John Mark (author of the second Gospel) established a congregation in Alexandria in the first century, and some of our greatest theologians (Augustine, Clement, Irenaeus, and Athanasius) served as leaders of African churches in the first few centuries. The Islamic invaders (and their forced conversions) didn't arrive until the seventh.

And then there's the date, in late December. Surely it must have some significance in African history or culture. The birth of a king, the founding of a nation, a military victory over an invading army? Such, after all, is the stuff of national holidays. Well, how 'bout it? Not even close.

Interestingly this holiday seems to be indistinguishable from the personality of Dr. Everett. It is described as an enterprise of the National Association of Kawaida (African culture) Organizations, and its official publications are produced by the University of Sankore Press. This might sound impressive until we consider that both of those organizations were established by (and continue to be headed by) Everett. Plus, the publishing company is named for an institution that doesn't exist.

Ultimately the tragedy of Kwanzaa, or the Black Nationalism, is that they will never achieve the ends that they seek. No one has ever empowered a downtrodden people by inventing a false heritage for them. No society has ever advanced itself by embracing a self-identity based on eternal victimhood. And will they ever reconcile with the White population of our nation? Their fiery rhetoric and exclusivist teachings seem to imply that they don't even desire to try. Their loss."

Perspective: Why I Quit Kwanzaa
By Robbyn Mitchell - 2015

I discovered an interesting and fresh perspective, written by Robbyn Mitchell, Staff Writer of The Tampa Bay Times. She stated, "It was just a small Baptist church on a nondescript corner of Washington, D.C., but every year after Christmas it could have very well been another country. Folks called out to one another "Habari Gani!" and strutted through the doors in their best Kente suits.

Kwanzaa felt special then. Early '90s black culture was rife with African iconography. In 2015, I cannot remember the last time the holiday held any personal importance. Speaking Swahili and wearing dashikis looked cool as a child, but now it's hard not to see it as a grasp at straws – an annual love letter to a continent that hasn't ever written us back. Black Americans are aware of their African ancestry in the universal sense. But trying to find a person whose forefathers came here in bondage who can also name his or her country of origin is easier said than done.

So, whom does Maulana Karenga's holiday connect us to? Africa is expansive, with many countries, people, and beliefs. There are 1.1 billion people spread across the continent's 54 countries. Who are we as black Americans trying to reach when we preach cooperative economics and self-determination around a row of red, black and green candles?

It's a relic of time when black power fists got Olympic champions sent home and not a T-shirt design; when wearing your hair how it grew out of your head was a political statement and not the latest fashion trend. Karenga, a professor of African studies, sought to create a holiday that would not only give black America a distinct celebration but push forward an agenda of advancement through separatism and reliance on working together to overcome overt oppression.

In a word, Kwanzaa became unnecessary. What part of drumming and African dance spoke to the black experience in America? For 200 years, an estimated 20 million Africans were transported from their homelands, 400 at a time, in cramped ships via the Middle Passage to be slaves in the Americas. Nearly half died during the journey. How did writing poems and crafting little pictures in pan-African colors generate more pride in people who might never set foot on that supposed motherland? African immigrants in my hometown were quick to remind us that they were the real African-Americans – a different class of people distinguished by different values, languages, and culture than black Americans.

The Law of First Mention

I remember the time, when Pastor Edward L. Haygood, Ph.D., Founder and Senior Pastor of Agape Christian Fellowship, in Los Angeles; was teaching his congregation, about the importance of 'The Law of First Mention;' as it pertains to the interpretation of Bible Scriptures. Dr. Haygood's teaching proved to be profound; in the writing of this book.

Let's look at the definition of The Law of First Mention: Anytime, that you see an original word, being used anywhere, that original word, is recorded and becomes, the best way to understand, the context and environment, from which, the word, was originally used. It sets a precedent, for anytime, the word is used. From then on, whenever they use, that same word, they may enlarge, upon it, for another situation, but, the way it was, FIRST used, was always, an important foundation. The Law of First Mention can help us, to understand, a point that a later writer might be trying to make.

The Law of First Mention; as it pertains to political terms, can best be described, as 'Vetting.' Vetting is the process, whereby, one investigates (someone) thoroughly, especially, to ensure that, they are suitable for a job, requiring secrecy, loyalty, or trustworthiness.

Let's take a close look at **(just a few examples for the sake of space)** The Law of First Mention; as it pertains to Kwanzaa. You will see when the Truth ended, and the Lying began. You will also see the Lies growing and growing and growing!

- 1966: I created Kwanzaa. People think it's African. But it's not. I wanted to give Black people a holiday of their own. So, I came up with Kwanzaa. I said it was African because, you know Black people, in this country, wouldn't celebrate it if they knew, it was American. Also, I put it around Christmas because I knew that's when a lot of bloods (Blacks) would be partying!" Ron Karenga **{FIRST MENTION}**

- 1968-1969: Karenga told me in the interview that I had with him when I joined US Organization, that he created Kwanzaa as an alternative to Christianity, The Ten Commandments, and Christmas; the White man's religion. Barbara A. De Loach **{FIRST MENTION}**

- 1966 - 2000: Kwanzaa was created, to be an "alternative to Christmas." Christianity was seen by, US Organization, at the time, as the handmaiden, of a pathological, Negro identity and a reconstructed, Black Nationalist consciousness: "Christianity is a White religion," Karenga stated. "It has a White God, and any Negro who believes in it is a sick Negro. How can you pray to a White man? If you believe in him, no wonder you catch so much hell. If we ask people, not to celebrate Christmas, then we must be prepared, to give them, an alternative, so we did." Ron Karenga **{FIRST MENTION}**

- 1978 "I created Kwanzaa. People think it's African. But it's not. I wanted to give Black people a holiday of their own. So, I came up with Kwanzaa. I said it was African because you know Black people in this country wouldn't celebrate it if they knew it was American. Also, I put it around

Christmas because I knew that's when a lot of bloods (Blacks) would be partying!" Hollie West, The Washington Post **{FIRST MENTION}**

- 2002: "Karenga wanted to design an alternative to Christmas for American Blacks. BigEye.com **{FIRST MENTION}**

- 2002: Why Was Kwanzaa Created? Kwanzaa was created: To reaffirm the communitarian vision and values of African culture and to contribute to its restoration among African peoples in the Diaspora, beginning with Africans in America and expanding to include the world African community. Kwanzaa: A Celebration of Family, Community, and Culture, Ron Karenga, Sankore Press, L.A., California. (Page 113).

- 2003: Kwanzaa was created in the midst of our struggles for liberation in the 1960s and was part of our organization US at first to create, re-create any and certainly African culture as an aid to building community, and enriching Black consciousness, and reaffirming the value of cultural grounding for life and struggle. Ron Karenga, The L.A. Sentinel Newspaper.

- 2014: "Celebrating Kwanzaa: Practicing Principles and Creating Good in the World" - "This seven-day holiday takes its name from the Swahili phrase matunda ya kwanza which means "first fruits," revealing the holiday's roots, in the first harvest celebrations of Ancient Africa, such as pert-en Min in Ancient Egypt, Umkhosi in Zululand, Odwira in Ashantiland and Odu liesu in Yorubaland

- The Kwanzaa celebration, thus, brings a central message of producing, harvesting and sharing good in the World, and as an agricultural celebration, it is earth-conscious and world-encompassing.

- In Addition to its roots, in ancient, African harvest, celebrations and culture, Kwanzaa also, has modern origins, in The

Black Freedom Movement in the 1960's." Ron Karenga, L.A. Watts Times.

- 2015: Kwanzaa is a historical record of Black people's tradition and social ethics, and culture. Kwanzaa: A Celebration of Family, Community and Culture, Ron Karenga, Sankore Press, L.A., California.

- 2016: Karenga said, "After all, Kwanzaa was born in struggle, in the midst, of The Black Freedom Movement. And it was, and remains, an act of, freedom and a celebration of freedom, the culturally grounded and empowering practice of self-determination, in the elevation, advancement, and liberation of our people." The L.A. Sentinel Newspaper.

- 2016: "I created Kwanzaa as an intellectual product and cultural practice, a tradition born of study, legacy, and struggle." Ron Karenga, L.A. Sentinel Newspaper.

- 2016: According to the Official Kwanzaa Website — as opposed, say to the Hallmark Cards Kwanzaa Site – "this celebration was designed to foster conditions that would enhance the revolutionary social change for the masses of Black Americans and provide a "re-assassinate, reclaiming, recommitment, remembrance, retrieval, resumption, resurrection, and rejuvenation of those principles (Way of Life) utilized by Black American ancestors." The Jewish World Review.

- 1966: The extra 'a' was added, Karenga has said, "simply to accommodate seven children at the first-ever Kwanzaa celebration in 1966, each of whom wanted to represent a letter." {FIRST MENTION}

- 1997: Dr. Karenga said, "He added the extra 'a' to give the word greater significance, according to the book, written by, Dolores Johnson, entitled, The Children's Book of Kwanzaa, (How Did Kwanzaa Begin? Pg. 10).

- 2003: A second 'a' was added to the end of the original spelling by, Karenga to distinguish the Afro-American celebration from the African one, according to The Book of American Traditions, By Emyl Jenkins.

Did you see the progression of his Lying? He even Lied about the extra 'a' - something as small as an 'a' - which didn't make any sense. The Lie Got Bigger, and Bigger, and Bigger! Karenga has taken Lying to a whole new level! This causes one to pause; to take a close look, at the description of a Sociopath.

The Definition of A Sociopath: Sociopaths are marked by an artificially enlarged self-concept, notes Cooper-White. They feel entitlement and are extremely narcissistic. When things go wrong they tend to blame, the people around them instead of taking responsibility for the situation. They also lack the inner sense of emotion that most people develop which means, they do not have a sensitivity for the inner emotional loves of others. This keeps them from being able to feel, let alone express empathy.

Sociopaths also tend to lie, but the most puzzling part is, the lies do not always serve any particular purpose, reports Cooper-White. In some cases, they just lie, to see if they can get away with it, or deceive people.

Sometimes, they use the lies to manipulate other people. When they are caught though, they do not show any sense of remorse. This may also explain why sociopaths have the ability to keep an extreme calm when in the middle of a frightening or perilous situation.

I'm just saying ...

CHAPTER 5

Kawaida (Revolutionary): A 'New' Black Value System (Philosophy) & The Black Arts Movement <u>Fighting For US, Maulana Karenga The US Organization, And Black Cultural Nationalism</u>

By Scot Brown- 2005

According to how Karenga explains things, he makes it sound like Kawaida came before Kwanzaa. For example, he states, "Maat is the basis for Kawaida, which is the basis, for Kwanzaa. When I was a member of US Organization, from 1968 – 1969, Kawaida had not been created. There was only Kwanzaa, at that time.

I never heard of Kawaida until 1992, when I looked up Kwanzaa on the internet; after my friend sent me that Kwanzaa card in the mail. Later, I bought and perused his book, entitled, Kawaida And Questions of Life And Struggle; it was published in 2008. I found it to be a pathetic book of commentaries.

Kwanzaa: The Holiday Given By The FBI

By Ann Coulter - 2016

While researching, I found an interesting article, by Ann Coulter, Author of, In Trump We Trust. She stated, "When Karenga, was asked to distinguish Kawaida, the underlying philosophy of Kwanzaa from, "Classical Marxism," he essentially said, that under Kawaida, we also hate Whites."

Kawaida: James Mtume & Jazz <u>Fighting For US, Maulana Karenga</u> <u>The US Organization, And Black</u> <u>Cultural Nationalism</u>

By Scot Brown - 2005

While the US/Panther conflict subverted the efficacy of the Taifa Dance Troupe, it helped catapult the organization's brief, but nonetheless significant, influence on several key jazz musicians and their works. The seeds for this development were planted before the deadly events of, January 1969 took place. James Mtume, who had become an US advocate in 1966, along with a group of fellow students from Pasadena City College, is the son of renowned jazz saxophonist Jimmy Heath and was raised by James "Hengates" Forman, a jazz pianist, and his mother, Bertha Forman, a jazz enthusiast.

As an US advocate in the late 1960s, Mtume embraced the group mandate of spreading Kawaida by influencing others to accept the doctrine. His personal acquaintance with many jazz musicians, because of his family background, offered opportunities to introduce them to his cultural-nationalist philosophy. "When jazz groups would come and perform at Shelly's Manhole or The Lighthouse [jazz clubs in Los Angeles], Mtume recalled, "I would go out and talk to them."

Sometime in 1968, Mtume began to have a major impact on the Herbie Hancock sextet in which his uncle Albert Heath was the drummer. These musicians' interest in US's ideology was further extended when they decided to take on Kiswahili names that Mtume provided for them."

The Rodney King Beating:
The Mtume Beating <u>Fighting For US,</u>
<u>Maulana Karenga The US Organization,</u>
<u>And Black Cultural Nationalism</u>

By Scot Brown - 2005

James Mtume was among a group of Saidi who had left the organization to join forces with the CFUN in Newark – in the hope that they could continue their cultural-nationalist mission there.

Earlier in 1969, "Mtume wrote all of the songs on an album called, Kawaida, except for one. The jazz group also wrote an album called, "Maulana" which by the time of this recording session, in December 1969, Mtume had already departed from US and had been assaulted, by a group of his former comrades!"

Brown further stated, "He had serious doubts about the quality and conduct of US's leadership during this period of strife. Nevertheless, the song ends with his voice humbly giving thanks to the Master Teacher, Maulana." This gesture, Mtume said, "Was my way of saying thank you for some very positive things that were given." By this point, he had shed, his exaggerated reverence for Maulana, and begun to "separate the principles from the person. That to me was my farewell."

Karenga has long ago proven that he is a person; which cannot be trusted. He has no loyalty or respect for anyone that disagrees with his evil plans. The Late, Dr. Myles Monroe, once said, "To educate a man in the mind and not in morals, is to educate a menace to society."

Kawaida Teaches

1) Everyone but the Negro has a God that looks like him.
2) We say life is a circle; you don't know where you came in or where you are going out.
3) Christianity is a White religion. It has a White God, and any Negro who believes in it is a sick Negro. How can you pray to a White man? If you believe in him; no wonder, you catch so much hell.
4) The Christian mind was the only one that created a hell.
5) Jesus was psychotic. He said if you didn't believe what He did, you would burn forever.
6) It never occurred to Christians that "white" wings would look funny on Black bodies.
7) The Christian Negro says loudly "We love everybody" and then under his breath, except Negroes.
8) We build our temples with love, not with stone.
9) Worship should be worship to power and retaining that power.
10) In Africa to be beautiful was to be good. It is both form and feeling that completes beauty.
11) Men who dare to say that they are Gods are men that dare to accept responsibility.
12) I am afraid, whether it hurts or not, that the Negroes sense of religious loyalty of life after death is overshadowed by the desire to keep on living even in the ugliness of this life.

13) We must concern ourselves more with the plans for this life, rather than the next life which has its own problems. For the next life across Jordan is much farther away than the growl of dogs and policemen and the pains of hunger and disease.

14) Christians do good because they feared; we do good because we love. They do good because God says so. We do good irrespective of God.

15) We are God ourselves; therefore, it is not good to be atheistic or agnostic. To be an atheist is to deny our existence and to be an agnostic is to doubt it.

16) Each man is the God of his own house. Therefore, our Gods belong to our homes, not to our temples. We say we have brought God from the sky and put him in our home.

17) The time we spent learning about Jesus, we should have spent learning about Blacks. The money we spend on Church should have been spent on our community, and the respect we gave the Lord should have been given to our parents.

18) Christians say everything has to have a beginning until we get to their God.

19) If you realize how human Jesus was you'd see he was no God.

20) If you can't change, it shows a lack in you and not in the other person. God is God who moves in power; God is God who moves in change and creates something out of nothing. If you want to be God just think about that.

21) We are all Gods of our own house and must strive for perfection.

22) Your house is the house of the Lord and guess who you are?

23) Christianity unconsciously teaches self-hatred.

24) Next thing Christianity deals with is spookism which is a degeneration of spiritualism.

25) Christian people become fatalistic; they don't believe they can change anything.

26) Christianity tells bloods (Black folks) to be non-violent, but Negroes are violent against themselves.

27) They taught us Christianity, so we could be like Jesus — crucified.

28) The more knowledge, wisdom, and understanding a man has the more of God he becomes.

29) God belongs to our home, not our temples.

30) Children are life after death. We could not live in any other way except through children and great works, but then children make our work and everything else worthwhile.

31) Our purpose in life should be to leave the Black community more beautiful than we inherited it.

32) Our morality is not one of guilt but a means of showing how one can improve.

33) A God must be three things: 1) Historical 2) Beneficial 3) And like you.

34) God, is he who moves in power and force.

35) We must carve out of our own being things that speak to us.

36) The Christian is our worst enemy. Quiet as it's kept it was a Christian who enslaved us. Quiet as it's kept it's the Christian that burns us. Quiet as it's kept it's a Christian that beats us down on the street; and Quiet as it's kept, when the thing goes down on the street it'll be a Christian that's shooting us down. You must face the fact that if the Christian is doing all this, there must be something wrong with Christianity.

37) Blacks cannot accept the religion of another people or the mythology of another people and expect that religion's God to defend them.

38) Negros want to be like Jesus; blond hair, blue eyes and pale skin.

39) Jesus said, "My blood will wash you white as snow." Who wants to be white but sick Negroes or worse yet — washed that way by the blood of a dead Jew. You know if Nadinola

bleaching cream couldn't do it, no dead Jew's blood is going to do it.

40) My brother told me Jesus didn't really get crucified, niggers begged him to death.

41) Jesus is as strong as the Negroes concept of him.

On practicing Kawaida: Karenga says, "Save yourself!" He further states, "You are the God of your family. You only need to practice, "Self-determination" and live by the 'Seven Principles' that our ancestors lived by."

Maat
(The Goddess of Truth)

Maat was the ancient Egyptian concept of truth, balance, order, harmony, law, morality, and justice. Maat was also personified as a goddess regulating the stars, seasons, and the actions of both mortals and the deities, who set the order of the universe from chaos to order in creation. Her ideological counterpart was Isfet.

The earliest surviving records indicating that Maat is the norm for nature and society, in this world and the next, were recorded during the Old Kingdom, the earliest substantial surviving examples being found in the Pyramid Texts of Unas (ca.2375 BCE and. 2345 BCE)

After her role in creation and continuously preventing the universe from returning to chaos, her primary role in Egyptian mythology dealt with the weighing of Souls (also called the weighing of the heart) that took place in the Underworld Duat.

Her feather was the measure that determines whether the souls (considered to reside in the heart) of the departed would reach the paradise of afterlife successfully. Pharaohs are often depicted with the emblems of Maat to emphasize their role in upholding the laws of the Creator.

Maat (The Goddess of Truth) 42 Laws

1) I have not committed sin.
2) I have not committed robbery with violence.
3) I have not stolen.
4) I have not slain men or women.
5) I have not stolen food.
6) I have not swindled offerings.
7) I have not stolen from God/Goddess.
8) I have not told lies.
9) I have not carried away food.
10) I have not cursed.
11) I have not closed my ears to truth.
12) I have not committed adultery.
13) I have not made anyone cry.
14) I have not felt sorrow without reason.
15) I have not assaulted anyone.
16) I am not deceitful.
17) I have not stolen anyone's land.
18) I have not been an eavesdropper.
19) I have not falsely accused anyone.
20) I have not been angry without reason.
21) I have not seduced anyone's wife.
22) I have not polluted myself.
23) I have not terrorized anyone.
24) I have not disobeyed the Law.
25) I have not been exclusively angry.
26) I have not cursed God/Goddess.
27) I have not behaved with violence.
28) I have not caused disruption of peace.
29) I have not acted hastily or without thought.
30) I have not overstepped my boundaries of concern.
31) I have not exaggerated my words when speaking.

32) I have not worked evil.

33) I have not used evil thoughts, words or deeds.

34) I have not polluted the water.

35) I have not spoken angrily or arrogantly.

36) I have not cursed anyone in thought, word or deeds.

37) I have not placed myself on a pedestal.

38) I have not stolen what belongs to God/Goddess.

39) I have not stolen from or disrespected the deceased.

40) I have not taken food from a child.

41) I have not acted with insolence.

42) I have not destroyed property belonging to God/Goddess.

Dr. Martin L. King Jr.'s "King" Jesus Christ, The Son of God

Dr. Martin Luther King, Jr.'s journey and vision came from Jesus Christ; the Son of God, for all humanity. Dr. Martin Luther King, Jr., was talking about all people in the World, coming into the unity of the faith in Christ Jesus. Dr. Martin Luther King, Jr., argued that Black Cultural Nationalism contained dangerous connotations of separatism.

Karenga hated Dr. King. Most people forget that Dr. Martin Luther King, Jr. was not just, a Civil Rights Leader. Dr. King was a Christian Pastor; he was a great man of God. Hence, Karenga saw Dr. King, as the enemy! Karenga stated, "Christians are our worst enemy."

Karenga would say, to the young men, in his training classes: "We have come to set a series of precedents, to do what the old men, of the Civil Rights Movement, didn't have will or ability to do!" God's Word Says It Best: "For everyone that doeth evil hated the light, neither cometh to the light, lest his deeds would be reproved. But he that doeth truth cometh to the light that his deeds may be made manifest, that they are wrought in God." (John 3:20-21) KJV.

I remember the time, which Karenga was mocking God and Dr. King, by saying, "Why didn't, Dr. King's White God, save him after he was shot? Why didn't, Dr. King's God raise him, from the dead? I know why He didn't save him; because He didn't know who he was! Dr. King, wasn't White, that's why! A White God serves White people, a Yellow God serves Yellow people, a Brown God serves Brown people, and a Red God serves Red people! We Black people need our own Black God!" <u>God's Word Says It Best</u>: "Be not deceived; God is not mocked: for whatsoever a man soweth, that shall he also reap." (Galatians 6:7) KJV.

What Is Biblical Discernment And Why Is It Important?

In its simplest definition, discernment is nothing more than, the ability, to decide between truth and error, right and wrong. Discernment is the process, of making careful distinctions, in our thinking about truth. In other words, the ability to think, with discernment, is synonymous, with an ability to think Biblically.

First Thessalonians 5:21-22 - Teaches that it is the responsibility, of every Christian, to be discerning: "But, examine everything carefully; hold fast, to that which is good; abstain from every form of evil." The Apostle John issues a similar warning, when he says, "Do not believe every spirit, but test the spirits, to see, whether they are from God; because, many false prophets, have gone out, into the world" (I John 4:1). According to the New Testament, discernment is not optional, for the believer, it is required.

The key, to living an uncompromising life, lies in one's ability, to exercise discernment, in every area of his, or her life. For example, failure to distinguish between truth and error leaves the Christian, subject to all manner, of false teaching. False teaching then leads, to an unbiblical mindset, which results in unfruitful and disobedient living, a certain recipe, for compromise.

Unfortunately, discernment is an area, where most Christians stumble. They exhibit, little ability, to measure, the things they are taught, against the infallible, standard of God's Word; and they unwittingly, engage in all kinds, of unbiblical decision-making and behavior. In short, they are not armed, to take a decidedly, Biblical stand against the onslaught, of unbiblical thinking and attitudes that face them, throughout their day.

Discernment intersects the Christian life, at every point. And, God's Word, provides us with the needed discernment about every issue of life. According to, Peter, God "has granted to us, everything pertaining, to life and godliness, through the true knowledge, of Him who called us, by His Own Glory and excellence." (2 Peter 1:3) You see, it is through, the "true knowledge of Him," that we have been given, everything we need, to live a Christian life, in this fallen world. And, how else, do we have, true knowledge of God, but through the pages, of His Word, the Bible? In fact, Peter goes on to say, that such knowledge, comes through God's granting, "to us, His precious and magnificent promises." (2 Peter 1:4).

Discernment, to think Biblically, about all areas of life – is indispensable, to an uncompromising life. It is, incumbent upon, the Christian, to seize upon the discernment that God has provided, in His precious truth! Without it, Christians, are at risk of being "tossed here and there by waves, and carried about, by every wind of doctrine." (Ephesians 4:14).

CHAPTER 6

MY PERSONAL EXPERIENCES: A FORMER MEMBER OF US ORGANIZATION

The Members of US Organization

Some of the members, I found to be interesting people. For example, Shahidi Hekima, a dear friend while I was a member of US Organization. He held the title, Shahidi, (Protector of The Faith). He was Second Vice-Chairman. Then, there was Tadakiki. She was a pretty woman, with a large natural hair style. She had a gift of fashion design; and was very talented. Tadakiki also had a love for Hispanic music. She liked to talk, as I did. We had a lot of interesting conversations. She was like the younger sister, I never had.

Tadakiki and Charles Massengale-Sigidi had a strong love connection. Sigidi had a brother, named Oliver Massengale-Heshimu. They looked to be about, two to three years apart; with Sigidi being the oldest brother. They both were Tree Trimmers for the City of Los Angeles. Sigidi's love affair with, exotic fish made a profound impact on my life. I became, interested in tropical fish and raising Oscars. I raised them from little babies to full grown fish. I trained one of my

Oscars, named Simba, to jump out of a 100-gallon tank, and eat the goldfish out of my hand!

Heshimu was the reserved one. He and his wife, Staajabu were always, in a world of their own. They seemed to have such a loving and private relationship. I learned from my research, that Heshimu had become a High Priest in the organization, before Karenga went to prison. I'll never forget the sister named, Tasamisha. She was the member that could holler like an African Bush Woman. She sounded like, 'the real deal.' After talking with her at length, about different topics, she impressed me; with her sense of self.

Another thing, which impressed me about Tasamisha; was the way, she treated her boyfriend. She showed him so much respect! Her boyfriend was Amiri (Commander) Jomo. She hung on his every word, as if he were, The President of The United States of America! He had her undivided attention, all the time! And, the best part, about their relationship was; he also treated her with that same level of respect, all the time! They were a joy to be around.

Samuel Carr-Damu was later known, as Ngao (Shield) Damu. He was an, 'ex-army sergeant,' Korean War Veteran. He had lots of influence on the US paramilitary wing, called the Simba Wachunga (young lions). You could always get a friendly conversation with him. Ngao Damu's wife was just the opposite. She was a teacher to the woman in the Organization. She knew her stuff; and presented it well. They were a cool couple; and the eldest in the Organization. Moreover, the members that I met, were always respectful and friendly toward me. There are too many people to mention, that made a positive impact on my life; however, you know who you are.

My overall view of The US Organization Members is this: Each and Every one who played a Character Role in the Synthetic US Organization, deserves to Win An Academy Award for the Best Supporting Actor and Actress to the Leading Man played by Ron Karenga!

The Thriller In Manila (Ali vs. Frazier Fight): Haiba vs. Karenga Fight - 1969

One weekend, I invited Hekima, Haiba, Karenga, and another couple, over to my home for dinner. The dinner was going well, everyone enjoyed the food, and the conversations; except for Haiba and Karenga's conversation was noticeably strained. Karenga wasn't acting like his usual self. He was acting as if, he wasn't in a mood to socialize.

And, Karenga sounded like; he had been drinking or using drugs. When I first joined US Organization, I was told that, members of US Organization, were not supposed to drink alcohol, use drugs or smoke cigarettes. Well, we all were still sitting at the dinner table, talking and laughing, when Haiba leaned over and asked Karenga, could she speak with him for a few minutes? Haiba asked me, if it would be alright, if they went into my bedroom to talk; and I replied, sure it's fine.

After they went into the bedroom, we all continued eating, talking and enjoying the evening. It was almost a good five minutes, of them being in the bedroom, before we heard them arguing! Then, they got a little louder, to the point that we could plainly hear what they were talking about.

Haiba asked Karenga about, the drugs which he was taking. At first, he didn't reply, and then she kept asking him. He finally said, "It wasn't a lot of drugs." Then, she started questioning him, about the reason; he had his Doctor friend's office bombed! Karenga said, "He wouldn't give me any more prescriptions; and I needed them to rest."

Then they kept bumping-up against the door, the wall, and you could hear licks being passed to one another, as they continued to fight! I asked Hekima to go tell them; that I wanted them to go home and fight! And, when Hekima opened the door to tell them; outcomes Karenga!

I felt embarrassed for him. And, I don't know why, I asked him a question. However, I said; how do you feel Maulana? If looks, could kill, I would have been dead for sure! He said, "Tikisa, how does it look like I feel?" I gathered my wits and decided not to answer that loaded question. I didn't want to tell the brother; that he looked **Tore-Up From The Floor-Up!**

This was the first time that I had personally witnessed Haiba and Karenga fighting. However, I did suspect something was going on in their marriage, that didn't make much sense to me. For example, I remember several occasions, when I wouldn't see Haiba at the Soul Sessions for a while; and she would also miss coming to the Afro-American School of Culture on Saturdays, for quite some time. When I inquired about her absence, I was always told that she was tired, and went to the hospital, to get some rest, from the kids and housework.

I personally, would not choose going to a hospital to rest. For example, nurses are in and out of your room all day, and night. You are punished by having to eat their food; not to mention, all the sick people around you, the smell of a hospital, the water is terrible; and lots of germs everywhere! I would rather go to another place, like a resort to rest; and leave going to a hospital to rest, for people who are involved in domestic violence, and mental abuse from their husband.

The UCLA Murders:
US Members - 1969

From the moment, I opened the front door, of my apartment, on January 19, 1969; my whole life changed! I remember, feeling knots in my stomach! My mouth, flew wide-open in shock! Some, US members had broken into my home! They were all over the place! Some were in my kitchen, and in my sons' bedroom, and in the living room! But, more importantly, the two brothers, George and Larry Stiner, were sitting in my living room! One of them was bleeding, from a gun-shot wound! I screamed at them, asking, how did you guys get into my apartment? One of the brothers responded, "We came through the front window."

I asked, what are you doing here? He said, "We received orders, from Maulana to come here; and go through the front window." Then he said, "Tikisa, didn't you hear the news today?" I replied, no I didn't! I've been at work all day! We don't listen to the radio; we work! He said, "Alprentice (Bunchy) Carter, and John Huggins, two members of the Black Panthers were killed today at UCLA." He further said, "We're waiting for them to be picked-up." I remember thinking that, this wasn't the Movement, I thought it was! I could barely gather my thoughts, to ask any more questions.

The reality, of the horrific incident, blew me away! I was overwhelmed by the news. As I sat there, in my kitchen listening; I realized that I had heard enough. I said, (pointing at the two brothers); they just killed two men, and you were ordered by Maulana, to bring them to my house?!! I said, why didn't he order you guys, to take them to his house?!! I jumped up from the table and screamed at everyone, to get the hell out of my house! And, they quickly left. The story was well reported, on television, radio and in the newspapers.

US Meeting:
US Headquarters - 1969

The next day after, the UCLA murders, Karenga called a meeting for all members. I remember going to the meeting, because I wanted to hear what he had to say about this horrific murder. In other words, this was the straw that broke this camel's back. This was a confirmation, that it was past-time to leave US Organization. While I waited, for the meeting to get started, I decided to see what was cooking in the kitchen.

When I got to the entrance door, leading to the kitchen, a Simba (young man) was standing at the door, and stopped me; before I could enter the room. He said, "Tikisa, you have to bow-down to Maulana's picture, before entering into the Kwanzaa Temple."

I responded, what Kwanzaa Temple? He said, "Maulana named this room, our Kwanzaa Temple. And, before entering the Kwanzaa Temple, we must bow-down; to give all praises to Maulana, our Leader." And, when we come before him, we also have to bow-down, to give all praises to our Leader." I told the brother that, I wasn't going to bow-down to no man or his picture!

I returned to the room, where the women were and asked them did they know, about bowing-down to Maulana, and his picture over the door? To my surprise, they said, "Yes, we know." As if it were no big thing! After, a few minutes, a brother came into the room, and announced that, Maulana had to cancel the meeting for today; and it is rescheduled for tomorrow, at his home.

On the next day, Haiba called me, to make sure that I would be attending the meeting at her home. I started to tell her, that I wouldn't be attending the meeting, because I had decided to end my membership in US Organization. Then I changed my mind and decided to make this, the last meeting that I would be attending, before ending my membership. I was curious to hear what Karenga had to say about the murders at UCLA; and bowing-down to him and his picture. [I didn't realize at the time; that inquisitiveness can sometimes lead one into dangerous situations. It was like the old expression: curiosity killed the cat.]

I told her, that I would come. Then she said, "Someone would pick me up in one hour, so that I wouldn't have to drive. She also said, "There will be other sisters that he's picking-up to bring to the meeting." The brother was on time picking me up, and there were three other sisters in the car. We were taken over to Karenga's home in Inglewood.

The Sexual Assault:
Tikisa vs. Karenga - 1969

Again, I should have ended my membership in US Organization, when I first decided to leave, months ago. However, I did not; and the price I paid for being indecisive, cost me 'Big Time!' I thought he was going to talk about the UCLA murders, and the bowing-down to him and his picture, at the meeting. When we arrived at Karenga's home, everyone was eating, drinking refreshments, talking and laughing! There was no meeting! The living room furniture had been completely removed, except for one chair remained in the room; and Karenga was sitting in that chair. There were pillows thrown all around the floor.

The brothers and sisters were sitting, on the front pillows according to their rank in the organization. Sitting behind the highest-ranking men were a few young brothers. Then sitting behind the young brothers, were some of the sisters in the organization. I noticed that Haiba was not in the room. I thought that she was probably in her bedroom. One of the young men, motioned to us, as we entered the room to have a seat on the pillows.

As we sat down, African music started playing real loud from the kid's bedroom. Then a sister, dressed as an Arabian dancer, entered the room! She was smiling at Karenga and focused her eyes; at him throughout the dance. She started moving her body in ways which were shameful. The men in the room were clapping their hands and laughing; to show their enjoyment of the performance. After the dance had ended; the dancer got a big hug from Karenga. Some of the people left right after the dance was over.

A sister was talking with me about Karenga's use of drugs, when a brother tapped me on my shoulder and said, "Tikisa, Haiba wants to talk with you in her bedroom." I got up and went to the bedroom, thinking that Haiba was in the room; so, I didn't suspect anything was wrong, when I knocked on the bedroom door. The door opened, and I walked in. Karenga shut the door behind me and locked it! That's when I saw that Haiba was not in the bedroom. He quickly grabbed my arm and threw me down onto the bed!

He said, "I want you to give me a massage and then we can laugh!" (He calls having sex laughing). I said, no, what are you doing?!! And, then I started yelling for Haiba! We wrestled on the bed, and I was fighting him off of me; and still yelling for Haiba to help me!

We fought and wrestled on the bed, until we fell onto the floor! That's when I had the presence of mind; to use the Karate that I had learned. So, I jabbed him hard in his eyes; then I hit him hard in his jugular with my fist! I jumped-up and kicked him hard in his groin! He balled-up in a knot and started hollering! In other words, **I KICKED HIS BUTT!** I unlocked the door and ran out of the room into the bathroom; and locked the door! Tadakiki and Tasamisha, knocked on the door; and I let them in. They said, "Tikisa, are you alright?" I said, Maulana tried to rape me! I told them, that they were not my friends, because they didn't help me! They said nothing! They just stood there, with their heads hanging down!

I left the bathroom and went into the children's bedroom. I found Haiba sitting on the bed, brushing her little daughter's hair!!! I said to her, I thought you were my friend! She couldn't even, look me in my eyes. She just dropped her head and said nothing! Then, I went up to the Brother that brought me there; and told him to take me home – right now! There were approximately, ten members still in the house; and no one tried to stop Karenga from Sexually Assaulting me! Everyone, in the living room, suddenly paused, when I entered the room; as if someone pushed the pause button. The Brother and I ran out of the house; and got away before Karenga could recover!

The New Rule:
US Organization

The next day around noon, I heard a loud knock on my front door. I opened the door, and there were two brothers from US Organization. One of the brothers said, "Maulana, told us to tell you, that he has made a New Rule in US Organization; to begin immediately.

The New Rule is for all US Members from the Los Angeles and San Diego Headquarters, to sign over your paycheck to him on a weekly basis, or monthly, depending on when you get paid; because, the Revolution needs money.

He also stated, "Maulana said, you are to make a list of all your bills, and he will pay them for you; starting this coming Friday." I told the Brothers, to tell that _____he won't get a dime of my money! I told them to tell Karenga; that I was no longer a member of US Organization! And, I told the Brothers, to never come back, to my home again!

The Rodney King Beating:
The Tikisa Beating

The next morning, I took my sons to the babysitter; and I went to work at L. A. Southwest College. After working eight hours, I went to my evening class on campus. The day was pretty much uneventful. Upon leaving the College, I remembered that I had to get a few things from Kmart; before picking-up my sons from their babysitter's home.

As I was driving to Kmart, a car came alongside my car, and I recognized the two women in the car; as Tamu and Didisi from US Organization. Didisi was waving, to me to pull over. I made a left, into Kmart's parking lot and parked. They drove up next to my car and parked.

Both women jumped out of the car and ran over to my car! Tamu opened the driver's side of my car, and Didisi opened the door, on the passenger's side! I was taken by surprise because I had been close to both women; thus, I thought they were still my friends. These two women were not at Karenga's house when he tried to rape me.

As, a matter of fact, Tamu was a Black Belt in Karate. Didisi was pretty good in Karate; and I was, also pretty good in Karate. Anyways, they pulled me out of the car! I was holding onto the steering wheel, trying to collect my thoughts; that I had to fight both of them!

Tamu and I started fighting! I did pretty good, defending myself, until Didisi jumped into the fight! Didisi started hitting me from behind, and I went forward into Tamu. Then Didisi tripped me, and I fell to the ground!

They started kicking the top of my head, my face, and my sides! They were stomping on my legs and my back! And, they were wearing Biscuits! These shoes were fashionable in the '60s. They had a big hard toe and a tall heel; this kind of shoe never wears out!

Every time, Tamu kicked me, she would tell me, what Karenga told her to say to me. For instance, she said, "Maulana said, the next time he asks you for money; you better give it to him! She said, "Maulana said, the next time you go into the Kwanzaa Temple; you better bow-down to his picture, and you better bow-down to him!"

After, they finished beating me and leaving me for dead; I tried to get up, but I couldn't! Then, I passed out for a while. When I came to myself again, I could not raise my head. I was shocked to realize, that I still couldn't get-up! I didn't have enough strength; and I was in too much pain to get-up. After lying there for a long while, I started to crawl on my knees, a little at a time.

After, what seemed like forever, I finally reached the pay phone booth; on the corner of the parking lot. I slowly pulled myself up; by holding onto the sides of the booth. I dialed the operator and made an emergency phone call to my older sister, Louise. I told her Karenga, had two sisters from US Organization to beat-me-up! I asked her to come and get me; because I couldn't drive my car.

When she got there, I was lying in the parking lot by the phone booth. We discovered they took the car keys. Therefore, I had to leave my car there; until the next day. That same night, Louise took me to the hospital. They kept me for one week! I had brain concussion, bruised ribs, hips, back, my face was black, blue, and swollen! The rest of my body, like my legs, and arms, were also black and blue.

While I was in the hospital, Karenga called me. He said, "Tikisa, everyone sends their love to you." I told Karenga that I was going to report him to the police, for sexually assaulting me; and for ordering the assault & battery by Tamu and Didisi. He said, "If I reported him to the police; then I wouldn't have any more Sons to raise." He said, "Tikisa, I plan on being around for a long time." I told him to go to hell, and hung-up in his face!

That same day, I received a dozen long-stemmed red roses. The card said, "Tikisa, we love you and wish you a speedy recovery! Maulana." I threw the roses in the trash. I was in pain, for a long time. I couldn't go back to work, for quite some time; simply put, I was messed-up. My babysitter kept my Sons; until I could take care of them again. After I recovered, from the beating, I and my Sons moved to another part of Los Angeles. That ended, my membership in US Organization; and I moved on with my life, and never looked back.

The Meeting Again:
Sixteen Years Later
Tikisa – Karenga - 1985

One day, I was visiting with my neighbor, who was a retired English Professor. She introduced me, to her house guests from South Africa. They were exchange students at USC in Los Angeles. We started talking, about some of the recent events in South Africa.

The conversation was fascinating, and after we talked for a while one of the students, asked me if I would like to attend a lecture about

South Africa, with them tonight? I told them, I would love to go. They said the lecture was being held in Los Angeles at a cultural center; and it started at 7 p.m. So, I went home and got ready to go to the lecture. By the time that we arrived, it was dark outside. So, upon arriving we parked down the street from the building. I didn't see the name on the building. We walked through the front door, and there was Karenga, standing in the front of the room; introducing the guest speaker!

I felt like fainting! My knees turned into Jell-O! We found some seats near the middle of the room. I was sitting there staring at Karenga; and Tiamoyo was sitting in the front row. When he saw me, he looked as shocked as I did! My first thought was to get out of there! I didn't want to be anywhere he was. But, then I remembered, I wasn't driving! I had come with the African students.

I was sitting there feeling trapped. So, many thoughts were rushing through my mind; and I started, having flashbacks of the sexual assault and the beating; it was crazy! It must've shown on my face; because the Sister that I came with asked me if I were okay? I said, yes, I'm okay. And, I asked her if she would please; get me a glass of water. She said, "Certainly I'll get you some water."

The lecture finally ended, in about 55 minutes; and they opened, the floor for questions and answers. When the Q&A ended, I quickly got up and started walking to the rear of the building to get out of there. I went over to the table and sat my glass down. When I turned around, Tiamoyo was in my face! She grabbed me and hugged me!

She said, "Tikisa, it's so good to see you!" I didn't say anything. **She said, "Tikisa, I'm an Assistant Professor at California State University, in Long Beach!"** I didn't say anything. Then she said, "I'm Maulana's Assistant! He's the Professor, of the Black Studies Department!" I still didn't say anything.

By this time, Karenga came over and joined us. I didn't say anything. He looked at me, with a sinister grin on his face, and said, "See Tikisa, I told you that I would still be around!" He was bragging!

I didn't say anything. I had nothing to say to Tiamoyo or Karenga; I just didn't want to be in the same room with them!

In retrospect, I think that was an excellent opportunity for Karenga to show some remorse for Sexually Assaulting me, and for Ordering the Assault & Battery against me. I learned from my research, that Karenga has a Ph.D. in Social Ethics. That said, one would think, that his behavior would, certainly show some signs of civility. He didn't surprise me, by not apologizing; because, he wasn't sorry for his violent behavior towards me. Maybe, he doesn't really, have a Ph.D. in Social Ethics; maybe he is lying about that too.

Before, he could say another word, two of the African students, that I came with joined us; and started talking with Karenga. When they started talking with him, I told the African Sister, that I would be waiting for them at the car; and then I left. I stopped, to say hello to Wesley Kabaila; who was standing in the back of the room. We talked, for a few minutes; and then, I went to the car to wait for the students. God's Word Says It Best: "These teachers will tell lies with straight faces and do it so often that their consciences won't even bother them." (1 Timothy 4:22) TLB.

CHAPTER 7

Bonnie & Clyde
Tortured Two Women:
Tiamoyo & Karenga
Tortured Two Women

The Grand Jury: Karenga, Tiamoyo, & Two US Members Charged: Conspiracy & Assault - 1970

Shortly after Karenga Sexually Assaulted me; and Ordered the Assault & Battery on me; and Ordered the Assault & Battery on James Mtume; he turned even more paranoid and dangerous!

In May 1970, Ron Karenga, Luz Maria-Tiamoyo, (Karenga's 2nd Wife) Louis Sedu-Smith, and Fred Sefu-Glover of US Organization, were reported to the LAPD by Deborah Jones, for commenting crimes against herself, and Gail Davis. The Filed Complaint went to a 'Secret' Grand Jury, and they indicted all the persons involved in the crime for Conspiracy & Assault and required them to be put on trial. (See: Black Militant Karenga Held In Torture Case - Newspaper Article)

Let's take a closer look at the Grand Jury: The Grand Jury is a legal body empowered to conduct official proceedings and investigate potential criminal conduct and determine whether criminal charges should be brought. A Grand Jury may compel the production of documents and compel the sworn testimony of witnesses to appear before it. A Grand Jury is separate from the courts, which do not preside over its functioning.

The function of a Grand Jury is to accuse persons who may be guilty of an offense, but the institution is also a shield against unfounded and oppressive prosecution. It is a means for lay citizens, representative of the community, to participate in the administration of justice. It can also make presentments on crime and maladministration in its area. The traditional number of the Grand Jury is 23. No indictment or presentment can be made except by the concurrence of at least twelve of the jurors.

The Grand Jury may accuse upon their knowledge, but it is done upon the testimony of witnesses under oath, and other evidence heard before them.

If the Grand Jury returns an indictment as a true bill, the indictment is said to be founded and the party to stand indicted and required to be put on trial.

Fighting For US, Maulana Karenga, The US Organization, And Black Cultural Nationalism

By Scot Brown - 2005

I again refer, to the interesting book, by Scot Brown. He stated, "In June 1971, Karenga was convicted, of 'Assault-Torture and False-Imprisonment;' and was sentenced to a one-to-ten-year prison term. The charges were that Karenga along with three other US members – Fred Sefu-Glover, Louis Sedu-Smith, and Luz Maria Tiamoyo

(Karenga's 2nd Wife) had subjected Deborah Jones and Gail Idili-Davis to various forms of torture in May 1970.

Glover was convicted, on only the False-Imprisonment charge while the other three co-defendants were found guilty of both charges. Key testimony against the US chairman came from his estranged wife, Brenda (Haiba) Karenga; the former head of US's Simba, George Weusi-Armstrong; and his wife, Carletta Weusi-Armstrong.

During the trial, Karenga's wife testified, that her husband had, come to the conclusion that Idili and Jones, were engaging in an assassination plot, to poison and drug him, and he, therefore, ordered as well as; participated in their beating and torture.

The goal was, to get information, from them about the location, of "pills" and "crystals" that were present in his food, and drinks. Jones, also testified, that she and Idili, were held captive, at Karenga's residence, in May 1970, beaten and tortured, with a water hose, soldering iron, and caustic chemicals. Gail Idili-Davis did not testify at the trial."

Professor Brown, further stated, "Gail Idili-Davis's recollections, corroborate much, of the testimony at the trial. Her silence at the time of the trial, she stated, was a response to a US ultimatum, threatening violent retaliation, against her and family members. She found solace, in the fact that Jones' testimony – along with that, of others succeeded, in convicting Karenga.

While Idili, also believed, that the organization had been infiltrated, during the course of a government campaign to destroy US. She noted that Karenga's own destructive response, to this pressure, brought about a terribly horrific ordeal.

She recalled that Karenga, succumbing to paranoia and drug abuse, accused her and Jones of being agents. As she remembered, the events, Karenga ordered, and directed others, at the Sun House, to brutally torture the two of them, in an attempt to extract nonexistent information.

That's how the torture started, because he was, trying to get me to talk; who sent me. I'm naïve, and I'm saying, 'I don't know, what he's talking about.' All I know is that he's tripping." After barely escaping, with her life, Idili sought refuge among family members, in the Bay Area.

On Dr. Maulana Karenga: An Open Letter

By Wesley Kabaila - 2010

Greetings,

For those who don't know me, my name is Wesley Kabaila, and have been an advocate of Kawaida since 1967, a member of the Us Organization from 1967-1985, and served as its Vice Chair from 1979-1985. During the years that I served in the Us Organization, I was trained as a Simba Wachanga, (young men) our defense and security arm. During 1979-1985, I also served as Chair of the Simba Wachanga, (young men). Lastly, I went through a 3-year training period to become a Sebati, a student-priest in the Maatian tradition.

During my entire tenure in Us, I was often assigned to Dr. Karenga's personal security. I state the above as qualification, for what I'm about to write. I write the following in the spirit of Maat, and the truth embodied in it. I also write it as a matter of corrective history that has too long endured as lies.

I too, applaud Geronimo Pratt for his forthrightness and honesty in speaking truth about the Us Organization being an equal victim of Cointelpro and dispelling the lies about any of its leadership being complicit with police agencies in any way. I wish to be unambiguous and state clearly, that it is my belief and knowledge, that no one in the inner circle of the Us Organization were agents.

I feel, however, that it is equally important, that Dr. Karenga be open and honest about the demise of the Us Organization, 1969-1971. For too long now, he has incorrectly asserted that members of the organization left him and that his jail time was served for "trumped-up" charges. It is my opinion that one of the reasons it remains believable that Dr. Karenga is a police agent in some circles, is because he has been dishonest about his involvement in the torture of two sisters, for which he served four years and his current wife, Tiamoyo served a stint also.

I wish to state here, unequivocally, that he and his wife not only tortured these two sisters for a period of over three weeks but also directed two young brothers in the torture also. Prior to this period of torture, he also locked up his first wife, Haiba, in a tiger cage that was housed in the garage of a home he leased in Inglewood, California.

Dr. Karenga also hit on wives of some of his closest confidantes, and I personally know of one sister, who is writing a book, in which she asserts that he attempted to rape her. Now, those of us who still proclaim to be Kawaida advocates can say that the pressures of Cointelpro, the US\Panther conflict all contributed to this abhorrent behavior. But the fact is, there was evidence of this kind of behavior long before the UCLA shooting, January 19, 1969. In fact, there are those I've talked to personally, that state this behavior started in the Afro-American Association which pre-dated the Us Organization of 1965; when then Ron Karenga had an affair with his Vice Chair's wife. At that time, his Vice Chair was Ahyum Palmer, who later became President of Marcus Garvey School, here in L.A.

Many will ask, why raise these issues now. For one, the truth of Maat demands it. Second, there are lessons about leadership that we should and must pass on to the next generation, and most of all, there are victims who still need to be apologized to and atonement done by the victimizer.

I had never heard of atonement before the Million Man March, for which Dr. Karenga authored the Mission Statement, which admonished Black men to atone for their past treatment of our women. My respect for Minister Farrakhan was greatly enhanced when he took responsibility for his role in creating the atmosphere for the assassination of Malcolm.

How could he ask us, as Black men, to atone if he did not? The same principle applies to Dr. Karenga. My question is, how can Dr. Karenga continue to call himself a High Priest of Maat or Master Teacher, when the very principles he writes about, seemingly do not apply to him?

In sum, I challenge those of us who still consider ourselves Kawaida advocates, to demand from Dr. Karenga an apology for the continued lying, which has affected the credibility of those of us who have defended him.

But even more than that, he owes an apology and release to the sister tortured and to her family, which was threatened, if she broke silence about her true torturer. If we, who consider ourselves revolutionary, do not check and challenge this kind of behavior, then our revolution is not even worth fighting for.

I respect and recognize Dr. Karenga, for his theoretical and practical contributions to our struggle, but that does not excuse his torture tactics of young Black woman, lying about it to his followers or the masses, and the continuing cover-up of it, although he has already been convicted and served the time.

Before writing this, I had to ask myself, what have I been fighting for, all of my life, if not to become a better African. I learned much of what I know about becoming a better African under the tutelage of Dr. Karenga, and feel it is my responsibility to hold him to the same standard and principles that he writes about for us.

I have spent all of my adult life as an Advocate of Kawaida and cultural nationalist, but not to see it all reduced to lies and miss-truths. We deserve more as a people, community and as comrades in struggle for a higher level of life and humanity. I challenge those who disagree with me, to state why we should demand less.

In Unity and Struggle,
Wesley Kabaila
Los Angeles Posted 9th July 2010

Comments:
On Dr. Maulana Karenga: An Open Letter

By Wesley Kabaila - 2010

Starting at: "… and that his jail time was served for "trumped-up" charges."

Comment: Karenga showed everyone that he has no integrity and no remorse for his crimes. He still tells lies, about his involvement, in the torture of the two sisters, instead of owning up to the error of his ways, by telling the truth. His current wife, Tiamoyo, served a stint in prison also.

Karenga said, "The Nguzo Saba, is a vital source of principles and practices to bring, increase and sustain good in the world." He further stated, "Indeed, the Seven Principles represent values and vital teachings of our ancestors, about how we are to live good lives, rightfully relate to each other and the world." So, what happened Karenga? Why didn't the Seven Principles work in your own life?

Starting at: "I wish to state here, unequivocally, that he and his wife not only tortured these two sisters for over three weeks but also directed two young brothers in the torture also."

Comment: My God! I thought the sisters were tortured for two days. But, Kabaila said that it was three weeks or more! Plus, the fact that Karenga was teaching the two young brothers, a lesson on how to successfully, torture your sisters, by using the Fourth Principle of Ujamaa (Collective Work and Responsibility).

Starting at: "Prior to this period of torture, he also locked-up his first wife, Haiba, in a tiger cage that was housed in the garage of a home he leased in Inglewood, California."

Comment: A Tiger Cage! Oh, my God! How crazy was that?! My heart hurts for her. I remember how sweet her spirit was. She was a good mother, to their children. Karenga is the one, who should be locked-up in a Tiger Cage!

The Seven Principles didn't work for Karenga's life; thus, it will not work in other people's lives; and especially our children's lives! To assist you to make the connection, and to bring more clarity to Karenga's devious mindset; I must tell you that, Karenga has a strong fascination with circuses; hence, the 'Tiger Cage.' I will be discussing the 'P.T. Barnum Concept,' further in Chapter 13. The Principle, Kuumba (Creativity) was evil and vicious!

Starting at: "I personally know of one sister, who is writing a book in which she asserts that he attempted to rape her."

Comment: Kabaila is talking about me. I love to see The Holy Spirit's timing unfold; He brought Kabaila and me across each other's paths at a store in Inglewood, at the same time! We had not seen one another in fifteen years; since I saw him, at the lecture with the African students in 1985. We stood, in the parking lot, and talked for over an hour. Another, Divine Appointment, arranged by The Holy Spirit.

Starting at: "Many will ask, why raise these issues now. For one, the truth of Maat demands it."

Comment: So, I wonder, what would Maat say, about Karenga's display of Kwanzaa's Seven Principles? I know, she would have been, pretty upset with Karenga; because he broke, over 22 of the 42 Laws of Maat!

Starting at: "Second, there are lessons about leadership that we should and must pass on to the next generation."

Comment: God Forbid! I don't want, this type of leadership, passed on to anyone, especially the next generation! Now, let's see, which one of The Seven Principles fits? Nia (Purpose) of course! Karenga says, "Nia speaks to us, of our collective vocation, to do good, in the world, and to restore our people to their traditional greatness; defined by this ongoing creation, and pursuit of the good." **Hogwash!**

Starting at: "And most of all, there are victims who still need to be apologized to and atonement done by the victimizer."

Comment: I don't need, nor do I desire an apology from Karenga. I have forgiven him, for the sexual assault, and for the assault & battery that he ordered. I have also, forgiven the two turncoats, Tamu and Didisi, because they were also victims, of Karenga's brainwashing. God's Word Says It Best: "Father, forgive these people, Jesus said, for they don't know what they are doing..." (Luke 23:34) TLB.

Starting at: "How could he ask us, as Black men, to atone if he did not. The same principle applies to Dr. Karenga. My question is, how can Dr. Karenga continue to call himself a High Priest of Maat or Master Teacher, when the very principles he writes about, seemingly do not apply to him."

Comment: Simple. He is the creator, and everyone who celebrates or practices Kwanzaa, are his people, or his followers, of his African Religion. It's like; he is above the law kind of thing. He believes that he is a 'god' of some sorts, and therefore, he can do what he pleases; but, everybody else must obey 'The Seven Principles!'

I believe, that Karenga's feelings were deeply hurt and damaged, based on Karenga's experience with Jesus Christ, as a child. His father, being a Baptist Minister, and having 13 other siblings, to share his Father with, plus his Mother; could have caused him, to have anger toward Jesus Christ.

Maybe his Father spent a lot of time, taking care of Church business, thereby, less time with him. And, the anger turned into resentment, then into hatred, hence; the hatred caused his 'Heart' to become 'Hardened,' toward Jesus Christ. Someone once said, "A hard heart, can be a dangerous weapon."

Something happened to Karenga; to make him, have such a horrific hatred, and anger toward Jesus Christ, White people and Jewish people. It reminds me of the adage, "The religion of a child, shapes the belief of a man."

Starting at: "Before writing this, I had to ask myself, what have I been fighting for all of my life, if not to become a better African."

Comment: Please, don't allow Karenga, to lead you straight to hell; because that is where you and he will end up, if you both continue, to reject Jesus Christ as Lord! Karenga is a "Wolf in Sheep's Clothing," and a "Black Blind Bully" leading the "Blind." All his Celebrants, who practice Kwanzaa, will go straight to Hell with Karenga; where Satan, wants everybody to spend Eternity in Hell with him, and his Demons! You need to move on, to a better way of life, without Karenga in it!

Starting at: "I learned much of what I know about becoming a better African under the tutelage of Dr. Karenga, and feel it is my responsibility to hold him to the same standard and principles that he writes about for us. I have spent all of my adult life as an Advocate of Kawaida and cultural nationalist, but not to see it all reduced to lies and miss-truths. We deserve more as a people, community and as comrades in struggle for a higher level of life and humanity."

Comment: Kabaila, how are you going to hold Karenga to

something that doesn't work? The Seven Principles of Kwanzaa didn't work for him, and they aren't going to work for you either. Everything, which he has taught you, were lies and miss-truths (which is still a lie).

Karenga can't give you something, that he doesn't have. For example, integrity, honesty, good morals, truth, good leadership and compassion for people! You have given, almost 20 years, of your adult life and for that; he gives you back Lies! I think you have been short-changed, "Big Time!"

Karenga is a grown man, so how can you hold him responsible, when he doesn't even hold, himself responsible, for ruining other people's lives! <u>God's Word Says It Best</u>: "In this way, we are like the various parts of a human body. Each part gets its meaning from the body as a whole, not the other way around. The body we're talking about is Christ's body of chosen people. Each of us finds our meaning and function as a part of His body. But as a chopped-off finger or cut-off toe, we wouldn't amount to much, would we? So, since we find ourselves fashioned into all these excellently formed and marvelously functioning parts in Christ's body, let's just go ahead and be what we were made to be, without enviously or pridefully comparing ourselves with each other, or trying to be something we aren't." (Romans 12:4-5) MSG.

Starting at: "I challenge those who disagree with me, to state why we should demand less."

Comment: Kabaila, I accept your challenge; although, I'm not an advocate of Kawaida. First, let me express to you, that I do understand the pain, you have in your heart. I know from, one year of membership in US Organization; I had the honor and pleasure, of meeting you. You were always, respectful to everyone; you are a good man, with a good heart. You are one of the members that were serious about your desire to serve the community, to help make things better, anyway that you could.

Karenga, not only lied to members of US Organization, but he lied to everyone around the Globe, via the Internet, public speeches, newspaper articles, university students and his books; about his phony holiday. He has a depraved mindset; and an immoral character. Second, The Black Cultural Revolution was only a reality in Karenga's head. It offers no solid foundation; for one to build their life on.

In conclusion, I hope that you don't demand anything from Karenga. Remember, all he has to give you are LIES and as you call it, MISS-TRUTHS! God's Word Says It Best: "Since they didn't bother to acknowledge God, God quit bothering them and let them run loose. And then all hell broke loose: rampant evil, grabbing and grasping, vicious backstabbing. They made life hell on earth with their envy, wanton killing, bickering, and cheating. Look at them: mean-spirited, venomous, fork-tongued God-bashers, bullies, swaggers, insufferable windbags! They keep inventing new ways of wrecking lives. They ditched their parents when they got in the way. Stupid, slimy, cruel, cold-blooded. And it's not as if they don't know better. They know perfectly well they're spitting in God's face. And they don't care – worse; they hand out prizes to those who do the worst best!" (Romans 1:28-32) MSG. And, because of God's unconditional love, and compassion, I'm praying for you, and your family's salvation, before it's too late. That said, I salute you!

It's The Principle of The Thing!

At this juncture, I would like to address, the fact that, Karenga did the crime, and has done the time. So, why am I talking about his prison time in the 70's? Because every time, that he opens his mouth, out comes a lie!

As a matter of fact, Karenga got out of prison early. Okay, why didn't he just, move on and be thankful? He knows, that justice prevailed; but, he wants to try and re-write history, as it were; by telling more lies! He says, "He was a political prisoner!" He states, "The charges against him were "trumped-up!" He states, "He was the victim!" Negro please! Just be honest!

Every year, when he writes his column in the L.A. Sentinel Newspaper, he goes back to the 60's. He is still trying to re-name, The Black Power Movement, by calling it, "The Freedom Movement." Another attempt to re-write history. In one of his articles, he stated, "… In spite of challenges, that destroyed other less durable, contemporary groups, in the Movement, in the 60's, US Organization survived." Everybody knows that he is talking about the Black Panther Party. However, he never mentions that; he was a part of the reason it didn't survive! He never mentions that; he was working with the FBI, to dissolve the Black Panther Party.

Karenga continues, every year to blame the former members, for the demise of US Organization; because, they left him. And, he also stated, "… they left their Blackness." However, he never mentions that during The Black Power Movement, he committed heinous crimes, against two women in his organization, and went to prison for four years!

So, you see, Karenga is the one to blame for the demise of US Organization. Karenga is the one that left his members, by going to prison; and Karenga is the one that left his Blackness; by Torturing and Assaulting the two Sisters! Like I said; It's The Principle of The Thing!

CHAPTER 8

THE GREATEST DECEPTION OF THE 20ᵀᴴ & 21ˢᵀ CENTURY!

The White House

My question is: Why is it that, President after President from Clinton, Bush, Obama, and Trump, have all sent "Shout Outs" to Kwanzaa Celebrants, every year; saying, "Happy Kwanzaa!" I'm amazed, and I wonder, why at least one of the Presidents, have their Chief of Staff or anyone, to vet Karenga?

My point is: It's not an ordinary occurrence for a person to create, a holiday in our society today. Therefore, why didn't anyone think: Who is this man? What is his background? Does he have a criminal record? Does he have a family? What are his motives, for creating this holiday, exclusively for Black people? What kind of character does this man have? The entire process, of investigating someone, isn't a big production.

Take, for instance, all the people that took time out from their busy schedules, to research Kwanzaa; which they discovered that Kwanzaa is a Religious Cult, made up by a convicted criminal felon! How Is It That Nobody Vetted Karenga? The Question Now Is: Why Not? **Thus, "We The People" Have To Listen To False**

Statements Every Year – From The President of The United States of America Praising A Lie! This Convicted Criminal Gets Praises From The Highest And Most Powerful Office In The World For Lying! Something Is Wrong With This Picture! And it needs to be **CORRECTED!**

President Bill Clinton, Started This Madness Of Sending Out False Statements Regarding Kwanzaa. For Example, The Following **FALSE** Tribute:

December 22, 1999

Kwanzaa 1999

"Warm greetings to everyone celebrating Kwanzaa. With roots in the ancient history and cultural traditions of Africa, and celebrating such fundamental American values, as unity and self-determination; this joyous annual festival reflects the diversity that gives our nation much of its strength from our diversity. As you gather with family and friends to celebrate your rich heritage, to reaffirm the bonds of family and community, and to give thanks to our Creator for the beauty and bounty of life.

As we look forward to the new millennium, we must not lose sight of the values and traditions that have strengthened and sustained us in the past. The seven principles of Kwanzaa – unity, self-determination, collective work and responsibility, cooperative economics, purpose, creativity, and faith – can be invaluable tools in teaching us how to live together in the 21st century as a community, in harmony with one another and our environment in humility before God.

Hillary joins me in extending warmest wishes for a joyous Kwanzaa and every happiness in the coming year."

Honestly, there is no excuse for the lack of professionalism in The White House, toward this important matter. And, whatever happened to Protocol? Not to mention, all the valuable time that it took away from, The President of The United States of America, taking care of more important issues; like focusing on homeland security, the economy, and the Failing School System in America!

Moreover, this Scandal is a 'cover-up' of Ron Karenga's heinous crimes which sent him to prison. He is not a good role model for our children! And, to have the Highest Office in the land, The President of The United States of America, turn a Blind Eye, is a Travesty of Justice!

It is our children's minds that are being poisoned, by the lies that Karenga made up for them to practice, study and celebrate in schools. And, The Presidents' of The United States of America, have given their stamp of **APPROVAL!**

The Highest Office in our government is NOT protecting our children and especially; Black American Children! For instance, if Karenga was a White man trying to brainwash and poison White children's minds with lies about their history; Karenga would have been like, The Shark Tank, Mr. Wonderful says, "Crushed Like The Cockroach That He Is!" And, to make matters worse – President Obama, appointed Karenga as Chairman over The Multi-Cultural Committee in The White House Administration!

Again, the entire Kwanzaa 'cover-up' from The White House to The Court House, to The Prison House, to The California State University House, and to The Millions of Black Families' Houses; is by far: <u>The Greatest Deception of The 20th And 21st Century</u>!

State Senator Glenn Grothman
Declares War On Kwanzaa

By Adam W. McCoy - 2013

In my research, I read an excellent article by, Adam W. McCoy, Patch. com. He interviewed, Senator Glenn Grothman, of Wisconsin, (now a Congressman).

Senator Glenn Grothman stated, "Why must we still hear about Kwanzaa?" The Republican lawmaker from West Bend asked in a press release. "Why are hard-core left wingers still trying to talk about Kwanzaa – the supposed African American holiday celebration between Christmas and New Year's?"

Starting the day after Christmas, the weeklong African American holiday was created several decades ago by now Africana studies professor at California State University, Long Beach.

In his release, Grothman called for the holiday to be slapped down. "Of course, almost no Black people today care about Kwanzaa – just White left-wingers who try to shove this down Black people's throats in an effort to divide Americans." Grothman further stated, "Irresponsible public- school districts such as Green Bay and Madison … try to tell a new generation that Blacks have a separate holiday than Christians."

Grothman adds, "Karenga didn't like the idea that Christ died for all of our sins, so he felt Blacks should have their own holiday – hence, Kwanzaa."

Grothman also advises; to be on the lookout for K-12 and college teachers trying to pass it off as a real holiday. "With tens of millions of honorable Black Americans in our country's past; we should not let a violent nut like Karenga speak for them. It's a fake holiday, aimed at dividing Blacks and Whites."

Did You Have A Happy Kwanzaa?

By Joseph Farah - 2002

In my research, I discovered an interesting, and humorous article by Joseph Farah, Commentator, WND.com. He stated, "I'm a little late in asking, forgive me. But, did you have a happy Kwanzaa? I know the celebration officially ended ten days ago, but the news has kept me busy until now. President Bush was quicker to the trigger than I was.

Back on Dec. 20 – a full six days before onset of this very spiritual weeklong rite – he sent "warm greetings to all who are celebrating Kwanzaa." It gave me a warm and fuzzy feeling all over – even though I don't personally celebrate this sacred event.

Why did Bush issue a proclamation on Kwanzaa? Well, he explained that this important holiday was established in 1966 as an African-American celebration of family, community, and culture. The seven-day observance, beginning Dec. 26 and ending Jan. 1, serves as a special time to recognize and reaffirm the Nguzo Saba, or Seven Principles, of African culture. These are "unity, self-determination, collective work and responsibility, cooperative economics, purpose, creativity, and faith."

Bush continued: "Kwanzaa provides an opportunity for people of African heritage regardless of their religious background or faith, to come together and to show reverence for their Creator and creation, to commemorate the past, to recommit to high ideals, and to celebrate the good life. These life-affirming traditions take on particular resonance this year, as the United States and the world face new challenges to peace. As individuals, families, and communities take part in the celebration of unity and enduring values, I extend best wishes to people throughout the globe for a wonderful and memorable Kwanzaa."

Touching, moving, multi-cultural. Bush was correct in pointing out that this new high holy day is a very recent invention. There are few holidays we can actually attribute to one man's vision. Kwanzaa is such a holiday – coined by Ron Karenga in 1966.

Who was Ron Karenga? Glad you asked. He is a convicted felon – sentenced four years after inventing Kwanzaa for torturing two Black women by whipping them with electrical cords and beating them with a karate baton after stripping them naked. He placed in the mouth of one of the victims a hot soldering iron, also scarring her face with the device. He put one of her big toes in a vise, and detergent and running water in both of their mouths. But that wasn't the beginning of the bizarre and violent behavior of Karenga, the patron saint of Kwanzaa – not by a long shot.

But no sooner did Karenga get out of prison on the torture charges in 1975 then all was forgotten about his criminal and violent past. He was proclaimed Saint Karenga. Four years later, he was running the Black Studies Department at California State University in Long Beach.

How did he get that job in academia with his record? Glad you asked again. Paul Mulshine, who has done an admirable job of chronicling Karenga's history for FrontPagemag.com, has a theory. Karenga had a jailhouse conversion.

No, he did not become a born-again Christian. He did not renounce violence. He did not even repudiate his past. But he did become a Marxist.

And, while becoming a Christian might have disqualified him for a role in the world of the modern U.S. University, a conversion to Marxism was perceived as a sign of rehabilitation. The one-time psychopath had seen the light.

In conclusion, I hope this little cultural and history lesson helps you see the light – about Kwanzaa. It's being taught to your kids in your government schools. It's become a commercial bonanza in Black communities throughout the United States. And, now, even the President of the United States is praising it as a legitimate holiday. Good grief. What's wrong with America?

On The First Day Of Kwanzaa ... It's Time For The Lazy Journalists To Finally Start Doing Their Research

By Paul Mulshine - 2013

During my research, I found a profound article by Paul Mulshine, of The Star-Ledger. He stated, "It's that time of year again – the time when lazy journalist's gout and write puff pieces about a fake African holiday created by a psychopath who tortured Black women.

If these characters would just do a Google search on Kwanzaa, they could find the truth about it. My in-depth article on this originally ran in FrontPage Magazine back in 2002. It's easily found on the internet by any journalist willing to do the tiniest bit of research into Kwanzaa. At the time I had to pore through a year's worth of microfilm to find the original Los Angeles Times articles on the case. That took hours. These days it's available online.

I also dug up the legal record of the case that included a mental examination that showed Karenga was delusional at the time of his imprisonment. It's all in that article. I like to link to it this time every year as a corrective to all of the dreadful journalism that occurs in every report of Kwanzaa.

If the media told the truth about Kwanzaa, then every right-thinking American would realize it's a fraud. Instead, we get the same silly endorsement of this "African" feast that has nothing to do with Africa and everything to do with California in the 1960s.

We then read the usual nonsense from some self-appointed spokesperson for African-Americans terming Grothman, a racist –

because he brought attention to all those awful things Karenga did to Black people.

Imagine if a White man had tortured those women in that way and then tried to market himself as some sort of a paragon of racial pride. If some Ku Klux Klan leader set-up a holiday to compete with Christmas, every editor in America would direct his reporters to research that leader's background before writing an article about how wonderful that holiday is.

But it's impossible to imagine an editor telling a reporter to include the truth about Karenga in these annual encomiums to him. If the journalists of America would only do their jobs and inform readers of the real nature of Kwanzaa, it would soon be a forgotten relic of a bad time in American history.

Maulana Karenga An Intellectual Portrait

By Molefi Kete Asante - 2009

During my research, I discovered a book, written by Molefi Kete Asante, a Professor in The Department of African American Studies, at Temple University; and Karenga's close friend. Professor Asante stated {in Chapter 5} - "The Press Promotes Division and Serves the Cointelpro." Professor Asante is trying to make Karenga's imprisonment seem like; it was for a **noble** cause.

Professor Asante further states, "No competing narrative, was allowed to emerge in the popular press, and unwittingly, some of the most popular figures in African American Studies, promoted the disinformation, received from the FBI campaign.

Not only was the truth blocked, but the narrative against Karenga was constructed in ways, to discredit the collective movement. Soon thereafter, in 1970, Karenga was arrested and convicted on trumped-up charges of assault and was not released until 1975. I call this period the interregnum, during which time, Kawaida ideas spread across the nation rapidly.

Like other African American leaders, who had seen, the inside of prisons – Garvey, King, and Malcolm – Karenga drew up plans, to promote his philosophy, while he was physically in exile. Invited by the editors, of the Black Scholar to write on the critical issues of the 1970's, Karenga used this opportunity, not only to address these issues, but also to present Kawaida, and develop it further, in the process. His essays written during his political imprisonment are published in his book, Essays on Struggle: Position and Analysis." (1978)

Comments:
Maulana Karenga An Intellectual Portrait
By Molefi Kete Asante - 2009

Professor Asante said, "Karenga, was arrested and convicted on "trumped-up charges of assault." Let's take a closer look at the words: Trumped-up Charges and Assault.

Trumped-up Charges: Faked, fabricated or falsely manufactured. Referring to legal accusations made for illegitimate reasons.

Assault: An intentional attempt using violence or force, to injure or harm another person. Tries to or does cause severe injury to another. Causes injury through the use of a deadly weapon.

On May 9, 1970, Dr. Karenga, assaulted Deborah Jones, and Gail Davis. Karenga was convicted, on two counts of felonious assault, and one count of false imprisonment. He was sentenced on

September 17, 1971, to one to ten years imprisonment. They were not trumped-up charges; even Karenga's wife, Haiba, testified against him; and the Jury was shown the scars on Deborah Jones' back!

In other words, the Prosecution presented enough evidence; to the Jury to prove that he was guilty! Professor Asante, further stated, "I call this period the interregnum..." Let's take a closer look, at the word: Interregnum.

Interregnum: Any period during, which a state has no ruler or only a temporary executive. Any period of freedom from the usual authority. This term has been applied to the period between the election of a new President of the United States and his or her inauguration, during which the outgoing President remains in power, but as a lame duck.

In some Christian Churches, "Interregnum" describes the time between vacancy, and appointment of priest or bishops to various roles.

Professor Asante, I beg to differ with you; I call this period; prison time! How could Professor Asante, in good faith, continue to use deceptive words; that do not fit the situations, that he is discussing? How dare, Professor Asante, compare Karenga's going to prison with Dr. King's going to jail! Let's take a closer look at the words: Jail vs. Prison.

Jail: A place of confinement for persons held in lawful custody; specifically: jail, is such a place under the jurisdiction of a local government (as a county) for the confinement of persons awaiting trial or those convicted of minor crimes. Some may stay less than one day or only for a few days until they are okayed for release in a court proceeding.

Prison: Is a secure facility that houses people who have been convicted of a felony criminal offense and are serving a sentence of (typically) 1 year or more. Prisons are operated by a state government or the federal government. "Penitentiary" is a synonym for prison. People released from prison may be released to parole supervision or some other type of community program.

Professor Asante, let me refresh your memory; about Dr. Martin L. King, Jr. He went to jail, fighting for justice, on behalf of people's civil rights being violated. He went to jail, for protesting and speaking out for peoples' Constitutional Rights. The Civil Rights Movement was a Non-Violent Movement. And, Dr. King was in jail for days not years. Dr. King's behavior contributed to him being awarded, a Nobel Peace Prize; for helping to bring about peace in the World!

Professor Asante, now let me refresh your memory, about Dr. Ron Karenga. He went to prison, for kidnapping two women, in his own organization, and torturing them for two days. And, Dr. Karenga was in prison for years not days. Dr. Karenga's behavior, contributed to him being awarded, a one to ten years' conviction; for helping to bring about violence in his own organization! So, please tell me how in the world, could you possibly compare the jail time of Dr. King to the prison time of Dr. Karenga?

How could you possibly compare the remarkable leadership, of Dr. King, to the corrupt leadership of Dr. Karenga? How could you compare Dr. King's non-violent reputation, with Dr. Karenga's violent reputation? The comparison is like: Good vs. Evil. Professor Asante, also said, "Karenga drew-up plans, to promote his philosophy, while he was physically in exile. Let's take a closer look at the word: Exile.

Exile: A person banished from his or her native land. Prolonged separation from one's country or home, as by force of circumstances; like wartime exile.

Who does Professor Asante think Karenga is; "St. John in Exile?" Professor Asante knows that Karenga was not in physical exile; he was physically behind bars in prison! Professor Asante also stated, "Invited by the editors, of the Black Scholar to write on the critical issues of the 1970's." The editors, at the Black Scholar, showed their lack of wisdom, by requesting Karenga, who was sitting in prison, behind bars, because of the critical issues {in his own life} in the 1970's.

So, how could Karenga possibly help someone else, when he couldn't even help himself? And, Professor Asante, called it an opportunity! What kind of an opportunity was that? The man was in prison! Professor Asante, further stated, "… essays written during his political imprisonment." How, did he get the word, Political out of Criminal?

Let's take a closer look at the words: Political vs. Criminal.

Political: Exercising or seeking power in the governmental or public affairs of a state, municipality, etc. of, relating to, or connected with a political party. of or relating to the government or the public affairs of a country.

Criminal: Pertaining to or involving crimes or the administration of penal justice. An individual, who has been found guilty, of the commission of conduct that causes social harm, and that is punishable by law; a person, who has committed a crime.

Professor Asante's choice of words is just more evidence, of the cover-up attempts, to hide the truth about Karenga's deceptive character and violent background! Hence, Professor Asante is just like Karenga; trying to re-write history. But, the Truth will always prevail over a Lie!

Maulana Karenga's Haunting Ghost

By Mukasa Afrika Ma'at - 2012

Again, I refer to the insightful information by Mukasa Afrika Ma'at. He stated, "Karenga was very displeased with Brown's, Fighting for US, and had his colleague, Molefi Asante, write a very lofty and flattering biography of him, entitled: Maulana Karenga An Intellectual Portrait.

Among other errors, Asante claims that Karenga was mentor to Jacob Hudson Carruthers on matters related to the study of KMT (Ancient Egypt). The opposite is true. While Karenga was in jail for kidnap and torture of two Black women, Carruthers was in Senegal meeting with Cheikh Anta Diop discussing the need to teach the history, literature, and culture of KMT. Of course, Asante doesn't mention this fact.

Asante gloats about Karenga being a founder of ASCAC, but he doesn't address the fact that Karenga's ego got him voted out of ASCAC in 1988. He was also removed from the Republic of New Afrika in 1969.

Members of the Black Radical Congress has long thought of him as an agent of the FBI. Asante did a biased, gloating, oftentimes false, and very poor job on the facts about Karenga."

8—San Mateo **The Times** Wednesday, May 2, 1973

No Parole For Acid Bath Killer

SACRAMENTO, Calif. (AP)— The California Adult Authority has denied parole to Dr. Geza de Kaplany, convicted in 1963 of killing his young bride by bathing her in acid.

In turning de Kaplany down Tuesday, the Adult Authority, which serves as the state's parole board, said de Kaplany would not be eligible for parole again until March 1976.

Among the reasons given by the board were the seriousness of the crime, de Kaplany's mental state and his alleged lack of understanding concerning the killing.

De Kaplany, a onetime Hungarian freedom fighter, was 47 in February 1963, when he was convicted of first degree murder in the death of Hajna, his 25-year-old bride of five weeks. Authorities said she had been slashed with a knife, then trussed and bathed with nitric acid. She died of burns on Sept. 30, 1962 in a San Francisco hospital.

During a widely-publicized six-week trial, the doctor admitted killing his wife—who was a beautiful ex-model and also an Hungarian refugee—but he pleaded innocent by reason of insanity.

The prosecution, however, argued that he had killed his wife in a jealous rage and de Kaplany was sentenced to life in prison.

In denying parole, the board said de Kaplany appeared to have "little insight or understanding" concerning his offense. The board referred to the killing as "a very diabolical crime" and said de Kaplany was a paranoid schizophrenic whose testimony before the board was "inconsistent and unbelievable."

The board also denied parole to Ron Karenga, convicted in September 1971 of ordering and directing what authorities described as the "torture-assault" of a woman member of the black nationalist organization, US, of which Karenga was a leader.

The board denied Karenga parole at least until next February, saying he had accepted "only partial responsibility" for the offense and "evades the seriousness" of the crime. Karenga, the board said, "remains a threat to the community and is not ready for parole at this time."

Both men are being kept at the California Men's Colony at San Luis Obispo, said Joseph A. Spangler, administrative assistant to the Adult Authority.

Write It Down, Says Kissinger

WASHINGTON (AP) — Henry Kissinger, the swinging member of the Nixon administration, has turned again to Hollywood for a White House dinner partner. He escorted ac-

Comments:
No Parole For Ron Karenga - 1973

Let's take a closer look at this article, entitled: "No Parole for Acid Bath Killer," Dated: May 2, 1973. Look at the second column, and the eighth paragraph, that starts at: "The board also denied parole to Ron Karenga, convicted in September 1971, of ordering and directing what authorities described as the torture-assault of a woman member, of the black nationalist's organization, US of which Karenga was a leader.

The board denied Karenga parole at least until February, saying that he accepted only partial responsibility for the offense and evades the seriousness of the crime. Karenga, the board said, remains a threat to the community and is not ready for parole at this time. Both men are being kept at the California Men's Colony at San Luis Obispo, said Joseph A. Spangier, administrative assistant to the Adult Authority."

Well, well, - what do we have here? It looks like a **CONFESSION** to me! Karenga has finally, for once in his lying life, told the truth about this matter!

He was **GUILTY AS CHARGED!** The Adult Authority Board said, "He accepted only partial responsibility for the offense." Therefore, that means, he took no responsibility for ordering and directing his members to commit these heinous crimes. He just merely abandoned them! That speaks volumes about his unheroic traitorous activities, character, trustworthiness, loyalty, integrity, honesty, respectability, sense of justice, faithless and lack of compassion, shown toward his members!

It wasn't surprising to learn that Karenga was evasive, to the seriousness of the crime. It is obvious that Karenga has a problem giving women; the same respect which he gives to men. His disrespect for women is one of the reasons he didn't see the torture-assault of the two women; as no big thing.

I do believe that it is safe to assume, that in the next two-year review, with the Adult Authority Board; Karenga told the truth, by accepting full responsibility of ordering and directing what authorities described as the torture-assault. Also, Karenga had to admit the truth, by acknowledging the seriousness of the crime, in order, to have been Paroled in 1975!

Now, Ladies and Gentlemen, Karenga can no longer hide behind the **LIE:** The charges were trumped-up! Because this newspaper article is **EVIDENCE** that Karenga did in fact, admit that he was **GUILTY AS CHARGED** to the Adult Authority Board!

CHECKMATE!

CONFIDENTIAL
THIS DOCUMENT IS LOANED TO YOU BY THE FBI
AND NEITHER IT NOR ITS CONTENTS ARE TO BE DISTRIBUTED OUTSIDE THE AGENCY TO WHICH LOANED
COPY
DECLASSIFIED BY UC60322LP/PJ/bes
ON 03-25-2008
"Anywhere we are, US is."
US
FEDERAL BUREAU OF INVESTIGATION
UNITED STATES DEPARTMENT OF JUSTICE
JOHN EDGAR HOOVER, DIRECTOR
FILED
MAR 9 1968
CONFIDENTIAL
GROUP 1
EXCLUDED FROM AUTOMATIC
DOWNGRADING AND
DECLASSIFICATION

CHAPTER 9

THE FBI MONOGRAPH: US J. EDGER HOOVER, DIRECTOR APRIL 1968

The following excerpts are from The Federal Bureau of Investigation (FBI), U.S. Department of Justice, in Washington, D.C. 20535.

The F.B.I. Monograph consists of forty-five (45) pages. I have used excerpts from the Monograph. To view, the entire Report: www.governmentattic.org.

FBI Summary

It has been said wisely and proved sadly that 'organized minorities' always defeat unaroused majorities. These words of warning are particularly pertinent today as extreme black nationalists in the United States, preaching hatred and anarchy, attempt to enlist the sympathy and support of all Negro Americans. It is with one numerically small segment of the organizing radical minorities that this paper is concerned.

There is on the west coast of the United States a small but dangerous Black Nationalist extremist group under the direction of a 26-year-old, highly educated American Negro, Ronald McKinley Everett, now known by the Swahili name, Maulana Ron Karenga. "The Blackest Panther," as he is called by his followers, from his group in Los Angeles, California in 1965, and named it US, representing the pronoun. He claimed to be working toward the establishment of an ethnological base in Africa to which the American Negro could adhere in his search for historical identity and dignity. Within one year, Karenga's increasingly violent statements belied his "cultural" intent.

As an organization, US is small and unstructured. Besides the "center" in Los Angeles, it has but one chapter, in San Diego. Although other individuals comprise a "staff," Karenga, an opportunist, and an aspiring dictator is the undisputed guiding light. With the motto, "Anywhere we are, US is," Karenga is attempting both to spread his ideas and to expand his organization in Black communities throughout this country.

He holds meetings, at some of which only he and a few leaders, wearing mixed alien symbols, are allowed to speak. He holds "classes" where Swahili, karate, and Afro-American history are taught. Hoping to gain prestige and protection, he surrounds himself with armed, costumed guards. Karenga is anti-American, anti-white, and anti-Christian.

What Karenga has brought to the 60-odd members who cluster around him and to the hundreds of listeners who give him their time and attention at public gatherings is a guidebook or a risky journey to a no man's land. With a Messianic complex, he parrots a Mau type of racial extremist that is cropping up among radical Negro elements in the United States today, and that portends a tragic delay in the democratic settlement of social difficulties.

Ron Karenga is a dangerous man; not because he has a large following. He does not. Nor are his borrowed ideas, nor his promises, nor the fanaticism he preaches so powerful that substantial numbers of intelligent American Negroes will be swept up by their force. Ron

Karenga is dangerous because he is a vocal part of a larger conspiracy striving through the deception of a fraternity of blackness to divide this house against itself. He and the comparatively small number of Negroes who selfishly join him in the hope of a violent revolution to affect Negro autonomy are not interested in the alleviation of injustice or the correction of existing wrongs. They are interested only in a lawless blood feud to pacify their lust for vengeance and power.

"... US Is"

In the midst of the racial tension that finally boiled over in the Watts area of Los Angeles, California, in the summer of 1965, there arose a Black Nationalist Organization called US. Founded by "Maulana Ron Karenga" in July 1965. US was formed initially, according to Karenga, to seek a "frame of reference" from which American Negroes could derive pride in their race and confidence in their ability to assume a rightful, respectable place in the 20th Century United States society. The group purportedly held no penchant for violence and sought solely to spread its ideas in Black communities throughout the country. Karenga's true militancy became increasingly evident, however, and the tenure of his remarks began to reflect his real position as a Black racist calling for nothing less than Negro autonomy. "Power yields only to power," Karenga said during an interview for an article published in The Saturday Evening Post, July 1966.

According to Karenga, known to his followers as "the Blackest Panther," the name of his organization represents the personal pronoun "us" and is not an abbreviation of any words or theme.

Articles of Incorporation

The Articles of Incorporation, which were filed September 14, 1966, with the State of California, indicate that US is a nonprofit organization maintaining offices at 8211 South Broadway, Los Angeles, California. The actual name of the group is recorded as "US" Incorporated.

There are set forth below selected "purposes," as stated in the Articles of Incorporation for US, followed by statements Karenga has made in, The Quotable Karenga, which reflect the true inflammatory, revolutionary racism of his Organization:

"The specific and primary purposes are to advise and by every lawful means to assist the Afro-American people in their efforts to unite as persons and groups."

"If you don't band together you'll die alone. And as a monument to your ignorance perhaps the white boy will treat you as he did the Indian, kill you, and put your head on a nickel."

"To instill in the Afro-American people, the need and value of creativity by education and demonstration."

"Our creativity motif must be revolution; all art that does not discuss our contribution to revolutionary change is invalid. That is why the "blues" are invalid, they teach resignation, in a word, acceptance of reality — and we have come to change reality."

"To research, teach, instruct and re-educate the Afro-American people to African Religion, and to add new values to said Religion..."

"Worship should be worship to power and retaining that power."

Maulana of US

"Maulana" (Swahili for "master teacher") Ron "Karenga" (Swahili for "continuation of culture") known more frequently as Ron Karenga, is the founder, chairman, and undisputed leader of US. The youngest in a family of 14 children, he was born July 14, 1941, in Parsonsburg,

Maryland, to a family named Everett. His parents named him Ronnie McKinley, but he later used the name, Ronald McKinley.

He graduated from William Penn High School in York, Pennsylvania, in 1958. From 1959 through the spring semester of 1961, he attended Los Angeles City College. In 1962, he entered the University of California at Los Angeles as a political science major. He was graduated with honors, receiving a Bachelor of Arts degree in July 1963. On September 11, 1964, the same University conferred upon him a master's degree in Political Science. It is reported that he took many courses relating to African culture and languages, becoming fluent in Swahili, Zulu, an Egyptian Arabic, in addition to French and English.

Karenga allegedly has strong ambitions to obtain a doctorate in African languages from Howard University in Washington, D. C. Karenga was employed as a clerk for the Los Angeles County Department of Public Social Services from November 1961, until October 1965, when he assumed the duties of a Social Worker.

The Pursuit of Blackness

In order to build his nonwhite culture, Karenga is attempting first to create a Black Psychology. At a Black Power Conference in San Diego in August 1967, Karenga told his audience, "To stop killing Black people. This doesn't mean you must not kill, but just don't kill Black people."

During a question-and-answer period at the end of this conference, concerning the type of society that Negroes were going to establish when they succeeded in taking over the United States, Karenga was asked, "What are you going to do with the White people when the Black man takes over?" Karenga expounded, "Some of you who like dogs will be allowed to keep a few White people around the house as pets."

Even God Is Wrong

Borrowing the idea, prevailing among some Black Nationalist, that even God must conform to the psychological needs of the Negro radicals, Karenga laments that "Everyone but the Negro has a God that looks like him." Therefore, he concludes, it is essential that the Negro reject Christianity as a White man's religion, discard a belief in life after death, and start his own "mythology." Jesus said, "My blood will wash you white as snow. Who wants to be White but sick Negroes, or worse yet — washed that way by the blood of a dead Jew. You know if Nadinola bleaching cream couldn't do it, no dead Jew's blood is going to do it."

As a paper gesture to establish a doctrinal footing for US, Karenga included in the Articles of Incorporation the setting-up of edifices for practice, teaching, instruction, and promotion of African Religion. Verbally, he has preached an atheistic doctrine based on the premise that each man is his own god. Your house is the house of the Lord and guess who you are?" Karenga asked.

In some of his public appearances, Karenga has lashed out viciously at Christianity. His remarks have been sacrilegious and obscene and, on occasion, have not been well received by his audiences.

Underlying these anti-religious preachments may very well be an effort to channel Church contributions into the coffers of US. In The Quotable Karenga, he suggests that "we must gear the money going from the Church to the support of the revolution. Revolution cannot succeed without finance."

Revolution In The '70's

The functions of advocates will be to raise funds for the Organization and to train potential revolutionaries who are sympathetic to US doctrines. "Blacks live right in the heart of America. That is why we are best able to cripple this man. And once you understand your role you won't talk revolution, but you'll make it."

When the minds of the Negro people in the United States have been won, US plans to take advantage of a small-scale riot that might be sparked by what Karenga describes as "average non-revolutionary Negroes." At such time, US, plans to enter the rebellion using guerrillas trained in the use of firearms as sophisticated as fire bombs. Special "hit team's assignments" are planned to liquidate various local and national governmental key figures.

There has been an allegation that Karenga is seeking allies and financial assistance for his revolution from Mexico, Latin-America, and Cuban leaders.

Never Pity The Honkie

Though small in membership, US is a dangerously violent, subversive group that would take advantage of any opportunity to create or profit from racial trouble. Leaders of this organization preach a bitter, compassionless hatred reminiscent of the bloody escapades of Kenya's Mau.

The audience at a Black action conference in Palo Alto, California, in September 1967, were told to teach their children to hate "Whitey" and never to pity the "Honkie."

"Redneck," "pigs," "devils," "peck," "whitey," and "Honkie" are overused epithets for White people. The only good Honkie is a dead Honkie, claimed Karenga at a US rally in August 1967, comprised of 800 to 1,000 people.

The Following Directive Appears in The Quotable Karenga

"When the word is given, we will see how tough you are. When it's burn, let's see how much you burn. When it's kill, let's see how much you kill. When it's blow up, let's see how much you blow up. And when it's take the White girls head too, we'll really see how tough you are."

On a television show in September 1967, Karenga stated that the White man in America was going to have to be eliminated for the Negro to obtain his goals.

The following remarks were made by Karenga at a Black rally held December 2, 1967, directly across from the United States Naval Hospital in San Diego, to protest discrimination at the hospital: "We're going to get to the point. We're going to take the White man's life. And don't turn to Jesus or the President. They can't help you."

"We've got to take the honkie's head. We must work at it every day, but mostly at night."

"We cannot be free until every White man is off this planet. They even train niggers to kill us."

"We're fighting the honkies, not the system. Take whatever you want and need now even his (White) life."

"The White man is free because he is oppressing us. You have to move on the White man even if it means violence and bloodshed."

"You shouldn't be afraid of death because you ain't living anyway."

"Your first job is to kill Jesus, and the other honkies will fall into line. And the White man dies."

"We just have to make them die faster than anyone else."

On White Liberals
And Hesitant Negroes

"All Whites are White," claims Karenga in discussing White liberals. "White doesn't represent a color," continues Karenga, "it represents a color that is anti-black." He cautions his "brothers" to watch out for Whites who are rebelling against their own society and uses the wave of Black revolution to push their cause."

"Negroes who are repulsed by the aims of the Black Power Movement and who prefer to approach racial difficulties in a different manner also come under Karenga's special wrath. "If some of our Black brothers get in the way," he warns, "eliminate him too."

Comments On:
The FBI Monograph: US J. Edger
Hoover, Director April 1968

At this juncture, I would like to refer you to The FBI Monograph. Under the subtitle of **Articles of Incorporation**, filed on September 14, 1966. It is cited as the **Primary Purpose** of US Organization:

"... US Is"

"To research, teach, instruct and re-educate the Afro-American people to **African Religion** and to add new values to said **Religion.**" (Page 31 of The FBI Monograph).

Even God Is Wrong

As a paper gesture to establish a doctrinal footing for US; Karenga included in the Articles of Incorporation, the setting-up of edifices for practice, teaching, instruction, and promotion of **African Religion.** (Page 17 of The FBI Monograph)

Kwanzaa was, in the beginning, an **African Religion**, with the added new values, to said **Religion**, which is called **Kawaida.** The Articles of Incorporation, does not say anything about celebrating Kwanzaa as an Ancient Cultural Firstfruit Harvest Festival From Africa! It is obvious, to see the truth: Kwanzaa is indeed, an **African Religion.**

As further evidence, that Kwanzaa, is indeed the **African Religion** that the Articles of Incorporation were alluding to; I refer you to Professor Asante's book entitled, Maulana Karenga An Intellectual Portrait. In Chapter 5, Professor Asante stated, "Kawaida ideas spread across the nation rapidly." He further stated, "Invited by the editors of the Black Scholar, to write on the critical issues, of the 1970's, Karenga used this opportunity, not only to address, these issues, but also to present, Kawaida and develop it further, in the process." In other words, while Karenga was in prison, he was working on Kawaida ideas; because it was in the formative stages. Professor Asante, also said, "Karenga drew up plans, to promote his Kawaida Philosophy, while he was physically in exile." So, you see, Kwanzaa came before Kawaida.

The Establishment Clause

I would like to reiterate my point: Kwanzaa is an African Religion/ Cult, made up by Ron Karenga. The Articles of Incorporation, cited as the Primary Purpose of US Organization is as follows:

"To research, teach, instruct and re-educate the Afro-American people to African Religion and to add new values to said Religion…" The new values are the Kawaida Philosophy, which was created in the late '70s. Therefore, in 1966 the said, African Religion is referring to Kwanzaa.

Thereby, the Kwanzaa Holiday, is in violation of The Establishment Clause. The First Amendment provides that "Congress shall make no law respecting an establishment of religion …"

The Establishment Clause for the Separation of Church and State: Prohibits government actions that unduly favor one religion over another.

The Three-Part Test enunciated in Lemon vs. Kurtzman, is used to assess whether a law violates, The Establishment Clause.

The Three-Part Lemon Test Asks:

1) Does the law have a secular purpose? If not, it violates The Establishment Clause.
2) Is the primary effect either to advance religion or to inhibit religion? If so, it violates The Establishment Clause.
3) Does the law foster an excessive governmental entanglement with religion? If so, it violates The Establishment Clause.

The Complaint:

To have the Kwanzaa Holiday: Practice, Celebration, Study and Rituals, taken out of all the Public Schools, Colleges, and Universities, in The United States of America, based on evidence that Kwanzaa is an African Religious Holiday; not a Cultural Holiday; which violates The Establishment Clause.

Kwanzaa's indoctrination of written study guidelines of practice, study, celebration, and rituals, starting from Pre-Schools, Elementary

Schools, Middle Schools, High Schools, Colleges, and Universities are **Exactly Like** the practices, celebrations, rituals, and study of the followers/believer's worshiping at Kwanzaa Temples, Kwanzaa Churches, Kwanzaa Schools, and Kwanzaa Celebrants' homes in The United States of America, and other places in the World. **The Three-Part Lemon Test answers are as follows: Question #1 – The answer is no. Question #2 – The answer is yes. Question #3 – The answer is yes.**

Also, the parents of students are not aware that their children are being indoctrinated by practicing, studying, and celebrating, an African Religion in their classrooms; without parental full-disclosure and permission.

The Kwanzaa Religion is celebrated for seven days, thus, demonstrating unduly favor of Kwanzaa Religion over another, and the rituals are practiced as a part of the regular school day.

The Rotten Roots of Kwanzaa

By Thomas Clough - 2001

I discovered, an interesting article written by Thomas Clough, Weird Republic. He stated, "The story of Christmas cannot be told in a government-run school. Teachers, acting as paid agents of the government, must avoid even the appearance of endorsing any religion. This constitutional restriction does not apply to pseudo-religions, however, so the dedicated adherents of even the most extreme pseudo-religion are free to gain a foothold in any government school.

Take, for example, the self-named Professor Maulana Karenga. Way back in 1966, when he was known as plain ol' Ron Karenga, this self-proclaimed radical black separatist had the distinction of creating history's most pathetic holiday: Kwanzaa.

It was pure Karenga, a seven-day celebration of crypto-Marxist values with racist overtones. According to the official Kwanzaa website, the celebration was designed to nurture "conditions that would enhance the revolutionary social change for the masses of Black Americans."

What makes Kwanzaa so pathetic is its total lack of authenticity. The name of Kwanzaa and each of its principles are all Swahili, a language not spoken by anyone brought to America in the days of the slave trade. The culture of East African Swahili speaker is profoundly alien to the cultures of West Africa.

As Christmas approaches, the pseudo-religious and historically rootless rituals of Kwanzaa are freely celebrated in countless government school classrooms. Karenga's blacks-only anti-Christmas is now an established tax payer-supported seasonal school event. The legacy of a racially divisive violent degenerate is kept alive with tax money taken from you by coercive government power. Any mention of the Prince of Peace in the same environment is a crime. Ours is truly a weird republic.

CHAPTER 10

CIA INFORMANT: RON KARENGA (RAT 416 – NZA) & KWANZAA EXPOSED

By Agent Filez - 2011

I discovered an explosive article and discussion in 'Conspiracy Alley' Agent Filez; which, the discussion was headed by Ruperta, December 26, 2015. Ruperta stated, "During the era of 1969-1972 a large-scale politicization of prisons throughout the U.S. flourished, particularly in California; and became The Prisoner's Rights Movement; was born out of imprisoned Afrikans consciously transforming themselves into revolutionary Afrikan warriors to serve the people. Their successes were noted and the CIA, in concert with Division Five of the FBI, the Stanford Research Institute, the California Bureau of Prisons, and the LAPD's CCS (Criminal Conspiracy Section) organized a project known as The Black Cultural Association (BCA). The BCA was a specific behavior modification and psychological experimentation unit housed within The California State Prisons and Medical Facility at Vacaville. Funding and directions for the BCA came from the CIA via the Stanford Research Institute (SEI) as well as the LEAA (Law Enforcement Assistance Administration of the U.S. Department of Justice). The cover story was "the development of black pride" for the Afrikan prisoners.

Heading up this department was a psychotic house **** by the name of Colton Westbrook. Westbrook came from a U.S. Army background as a specialist in Psychological Warfare and Terror Ops for the CIA's Phoenix Project in Southeast Asia. Westbrook provided logistical support for CIA's Phoenix Program, and his particular job was, the indoctrination of assassination and terrorist cadres also known as synthetic terror groups or pseudo-gangs. The Phoenix Project was a sustained policy of political assassinations, rigged elections, outright terror campaigns against civilians, political imprisonment in American-made tiger cages, torture and PsyOps propaganda by CIA agents. CIA Director William Colby promised at his Senate confirmation hearings in July 1973 that he would curb the CIA's activities at home and abroad. Instead, he has imported The Phoenix Program, directly into the United States.

Mae Brussell on Ron Karenga, originator of Kwanzaa: "Black leader of the US Organization. In December 1967, Detective Sergeant R. Farwell recruited Donald DeFreeze to work for the Public Disorder Intelligence Unit, of the CCS (Criminal Conspiracy Section), LAPD, as part of a "f**k-f**k unit," running guns to various black militant groups, hoping to set off a gang war between the Black Panthers and the US Organization. US member, Melvin Colton Smith, helped set up Black Panther busts for the police. The Steiner Brothers, working with Karenga and the LAPD, killed Panther leaders John Huggins and Alprentice Carter at UCLA. Members of Karenga's group were at Vacaville with DeFreeze.

Colton Westbrook co-opted the works and revolutionary writings of the genuine Afrikan Prisoners Movement and incorporated them into the teachings of the BCA. DeFreeze, his star pupil, was even allowed to set up a sub-group called Unisight to refine his programmed leadership role in the Symbionese Liberation Army. Earlier, Westbrook had invented Ron Karenga's United Slaves logo with the seven-headed cobra, along with accompanying Swahili principles incorporating each head: Umoja, Kujichagulia, Ujima,

Ujamaa, Nia, Kuumba, and Imani. You may know these now as the 7 Principles of Kwanzaa.

The Agent Filez also stated, "Ron Karenga was convicted of two counts of felonious assault and one count of false imprisonment for his role in the imprisonment and grievous torture of two Afrikan women, named Deborah Jones and Gail Davis. A May 14, 1971, article in the Los Angeles Times described the testimony of Deborah Jones, who once was given the Swahili title of an African queen. She said, "That on May 9, 1970, she and Gail Davis were whipped with an electrical cord and beaten with a karate baton after being ordered to remove their clothes. She testified that a hot soldering iron was placed in Miss Davis' mouth and placed against Miss Davis' face and that one of her own big toes was tightened in a vise. Karenga, head of US, also put detergent and running hoses in their mouths, she said."

Additional evidence and testimony surfaced that indicated that the following day, Karenga allegedly told the women, "Vietnamese torture is nothing compared to what I know." (CIA torture lessons from Westbrook and the Phoenix Project no doubt). One of two cohorts, Luz Maria Tiamayo reportedly put detergent and a caustic substance in the women's mouths, and the other, Louis Smith turned a water hose full force on their faces, with Karenga, holding a gun, and threatening to shoot both of them (Jones & Davis)." Karenga was also found to have burned Davis and Jones with lit cigarettes and inserted a water hose into them (their vaginas) and sadistically forced cold and alternately very hot water into them.

Seeing that this could lead to a real stretch in a real prison, Karenga didn't want to do hard time in a regular prison, so he feigned insanity and beseeched his covert masters for their help. Quoting from a transcript of Karenga's sentencing hearing on Sept. 17, 1971: "A key issue was whether Karenga was same. Judge Arthur L. Alarcon read from a psychiatrist's report: "Since his admission here he has been isolated and has been exhibiting bizarre behavior, such as staring at the wall, talking to imaginary persons, claiming that he was attacked by dive-bombers and that his attorney was in the next cell."

"... During part of the interview, he would look around as if reacting to hallucinations and when the examiner walked away for a moment he began a conversation with a blanket located on his bed, stating that there was someone there and implying indirectly that the 'someone' was a woman imprisoned with him for some offense. This man now presents a picture which can be considered both paranoid and schizophrenic with hallucinations and delusions, inappropriate affect, disorganization, and impaired contact with the environment."

Either he was faking for a reduced sentence, or some BCA programming was going haywire. In any event, he was sentenced on Sept. 17, 1971, to serve one to ten years in California State Prison named "California Men's Colony," in San Luis Obispo, California. His handlers stepped in once again, and he was later transferred to – get this ... The California Medical Facility at Vacaville (for possible de-programming or re-programming?) Brother Spartacus of GAP Radio asserts that it's possible that Karenga may have never even served the sentence in the prison at all. And that his masters in the FBI may have arranged for fake prison records to be generated at the facility of his alleged prison term. Which is something to ponder, considering how valuable he WAS to them then, and IS to them now. Since then, the FBI's Anti-Afrikan COINTELPRO strategy continued uninterrupted and has been expanded and instituted globally with new names such as TOPLEV, COMTEL, and THERMCON.

A brief account of the sentencing ran in several newspapers the following day. That was apparently the last newspaper article to mention Karenga's unfortunate habit of doing unspeakable things to black people. After that, the coverage came from the hundreds of news accounts that depict him as the wonderful man who invented Kwanzaa.

The Member Writer further stated, "Karenga was released a scant 3 years later in 1974, and his handlers in the CIA and FBI set him up to be Chairman of the Department of Black Studies at California State University. Now named Professor Maulana (Master teacher) Karenga, he later resurfaced with the resurrected SLA principles and dubbed them the 7 Principles of Kwanzaa complete with an Africanized Hanukkah menorah called the Kinara. **His handlers in the FBI thought that this would serve a two-fold purpose of the establishing and marketing a synthetic African holiday with a convoluted African origin, that would serve their financial agenda as an alternative Christmas marketed directly to black people. And two, to give their valued operative a new cover for a re-insertion into the Afrikan community.**

Primarily for intelligence gathering, gatekeeping and an assumed leadership role with complete absolution of his crimes against the Afrikan masses. That, in addition to the great laughter they enjoy watching us sanctify a sick, sadistic, predator of Afrikan people. A vile tool who delights in the continued destruction of our liberation. But let's hear from the man Karenga himself talking candidly in a May 9, 1978 article from the Washington Post: "People think it's African, but it's not." He continued, "I came up with Kwanzaa because black people in this country wouldn't celebrate it if they knew it was American. Also, I put it around Christmas because I knew that's when a lot of bloods (young black people) would be partying."

We need to make a revolutionary choice at this point, and either continue celebrating a holiday given to us by our enemies. A holiday that amalgamates Christmas and Hanukkah, with a synthetic African characteristic, inserted strategically for seven days right after Christmas.

Kwanzaa was an Afrikan Trojan Horse to continue an un-official celebration of the Christmas season, and redirect our hard-earned money back into the enemy's coffers. To depart a legend and give absolution to a traitor of the Afrikan masses should have been judged and given a death sentence for crimes against Afrikan people and our struggle. Kwanzaa is now as commercially viable a commodity as

Christmas, generating millions in greeting-card sales alone. "It's clear that a number of major corporations have started to take notice and try to profit from Kwanzaa," said a San Francisco State Black Studies Professor Oba T'Shaka.

Comments On:
CIA Informant: Ron Karenga (RAT 416 – NZA) & Kwanzaa Exposed By Agent Filez- 2011

At this juncture, I would like to refer you to (the 2nd paragraph, 4th sentence). **Start reading at**: "Westbrook provided logistical support for CIA's Phoenix Program, and his particular job was the indoctrination of assassination and terrorist cadres also known as synthetic terror groups or pseudo-gangs. The Phoenix Project was a sustained policy of political assassinations, rigged elections, outright terror campaigns against civilians, political imprisonment in American-made tiger cages, torture and PsyOps propaganda by CIA agents."

This 'Ah-Ha Moment' was profound! Yes, Karenga does have a fascination with Circuses; but, I didn't know that the **Tiger Cage Torture**, originally came from the terror mind-control programming by The Phoenix Project! In other words, when my research led me to this information; **instantly, everything fell into place!** For example, Karenga Locking-up Haiba in a **Tiger Cage** housed in his garage! He got the American made Tiger Cage from The Phoenix Project!!! Another example is Karenga's bragging to the two Sisters that; "Vietnamese Torture" is nothing compared to what I know." Karenga is confirming, that he has received, torture-training from Colton Westbrook!

I would also like to refer you to (the 9th paragraph and 4th sentence). **Start reading at:** "His handlers stepped in once again, and he was later transferred to —get this— The California Medical Facility at Vacaville (for possible de-programming or re-programming?) I believe, after all this de-programming or re-programming, is one of the main reasons why Karenga is so messed-up and confused in his evil mindset. It appears that Karenga's behavior is from the modification and psychological experimentation unit housed within the California State Prison and Medical Facility at Vacaville! The article also states that Members of Karenga's group were at The California Medical Facility at Vacaville with DeFreeze.

Now, I refer you to (the 11th paragraph, 1st sentence). **Start reading at**: "The Member Writer further stated, "Karenga was released a scant 3 years later in 1974, and his handlers in the CIA and FBI set him up to be Chairman of the Department of Black Studies at California State University." This information confirms that, the FBI and the CIA were the ones who got Karenga, and his second wife, Tiamoyo hired at California State University, Long Beach!

Last, but not least, the **Tiger Cage** information is **evidence** that Karenga is a CIA RAT. **And, this CIA RAT is Teaching our Children, Youth, and Young Adults in The United States of America's Educational System!**

CHECKMATE!

CHAPTER 11

UNIVERSITIES, COLLEGES, & THE DEPARTMENT OF EDUCATION: HAVE SET A DANGEROUS PRECEDENT OF HIRING QUALIFICATIONS FOR EDUCATORS IN THE UNITED STATES OF AMERICA

The Liberal Memory Hole
The Monster Who Made Up Kwanzaa

By Thomas Clough - 2001

Again, I refer to the interesting article written by Thomas Clough, Weird Republic. He stated: {**This is the sadistic ex-con torture-squad commander who invented America's most laughable celebration: Kwanzaa. The liberal media have been hiding the truth about him for decades. Here, at last, is the truth.**}

Using the same technique that Joseph Stalin employed to

refashion history, the keepers of America's newspaper archives have rehabilitated the depraved inventor of Kwanzaa. Unpleasant references to torture sessions, blazing campus gun battles, Marxist ideology and the brutal beatings of Karenga's campus political competitors have been erased by sympathetic leftists. The truth would have been lost forever were it not for the diligent research of Paul Mulshine of the Newark Star Ledger. It took Mulshine two days to ferret out the truth from the dusty microfilm archive of the Los Angeles Times. The computer data bases had been scrubbed of all references to Karenga's violent past. The women he tortured have dropped out of sight. The court records of Karenga's trial are unobtainable. Only a handful of newspaper accounts of what really happened are still unavailable to us. What is clear is that America's "journalists" cannot be trusted to tell us the truth for it is they who have toiled to sanitize the history of Kwanzaa's depraved inventor.

Happy Kwanzaa

By Paul Mulshine - 1999

In my research, I found an eye-opening article written by Paul Mulshine, in Heterodoxy. He stated, "Profiting from the absence of memory, he remade himself as, Maulana Ron Karenga, went into academics, and by 1979 he was running the Black Studies Department, at The California State University, in Long Beach. This raises a question: Karenga had just 10 years earlier proven himself capable of employing guns and bullets in his efforts to control hiring in the Black Studies Department at UCLA. So, how did this ex-con, fresh out of jail, get the job at California State University, in Long Beach? Did he just send a resume and wait by the phone?

The officials at Cal State University don't like that type of question. I called the university and got a spokeswoman by the name of Toni Barone. She listened to my questions and put me on hold. Christmas music was playing, a nice touch under the circumstances.

She told me to fax her questions. I sent a list of questions that included the matter of whether Karenga had employed threats to get his job. I also asked just what sort of crimes would preclude a person from serving on the faculty there at Cal State? And, whether the university takes any security measures, to ensure that Karenga, doesn't shoot any students.

Barone faxed me back a reply stating, "That the university is pleased, with Karenga's performance, and has no record of the procedures, that led to his hiring." She ignored the question, about how they protect students.

California State University, Long Beach

According to the information in the article, by Agent Filez, Karenga's handlers in the **CIA and FBI set him up to be Chairman of the Department of Black Studies at California State University, Long Beach**. Now named Professor Maulana, and his wife, Tiamoyo, was also hired as an Assistant Professor, in the Black Studies Department. **Therefore, the Hiring Policies and Procedures for The Educational System in America, needs to be Investigated, and Transformed**.

Professor Ron Karenga, PhDs. has told LIE after LIE about Kwanzaa, and the Universities, Colleges, and The Public-School Districts in The United States of America have allowed this LIE to be practiced, studied, and celebrated by our children and youth far too long. Enough is enough! What kind of a message is this **Travesty of Justice** sending to our Children and Youth? It is sending the message: That Criminal Behavior Pays Off! – Big Time! So, who is next to be hired to educate our Children and Youth? Maybe, someone like the Late Charles Manson?

Positions For:
Professor, Department Chair &
Tenure Qualifications

- Applicant must have twenty (20) years of experience as an FBI Rat\Stooge\Agent\ Informant\Snitch; along with two (2) Letters of Recommendation from the FBI.
- Applicant must have twenty (20) years of experience as an CIA Rat\Stooge\Agent\ Informant\Snitch; along with two (2) Letters of Recommendation from the CIA.
- Applicant must have created one (1) Religious Holiday; saying it is a Cultural Holiday from Africa; so, it could go, under-cover, into all Public Schools to be practiced, studied and celebrated; and to indoctrinate all the innocent children and youth, to become followers/believers in the Kwanzaa African Religion/Cult, without parental full-disclosure, and permission.
- Applicant must have hated White people and Jewish people over thirty (30) years.
- Applicant must be Extremely Narcissistic and a Believable Liar.
- Applicant must have the experience as a Chief Executive Officer of a Nonprofit Organization; that received and gave orders to Murder two (2) Black Panther Members at UCLA in 1969.
- Applicant must have Sexually Assaulted three (3) Black women, in his own organization, to qualify for Tenure.
- Applicant must have the experience of Ordering an Assault and Battery against one (1) Black woman, in his own organization.
- Applicant must have the experience of Ordering an Assault and Battery against one (1) Black man, in his own organization.
- Applicant must have the experience of illegally practicing Polygamy in America.

- Applicant must have previous experience of afflicting Mental Abuse and Domestic Violence against his Wife.
- Applicant must have the experience of Locking-up his **Wife in a Tiger Cage** and keeping her in his garage.
- Applicant must have the experience of holding a loaded gun aimed at two (2) Black women and ordering them to remove all their clothes and threatening to shoot them if they did not comply; then whipping them with an electrical cord and beating them with a karate baton.
- Applicant must have the experience of placing a **Hot Soldering Iron** in the mouth of one (1) Black woman; and against her face, in his own organization.
- Applicant must have the experience of Ordering and Directing three (3) people to Assault two (2) other people, in his own organization, to qualify for The Department Chair, in The Black Studies Department.
- Applicant must have the experience of tightening a vise on one (1) Black woman's big toe, in his own organization.
- Applicant must have the experience of putting detergent and running water from a hose in two (2) Black women's mouth, in his own organization.
- **Applicant must have the experience of burning Davis and Jones with lit cigarettes and inserted a water hose into them (their vaginas) and sadistically forced cold and alternately very hot water into them.**
- Applicant must have the experience of hitting two (2) Black women on their heads with a **Toaster**, in his own organization.
- Applicant must have been Convicted by The Grand Jury for: Conspiracy and Assault.
- Applicant must have been Convicted of Two (2) Counts of Assault-Torturer and must have successfully Kidnapped two (2) Black women for three (3) weeks or more and held them hostage in his garage.

- Applicant must have completed four (4) years of Prison in The Department of Justice System, in The United States of America, to quality for Tenure; **and to qualify a Convicted Criminal Wife; as Assistant Professor in The Black Studies Department.**
- Applicant must have been denied Parole one (1) time by The Adult Authorities Board for **Lying.**
- Applicant must be an Educated Fool holding a BA, MA, and two PhDs. to qualify as a Nutty Professor, in The California State University System, in The United States of America.
- Applicant must have the ability to write Text Books Full of Lies for Universities, Colleges and Public Schools in The United States of America.
- Applicant is Not Required to be Vetted for these Positions.

CHAPTER 12

PERSONAL MESSAGES TO:
Haiba Karenga

My Dear Sister, I am so sorry, to hear about the Barbaric Act, of Karenga putting you in a Tiger Cage; it broke my heart. And, I want you to know that I forgave you, for not helping me, when Karenga attempted to rape me, in your home, while you, your three children, and approximately ten members of US Organization were also at your home, during the attempted rape; and no one tried to stop him. <u>God's Word Says It Best</u>: "Father, forgive them; for they know not what they do." (Luke 23:34) KJV.

I truly understand, why you couldn't help me; because, at that time, you couldn't even help yourself. I believe that, Dr. Maya Angelo, said it best; "When you know better, you do better." It took a lot of courage, to testify against Karenga at his criminal trial. I believe, by your testifying against Karenga, you have redeemed yourself. You took a stand for justice; and that is, the kind of person, I remember you to be. And, because of God's unconditional love, and compassion, I am praying for you and your family's salvation; before it's too late. That said, I salute you!

Tamu & Didisi

My Dear Sisters, I have forgiven both of you, for the Assault & Battery which you did to me; and then, leaving me for dead. Tamu, I want you to know that, I did receive your message that you sent to me; and I accepted your apology. Thank you.

Didisi, I believe that you were, the one that surprised me. I treated you like, the younger sister that I never had. I forgave you Didisi, because I realized, that you were also, brainwashed by Karenga; and just didn't know it at that time. God's Word Says It Best: "Father, forgive them; for they know not what they do." (Luke 23:34) KJV. And, because of God's unconditional love and compassion, I am praying for both of you, and your families' salvation; before it's too late. That said, God bless you both.

Gail Davis & Deborah Jones

My Dear Sisters, I am so sorry to hear what happened to you; it broke my heart. Gail, I can relate to your not testifying at the trial; because Karenga also threatened to kill my family, if I reported him to the police. Gail, during my research, I learned that you are now a Born Again Christian! Glory to God! Deborah, great job! Therefore, Deborah Jones, because of God's unconditional love, and compassion, I'm praying for you and your family's salvation, before it's too late. That said, I salute you both!

Ron Karenga

My Dear Sick Brother, I want you to know, that I have forgiven you for Sexually-Assaulting me at your home in Inglewood; and for Ordering an Assault & Battery against me; in 1969, by Tamu and Didisi. Karenga, how could you torture those young women like that? And, putting Haiba in a Tiger Cage is just as sadistic, as the torturing of the two women! You are really crazy!

I have never in my life, heard of anything so demonic and demeaning; as what you have done to Haiba! How could you, disrespect her like that? **YOU DOG!**

This Barbaric Act, of your locking Haiba up in a Tiger Cage in your garage; reminded me of the Horror Mystery Shows on Television, back in the 60s. For example, Inner Sanctum, and Alfred Hitchcock.

Karenga, please tell me this: When you first got the evil thought, to put Haiba inside the Tiger Cage; why didn't **YOU** use, Self-Determination, from The Nguzo Saba, to stop yourself from commenting Domestic Violence, and Mental Abuse against your Wife? Karenga, you are the creator, of The Seven Principles; so why didn't they work for you; to bring good into your marriage? I thought you were the Master Teacher, who teaches Black Americans, how to be the best, of what it is to be African. I guess you'll blame everything on Jesus Christ and White people, **HUH?**

That said, there is nothing in that fake religious holiday that is going to work for anyone's life; you have proven that! Now, I see why you no longer do interviews, with the mainstream media. You don't want people to find out; who you are behind closed doors. People all over the World should feel **Righteous Indignation**, at this **Barbaric Act** that you committed against your first wife, Haiba!

It clearly shows the type of sick character that you have. You locked your wife, the Mother of your children, in a Tiger Cage and housed her in your garage!!! And, you claim to be a High Priest! People only know you by reading your articles, books, and your public speeches. They don't know the monster that you are on the inside; **but, now they do!** Karenga, you have absolutely, no compassion for anyone! Because, if you had any compassion; you would have included **LOVE** in your Seven Principles! <u>God's Word Says It Best</u>: "If I have the gift of prophecy and can fathom all mysteries and all knowledge, and if I have a faith that can move mountains, but do not have love, I am nothing." (1 Corinthians 13:2) NIV.

You are unfit, to teach our children anything! And, how did you get the position of a Professor at California State University? Oh yes, I forgot, you are an FBI Rat\Stooge\Informant\Agent\Snitch! Therefore, you didn't have to go through, the vetting process; before they hired you.

And, they gave you tenure! That is surprising indeed, because tenured Professors, can be dismissed, only for serious misconduct; or severe economic necessity. However, it was just the opposite, in your situation; you have a background, of very serious misconduct, of being a convicted felon, of violent heinous crimes; and you still got hired! Quite an accomplishment; for you and the FBI.

When I read, your column in the L.A Sentinel Newspaper, dated September 8, 2016 about Kwanzaa; it read like a fictional story. It sounded like, you were somewhere, on an island with people, like in the Wizard of Oz; and of course, you are 'The Master Oz.' The article, sounded like you were teaching people, how to be like you. You sounded like, you were 'God' speaking to your children, about how to handle being Black when White people, are trying to disrespect your Blackness. You talk about unity, but only with Black people! And, you want to take Black people, back to Egypt! Didn't you get the memo, that Almighty God already delivered us from bondage in Egypt!

You must learn how, to forgive people that have wronged you; for whatever reason and move on. It reminds me, of the famous words of Rodney King, "Can we all just get along?" Karenga, why are you, still teaching Black people, to **HATE** White people; just because there are some **Bad Apples** in their **Race-Basket? Every Race**, on planet earth, has some **Bad Apples** in their **Race-Basket**; but, you don't blame and condemn, all the other **Apples** just because, of those few bad ones. You remind me, of a **Bad Apple** in Black people's **Race-Basket**; simply because, you are a **Basket Case!**

I just want to cry, every time I visualize Haiba, all balled-up, with her knees up to her chin, her heart breaking, her crying, and remembering the times, that she had a loving, Marital Relationship with you! So, please tell me, and all the millions of Kwanzaa Celebrants, around the World, how an African American Man should treat his Wife, according to The Nguzo Saba; The Seven Principles of Kwanzaa in Maat; in order for us to glean, more clarity about your Tiger Cage situation:

- What did Haiba do, or say, to cause you to lock her up in a Tiger Cage?
- Where were your Children while you were playing **Black Kwanzaa Circus** in your garage with their Mother?
- Tell us how long, did it take you to research, study and intellectually put together a scholarly plan of action, to put her into a Tiger Cage?
- Did you intellectually discuss with Haiba, the reasons why she had to be put, into a Tiger Cage?
- Did you compare prices, or did you just buy, the first Tiger Cage, that you saw online?
- Who helped you use Ujima (Third Principle) Collective Work and Responsibility? I know you didn't put Haiba in that Tiger Cage all by yourself; because, she would have **Kicked Your Butt**; like she did at my apartment, remember?
- Did you beat her or drugged her, before putting her into the Tiger Cage?
- Did you feed her?
- Did you give her water?
- Did you let her out to go to the bathroom?
- Did you protect her like a Black African from the Zulu Tribe; by leaving a Simba Wachunga with her in the garage? Or did you leave her alone?
- How long was Haiba locked-up? Was it hours? Was it days?

Was it weeks? Never mind; you probably don't remember, because of all the drugs you were taking.

- Did you leave a light on, in the garage, so that she wouldn't be scared?

Now that you have successfully garnered, all this first-hand experience, research, and practice; you should write a thesis on: **Home Grown Terrorism Against Black Women In The United States of America; and get another Ph.D.!**

You have no remorse for what you did. I hope you know that, in the Real World, what you did to Haiba, is called, Domestic Violence and Mental Abuse! You have told so many lies, for so long, that you now believe them to be the truth! It's called, 'lying to yourself!' You think that you are a 'god' called to save all Black Americans from Jesus Christ and White people!

And, if you are trying to be a Historian; don't you know that, you are supposed to record history, not make-it-up-yourself! You were so busy thinking that you were such an Intellectual Genius. You became an Intellectual Madman. You became Dangerous. **And, you still are!**

You need to use your degrees on yourself; and leave our people and children alone! And, you are **NOT** a leader for our people, just because you, the FBI and the CIA, say you are! **And, for the record; Jesus Christ is our Leader!** Even the number of people, you say are celebrating Kwanzaa; all over the World, probably isn't true. First, it's 20 million, now it's 40 million! Who did the survey for you? I know; you probably did.

Karenga, I realized that you sold your soul to Satan out of ignorance and ego. But, I am praying that God will do for you, what He did for the Apostle Paul: "To Have An On The Road To Damascus Encounter With Jesus Christ!" God's Word Says It Best: "As he journeyed he came near Damascus, and suddenly a light shone around him from heaven. Then he fell to the ground, and heard a voice saying to him, "Karenga, Karenga, why are you persecuting

Me?" And you said, "Who are You, Lord?" Then the Lord said, "I am Jesus, whom you are persecuting ..." (Acts 9:3-5) NKJV.

Karenga This Is My Point: Kwanzaa Is Not The Truth! So Why Should Our Children Celebrate or Study A Lie? And, last, but not least, you and your fake religious holiday, are not worthy to represent Black Americans in The United States of America! And, the Kwanzaa Stamp doesn't measure-up to the High Moral Standards to Represent The United States of America! **Therefore, these concerns will be addressed.** And, because of God's unconditional love and compassion; I'm praying for your and Tiamoyo's salvation before it's too late. That said, God bless you both.

The Five-Fold Ministry

I remember, what seems like yesterday, when I was a member of, Crenshaw Christian Center, when it was located on Crenshaw Blvd., in Inglewood, California; where the Apostle, Dr. Fredrick K.C. Price, Sr. was the Founder and Senior Pastor. This was in the late 70's, when people were just beginning to talk about, the strange behavior of Pastor Jim Jones, at The People's Temple, in Los Angeles.

Pastor Jim Jones held degrees, from Indiana University, and Butler University, and was Ordained in the Christian Church\Disciples of Christ. It wasn't long, before someone, shared the negative feedback, with Pastor Price; about the bazaar things that were going on at The People's Temple.

Apostle Frederick K.C. Price, Sr., took time out, of his busy schedule, to go to Pastor Jim Jones' Church, to see what was going on. I would like, to point out that, Apostle Price, didn't have to do that. For instance, he could have delegated one of his Assistant Pastors, Elders, or Deacons, to go 'Scout out the Land.' In Biblical times, it was a common practice, for soldiers to be sent ahead, to spy on the enemy, and bring back a report.

However, being such an incredible example, of a concerned Shepherd for God's flock; he went to check out, this man for himself. After attending one of Pastor Jones' services; he brought back, a report to his congregation. The report, as I remember it, was more like a "warning" to stay far away, from Pastor Jim Jones, and his Church!

He also suggested, that we warn, our family members and friends, that Jim Jones's People's Temple was, in fact, a Religious Cult! Shortly after that, Pastor Jones, moved his People's Temple, from Los Angeles to Jonestown, Guyana. Later, on November 18, 1978, in Jonestown, Guyana, over 900 people died, of mass murder\suicide.

You know, one cannot help, but to admire, Apostle, Dr. Frederick K.C. Price's love, for his members; and wanting to protect them from, "Wolves in Sheep's Clothing." He is, indeed, an excellent example, for the Five-Fold Ministry, in the Body of Christ to follow; especially pertaining to this important matter of Spiritual Life and Death regarding Karenga, Kwanzaa, and Kawaida.

I would also like to take this opportunity to say that, you are doing an Amazing job! Your Assignment in The Kingdom of God, is such an Extremely Difficult Office To Occupy; but you make it look easy! In other words, without **YOU** we wouldn't have a **CLUE!** God's Word Says It Best: "How then shall they call on Him in whom they have not believed? And how shall they believe in Him of whom they have not heard? And how shall they hear without a Preacher?" (Romans 10:14) NKJV. Thank you so much, for your **LABOR OF LOVE!** That said, I salute all of you!

CHAPTER 13

KWANZAA: THE GULLIBILITY OF THE MASSES

The Definition of Gullibility: Is a failure of social intelligence in which a person is easily tricked or manipulated into an ill-advised course of action. It is closely related to criminality which is the tendency to believe unlikely propositions that are unsupported by evidence. Classes of people especially vulnerable to exploitation due to gullibility include children, the elderly and uneducated people.

P.T. Barnum was known as the Shakespeare of marketing; based on "The gullibility of the masses," and his innovative and impressive ideas. He knew how to draw patrons by giving them a thread of something that had never been seen before. He said, "Without promotion, something terrible happens… Nothing!" P.T. Barnum was at times, accused of being deceptive and promoting false advertising.

Like P.T. Barnum, Karenga is the Shakespeare of promoting a False African Holiday and false hope. Karenga knew how to draw Black folks into his **Black Kwanzaa Circus**, if you would; by deceiving the people.

So, based on lies, his ego, and his low estimation of Black folks, Karenga wanted to do the same thing, which P.T. Barnum did; trick the people into believing, that Kwanzaa had been celebrated by our Ancient Ancestors in Africa! He decided to give the Negroes, as he put it, a glimpse of something, which they had never seen before: **Black Kwanzaa Circus!**

See, if you want to 'hide' anything from the bloods; put it in a book!" And, he started laughing! My question is: Why would Karenga want to 'hide' anything from Black people? Karenga further stated, "The concept that P.T. Barnum created ... worked! The idea, of telling people, that an individual thing existed like a freak of nature in the circus would trick the people, into believing, and accepting it as truth just because they see it, with their own eyes; they would think it was truth." Karenga said, **"Anybody gullible enough to believe that Kwanzaa came from Africa, needs to be fooled!"**

The Culture War In The United States of America

The Culture War is a clash of ideas about what one believes to be true, and others with different viewpoints. Your experiences, family, friends, education and the media help to form your belief system or World View.

Your Worldview, determines where you stand, in the Culture War. Everyone has a Worldview: educated or uneducated, religious or non-religious, rich or poor, liberal or conservative. Your fundamental beliefs from your Worldview placing you on one side of the Culture War.

These basic beliefs, come from the following questions: Who am I? Where did I come from? What happens when I die? Is there a God? Where did the universe come from? What is truth? What are good and evil? What is my purpose? How you answer these basic questions forms a viewpoint or your reality from which you evaluate and make sense out of all data of life and the world.

For the past 150 years, new ideas and discoveries in science have challenged the traditional Christian World View; that God created the Earth, Sun, Moon, the Stars and all Life on Earth. Dr. D. James Kennedy has said, "The Culture War, is a difference in the World Viewpoints, between believers and unbelievers of Christ."

The Culture War has been formed and defined, by a number, of discoveries and new theories that were developed, in the 19th and 20th centuries that have molded, the present-day mindset of American Society. New discoveries in the past ten years are casting some doubt on theories of the past two centuries. While some are eager to latch onto the new ideas, many others are still holding onto the old ideas and values of the past.

A recent national poll that asked, "Do you believe there is a God? Eighty-five percent of Americans that answered the question said "Yes" they do believe in a supreme being, which becomes a central worldview defining the Culture War in America. The Culture War is one of the most important debates in our society today. In politics, it has become the Red States versus the Blue States.

The Long March Through The Institutions

By Tightrope - 2016

I found an explosive article, written by Tightrope. Tightrope stated, "While some might consider Ron Karenga's implausible triumph to be an illustration of P.T. Barnum's axiom regarding human gullibility, there is something much worse than foolishness at work.

Kwanzaa offers a potent illustration of Communist Theoretician Antonio Gramsci's strategy for overthrowing Western Society by conducting a "long march through the institutions" of culture, including educational and religious institutions. It is this urge to destroy and defile our Western patrimony that represents the true spirit of Kwanzaa."

The Long March Through The Institutions Is The Culture Way

By Lee Congdon, Ph.D. - 2015

I found, a profound article by, Lee Congdon, Ph.D., Professor Emeritus of History at James Madison University. He stated, "Too few Americans is Antonio Gramsci a familiar name. That is to be regretted because the work of the late Italian Marxist sheds much light on our time.

It was he who first alerted fellow revolutionaries to the possibility that they would be able to complete the seizure of political power only after having achieved "cultural hegemony," or control of society's intellectual life by culture means alone. His was incremental, rather than an apocalyptic, revolution-the-kind that we have been witnessing in the United States, and the Western world generally, since the 1960s.

With this in mind, we ought not, to treat the contemporary, "culture war" lightly; the fate of what remains, of civilized life, may well be decided, by its outcome. Following Gramsci, Leftists know, that Christianity, remains the greatest obstacle, to their total victory, in the culture war.

"The civilized world, had been thoroughly saturated, with Christianity for 2000 years," the Italian had written; something, he insisted, had to be done about that, and something has. The de-Christianizing of America and the West; that he advocated is by now, well underway.

Few thoughtful people, deny that we are living, in a time

of decline. "... The only question that remains is: Is the decline reversible? There are a few signs of hope, including the much, commented upon challenge, to the "mainstream" media presented by talk radio, bloggers, and Fox News.

That is something, but not enough. Gramsci counseled his side, to begin a "long march through the institutions," by which he meant, the capture of the cinema, theater, schools, universities, seminaries, newspapers, magazines, radio, television, and courts. It is past time, to begin a long march, in a new and better direction."

CHAPTER 14

THE SEVEN LETTERS OF ASIA MINOR: TO THE SEVEN CHURCHES OF JESUS CHRIST WORLDWIDE

A Prophetic Word To All Born Again Christians Especially The Five-Fold Ministry

I was in the Spirit, on the day that God, told me to write this Chapter to The Seven Churches in The World. He said, To wake you up and warn you, about the wickedness of Karenga, Kwanzaa, and Kawaida; and to remind His people that; you are surely destroyed for a lack of knowledge! Therefore, take heed, to what the Spirit of God is saying to you: **GET THE SIN (KWANZAA) OUT OF HIS FATHER'S HOUSE OF PRAYER!**

He said, locate your behavior and correct it if need be. He said, I change not; examine yourself and repent; do it quickly, as the time, grows short, and My return draws nigh.

Thus Saith The Lord

The Horns of The Altar (Excerpts)

By Pastor C.H. Spurgeon – 1884

The Lord's Words from Revelation 2:1-19 & Revelation 3:1-22 are quoted first. Following each Letter, to the Seven Churches, are excerpts of the Sermon, "The Horns of The Altar" based on, "And he said, Nay; but I will die here" (I Kings 2:30). This sermon was delivered by, Pastor C. H. Spurgeon, from the "Metropolitan Tabernacle Pulpit," on March 23, 1884. (No. 182)

Revelation 2
The Loveless Church

1) Unto the angel of the church of Ephesus write; These things saith he that holdeth the seven stars in his right hand, who walketh in the midst of the seven golden candlesticks;

2) I know thy works, and thy labor, and thy practice, and how thou canst not bear them which are evil: and thou hast tried them which say they are apostles, and are not, and hast found them, liars:

3) And hast borne, and hast patience, and for my name's sake hast labored, and hast not fainted.

4) Nevertheless, I have somewhat against thee, because thou hast left thy first love.

5) Remember therefore from whence thou art fallen, and repent, and do the first works; or else I will come unto thee quickly, and will remove thy candlestick out of its place, except thou repent.

6) But this thou hast, that thou hatest the deeds of the Nicolaitans, which I also hate.

7) He that hath an ear let him hear what the Spirit saith unto the churches; To him that overcometh will I give to eat of the tree of life, which is in, the midst of, the paradise of God.

"There are others who put their trust in religious observances of sundry kinds. Their visible altar-horn is something which they believe to be very proper and right, and which, indeed, may be so if wisely used, for the thing is good if used lawfully; but it will be their ruin if it be put out of its own place. For instance, there are, doubtless, some would think that they are all right because they frequent sermons. They delight to be found hearing the Gospel.

Now, in this you do well, for, "Faith cometh by hearing, and hearing by the word of God;" but, if you suppose that the mere hearing of a sermon with the outward ear can save you, you suppose what is untrue, and you build the house of your hope on sand. "Oh, sir, I have sat to hear the true Gospel of our Lord Jesus Christ these many years." Yes, and these many years you have rejected it.

The Kingdom of God has come nigh unto you, but I fear it will work your damnation through your unbelief; for it will be a savor of death unto you. I fear that in the last great day it shall be seen that I have ministered unto some of you to your hurt. It will not be laid to my charge, but to yours if I have been faithful in the declaration of the Word.

Oh, may God grant that no man or woman among you may ever put the slightest faith in the mere hearing of the Word! Except ye receive it by faith ye deceive your own souls; if ye are hearers only, what good can come of it?"

The Persecuted Church

8) And unto the angel of the church in Smyrna write; these things saith the first and the last, which was dead, and is alive;

9) I know thy works, and tribulation and poverty, (but thou art rich) and I know the blasphemy of them which say they are Jews, and are not, but are the synagogue of Satan.

10) Fear not of those things which thou shalt suffer: behold, the devil shall cast some of you into prison, that ye may be tried; and ye shall have tribulation ten days: be thou faithful unto death, and I will give thee a crown of life.

11) He that hath an ear, let him hear what the Spirit saith unto the churches; He that overcometh, shall not be hurt of the second death.

"Oh, but," says another, "I attend prayer meetings." I admit that it is not every hypocrite that will regularly come to prayer-meetings, but there are some that do; and, though you are so fond of prayer-meetings, yet, my dear friend, unless it can be said of you, "Behold he prayeth," you need not make sure of safety. Your being found in the place where prayer is won't be made to be no true sign of grace. "Ah, but I do more than that, for I have prayers in my own house." Yes, and very proper, too. I would that all did the same; I am grieved that any should neglect the ordinance of family prayer.

But, if you think that the reading of a form of prayer in your household, or even the use of extempore prayer, is a thing to be relied upon for salvation, you do greatly err. "He that believeth in Him hath everlasting life," but he that believes not in the Lord Jesus Christ does but offer unbelieving prayer to God; and what is that but a vain sacrifice which He cannot accept? Oh, do not rely upon the habit of outward worship, are you will lean on a bulrush!"

The Compromising Church

12) Add to the angel of the church in Pergamos write; these things saith he which hath the sharp sword with two edges;

13) I know thy works and where thou dwellest, even where Satan's seat is: and thou holdest fast my name, and hast not denied my faith, even in those days wherein Antipas was my faithful martyr, who was slain among you, where Satan dwelleth.

14) But I have a few things against thee because thou hast there them that hold the doctrine of Balaam, who taught Balac to cast a stumbling block before the children of Israel, to eat things sacrificed unto idols, and to commit fornication.

15) So hast thou also them that hold the doctrine of the Nicolaitans, which thing I hate.

16) Repent; or else I will come unto thee quickly and will fight against them with the sword of my mouth.

17) He that hath an ear, let him hear what the Spirit saith unto the churches; To him that overcometh, will I give to eat of the hidden manna, and will give him a white stone, and in the stone a new name written, which no man knoweth saving he that receiveth it.

"But I regularly read a chapter," says one. I am extremely glad you do, and God bless that chapter to you! I would that all were in the habit of reading right thoughts from the Bible regularly, and endeavoring to understand it; but, if you trust in your Bible-readings as a ground of salvation, you are resting upon a mere soap-bubble which will burst under your weight.

Faith in the Lord Jesus Christ, producing in the soul a change of heart, a new birth unto God, this is what is wanted; and, apart from that, all the Bible reading you ever practice can do you no good whatsoever. "Ye must be born again;" and if there be not this inward change, then vain is all outward observance. You may wash a corpse, you may clothe that corpse in the purest white shroud that was ever woven, but when all is done it does not live; and what are all the outward devotions of a carnal man but dead things which bring no life with them to men dead in sin?"

The Corrupt Church

18) And unto the angel of the church and Thyatira write; these things saith the Son of God, who hath his eyes like unto a flame of fire, and his feet are like fine brass;

19) I know thy works and charity, and service, and faith, and thy patience, and thy works; and the last to be more than the first.

20) Notwithstanding I have a few things against thee because thou sufferest that woman Jezebel, which called herself a prophetess, to teach and to seduce my servants to commit fornication, and to eat things sacrificed unto idols.

21) And I gave her space to repent of her fornication; and she repented not.

22) Behold, I will cast her into a bed, and them that commit adultery with her into great tribulation, except they repent of their deeds.

23) And I will kill her children with death; and all the churches shall know that I am he which searches the reins and hearts: and I will give unto every one of you according to your works.

24) But unto you I say, and unto the rest in Thyatira, as many as have not this doctrine, and which have not known the depths of Satan, as they speak; I will put upon you none other burden.

25) But that which ye have already hold fast till I come.

26) And he that overcometh, and keepeth my words unto the end, to him will I give power over the nations:

27) And he shall rule them with a rod of iron; as the vessels of the potter shall they be broken to shivers: even as I received of my Father.

28) And I will give him the morning star.

29) He that hath an ear, let him hear what the Spirit saith unto the churches.

"Some are foolish enough to put their confidence in ministers. It would seem to me to be the maddest thing in all the world for anybody to have confidence in me as to helping him in his salvation; and I trust that nobody is such a fool. I cannot even save myself; What can we do for you, dear hearts, if you will not have our Savior?

We can stand and weep over you, and break our hearts to think that you reject Him; but what can we do? Oh, if we could let you into heaven if we could renew your hearts, how joyfully would we perform the miracle; but we claim no such power, no such influence! Go you to Christ, and lay hold upon the true altar-horn; but do not be so foolish as to put confidence in us or in any other ministers."

Revelation 3

The Dead Church

1) And unto the angel of the church in Sardis write; These things saith he that hath the seven Spirits of God, and the seven stars; I know thy works, that thou hast a name that thou livest, and art dead.

2) Be watchful, and strengthen the things which remain, that are ready to die: for I have not found thy works perfect before God.

3) Remember therefore how thou hast received and heard, and hold fast, and repent. If therefore thou shalt not watch, I will come on thee as a thief, and thou shalt not know what hour I will come upon thee.

4) Thou hast a few names even in Sardis which have not defiled their garments; and they shall walk with me in white: for they are worthy.

5) He that overcometh, the same shall be clothed in white

raiment; and I will not blot out his name out of the book of life, but I will confess his name before my Father, and before his angels.

6) He that hath an ear, let him hear what the Spirit saith unto the churches.

"Ah, well, says one," I am free of that. I am a professor of religion and have been a member of a church now these twenty years." You may be a member of a church fifty years, but you will be damned at last unless you are a member of Christ. It matters not though you are a church-officer, a deacon, an elder, a pastor, a bishop, or even Archbishop of Canterbury, or an apostle, you will perish as surely as Judas, who betrayed his Master with a kiss unless your heart is right with God.

I pray you, put no confidence in your profession. Unless you have Christ in your heart, a profession is but a painted pageantry for a soul to go to hell in. As a corpse is drawn to the grave by horses adorned with nodding plumes, so may you find in an outward profession a pompous way of being lost? God save us from that!"

The Faithful Church

7) And to the angel of the church in Philadelphia write; these things saith he that is holy, he that is true, he that hath the key of David, he that openeth, and no man shutteth; and no man can shut it; and no man openeth;

8) I know thy works: behold, I have set before thee an open door, and no man can shut it: for thou hast a little strength, and hast kept my word, and hast not denied my name.

9) Behold, I will make them of the synagogue of Satan, which say they are Jews, and are not, but do lie; behold, I will make

them to come and worship before thy feet, and to know that I have loved thee.

10) Because thou hast kept the word of my patience, I also will keep thee from the hour of temptation, which shall come upon all the world, to try them that dwell upon the earth.

11) Behold, I come quickly: hold that fast which thou hast, that no man take thy crown.

12) Him that overcometh will I make a pillar in the temple of my God, and he shall go no more out: and I will write upon him the name of my God, and the name of the city of my God, which is new Jerusalem, which cometh down out of heaven from my God: and I will write upon him my new name.

13) He that hath an ear, let him hear what the Spirit Saith unto the churches.

"No, says one," but I do not trust in mere profession. I have great reliance upon orthodoxy. I will have sound doctrine." That is right, friend, I would have all men value the truth. "My confidence is in sound doctrine." That is not mine, friend, and I hope that it will not be yours long, for many lost souls have firmly believed orthodox doctrine. In fact, I question whether anyone is more orthodox than the devil, for the devils believe and tremble. Satan is no skeptic; he has too much knowledge for that.

The devils believe and tremble, and yet they are devils still. Put no confidence in the mere fact that you hold to an orthodox faith, for a dead orthodoxy soon corrupts. You must have faith in Christ, or else this altar-horn of a correct creed, on which you lay your hand, will bring you no salvation."

The Lukewarm Church

14) And unto the angel of the church of Laodiceans write; these things saith the Amen, the faithful and true witness, the beginning of the creation of God;

15) I know thy works, that thou art neither cold nor hot: I would thou wert cold or hot.

16) So then because thou art lukewarm, and neither cold nor hot, I will spue thee out of my mouth.

17) Because thou saith, I am rich, and increased with goods, and have need of nothing; and knoweth not that thou art wretched, and miserable, and poor, and blind, and naked:

18) I counsel thee to buy of me gold tried in the fire, that thou mayest be rich: and white raiment, that thou mayest be clothed, and that the shame of thy nakedness does not appear; and anoint thine eyes with eyesalve, that thou mayest see.

19) As many as I love, I rebuke and chasten: be zealous therefore, and repent.

20) Behold, I stand at the door, and knock: if any man hears my voice, and open the door, I will come into him and will sup with him, and he with me.

21) To him that overcometh will I grant to sit with me in my throne, even as I also overcame, and am set down with my Father in his throne.

22) He that hath an ear, let him hear what the Spirit Saith unto the churches.

"If I were in your stead tonight, I think that I should bless God to have this matter put so plainly to me. I know that years ago when I was under a sense of sin if I had heard even such a poor sermon as this, I should have jumped for joy at it, and would have ventured upon Christ at once.

Come, poor soul; come at once. You have heard the Gospel long enough; now obey it. You have heard about Christ long enough; now trust in Him. You have been invited and entreated and pleaded with; now yield to His grace. Yield to joy and peace by trusting in Him who will give you both as soon as you have rested in Him.

Look! Sinner, look! A look out of thyself will save thee. Look away from all thy works, and prayers, and tears, and feelings, and Church-goings, and chapel-goings, and sacraments, and ministers. Look alone to Jesus. Look at once to Him who on the bloody tree made expiation, and who bids thee look, and thou shalt live."

CHAPTER 15

SUMMARY

My personal motivation, for writing this book is; If just one person, reads the book, and sees the truth of the **Deceptive Spirit**, behind Kwanzaa and denounce it, and ask the Lord, to come into their heart, and become a Born Again Christian; then I will have, accomplished my purpose in life: To hear, The Heavenly Father, say to me, when I get back to Heaven: <u>God's Word Says It Best</u>: "His lord said unto him, well done, thou good and faithful servant: thou hast been faithful over a few things, I will make thee ruler over many things: enter thou into the joy of thy lord." (Matthew 25:21) KJV.

My prayers are that God will open your Spiritual eyes so that you will see, the diabolical mindset, of Ron Karenga's motives, behind creating a 'Religion' for Black people. And, taking it upon himself, to appoint himself, by naming himself, the 'Master Teacher,' of Black people, in the United States of America!

Too many Black people are still celebrating (practicing) Kwanzaa without knowing anything about its Roots! Too many Black people do not know who, Ron Karenga really is. Besides, just knowing, that he made up Kwanzaa and Kawaida; and a Professor at California State University, in Long Beach. Knowing where a person works, is not enough reason, for Black people to start living their lives, according to how he tells them to live it!

Do you honestly think, that Almighty God, forgot about your Culture? Of course, He didn't. Culture is essential; because God created it. God did not create Culture for you to base your entire life on. **GOD DECIDES WHO YOU ARE, AND YOUR ASSIGNMENT IN LIFE; NOT YOUR CULTURE! And, Salvation transcends Culture! Your Culture cannot get you into Heaven; but, your Salvation can!**

I'm reminded what Dr. Mike Murdock, The Wisdom Center; one of the most dynamic speakers in America today; and Author of, The Assignment, The Dream & The Destiny – (A 31 Day Mentorship Program of Wisdom). He stated, "Your gifts and skills were given to you by The Holy Spirit. Your gifts and skills are different from others around you. He said, You are sent by God into this generation. God has a plan. God has a plan for your life. His plan for your life will require your obedience. His plan for your life will require a personal decision on your part to cooperate. His plan guarantees His Blessing when completed. His plan gives life to you, while other plans will bring death."

Dr. Mike Murdock further stated, "God decides what He desires for you to do. You decide your obedience. Think for a moment. Did the automobile instruct Henry Ford and declare to him what it had decided to be? Of course not. Mr. Ford named it. Did the airplane inform the Wright brothers that it was going to fly and be called an airplane? Of course not. Orville and Wilbur Wright declared it so. The Creator decides. The creation discovers. The Creator decides what He has intended for you to become. The creation merely decides the degree of obedience and cooperation to make it so. Products do not decide. Manufacturers decide. You are the product of God. He is the only One who can reveal the Assignment He decided for you at your birth. Remember: Your Assignment Is Not Your Decision, But Your Discovery."

Unfortunately, if you are celebrating (practicing) the Seven Principles; that makes you a **Follower\Believer** of the Kwanzaa Religious Cult! Simply put, Ron Karenga, is a Black, Blind, Bully! It's a dangerous case of The Blind Leading The Blind! <u>God's Word Says It Best</u>: "In whom the god of this world hath blinded the minds of them which believe not," (2 Corinthians 4:4) KJV.

To those of you, who are celebrating Kwanzaa; you are being Blindly lead straight to Hell! And, to those of you, who don't know it by now; yes, there is a **Hell** to shun, and a **Heaven** to gain. I pray that you wake-up, to see the deception, without going into denial. You know what I mean? Just in case, you don't know what I mean, let me say, I hope you don't say, "Well, we can still get together, and celebrate anyways; just to be celebrating, our ancestors here in America." No, because what you will be doing is called, Compromising!

Remember in Chapter 13; I shared with you, that Karenga said, "He was so impressed, with the thinking of P.T. Barnum's experiment, of doing something, that people never heard of?" So, it inspired him, to try the same concept; and Kwanzaa was birthed! Therefore, please do not choose to be a part of Karenga's **Black Kwanzaa Circus!**

I decided, to terminate my membership in US Organization, based on a lot of reasons. For instance, it was **NOT THE MOVEMENT** that I thought it was when I joined; it was finding out the **TRUTH** about US Organization's involvement in the **UCLA MURDERS**; it was the way Karenga started thinking, that he was **GOD**; and wanting everyone to **BOW-DOWN TO HIM AND HIS PICTURE**, which he placed over the Kwanzaa Temple's doorway; it was the **SEXUAL ASSAULT**; it was the **ASSAULT & BATTERY**; and it was the **THREATENING TO KILL MY TWO SONS IF I REPORTED HIM TO THE LOS ANGELES POLICE DEPARTMENT**; just to name a few.

I understand, why you might not want, to acknowledge that; Kwanzaa is a Lie; but, **IT IS WHAT IT IS!** And, I would be lying, if I said that; I don't care what you decide to do about Kwanzaa; it's not my life, it's yours! However, I must be real, and true to my core values, based on God's Holy Word; and that is why I must tell you the Truth. I do care! I care about you and your family, and especially your children! So, please think about everything, which you have read; and then do your research, if necessary.

And, for those of you, who already know the Lord; please ask Him, what He wants you to do about this diabolical, so-called stinking holiday; that's trying to **STEAL HIS GLORY!** I am pretty sure, He will tell you to: **Kick It To The Curb! Quickly!**

In conclusion, now that all the pieces to the puzzle are in place; the picture shows, a clear case of a conspiracy strategy for overthrowing Western Society; by conducting a long march through the institutions. And, the "de-Christianizing of America" and the West; including educational and religious institutions that Gramsci advocated. In other words, I agree with Tightrope, and Professor Lee Congdon, Ph.D. **I also agree, that there will always be HOPE in the World; as long as Jesus Christ is Lord!** Let's take a closer look at the word: Conspiracy.

Conspiracy: A secret plan by a group to do something unlawful or harmful. For example, 'a conspiracy to destroy the government.' The action of plotting or conspiring. For example, 'they were cleared of conspiracy to pervert the course of justice.'

A Conspiracy of Silence: An agreement to say nothing about an issue that should generally be known. For example, 'the ministers took part in a conspiracy of silence over the decision to close the steelworks.'

The Elements of Conspiracy Agreement: The essence of conspiracy is the agreement between two or more persons. A single person acting alone cannot be guilty of conspiracy.

I Rest My Case

HE'S DOING A NEW THING!

Based on: Isaiah 43:18-19
"Remember ye not the former things,
neither consider the things of old.
Behold, I will do a new thing: …
now it shall spring forth:
shall ye not know it?
I will even make a way
in the wilderness, and
rivers in the desert."

He Said Remember Ye Not
The former things
Neither consider
The things of old
Behold!

He's Doing A New Thing!
Look around you can't you tell
Oh, don't put Him in a shell
It's time to snatch people
From going to Hell
So, come on now Church
Get on the right trail
It's called the Latter Rain

<u>Do tell!</u>

He's Doing A New Thing!
Yes! It's time for the Church
To do the greater works
Yes! He's turned-up the heat
So, come on and
Get on your feet
And get ready
<u>For The Grand Finale!</u>

He's Doing A New Thing!
Unfolding signs
And wonders galore
Like you've never seen before
<u>So, come on and yield</u>
To His appeal!

He's Doing A New Thing!
So, roll-up your sleeves
And get-up off your knees
Oh - Come on now Church
Get out of the pews
<u>Cause His Anointing is upon You</u>!

He's Doing A New Thing!
With the Young and with the Old
So, go ahead get out front
And take your stand
And get ready
<u>For The Greatest Revival</u>
<u>Known To Man!</u>

He's Doing A New Thing!
He will use You to win Lost Souls
So, dress to impress
<u>Yes! Put on the Whole Armor</u>
<u>Of God to look your Best</u>
Now go storm the gates of Hell
And Fight! Fight! Fight!
With all your Supernatural Might!

He's Doing A New Thing!
<u>Oh - It Doesn't Matter</u>
<u>What Color You Are</u>
<u>No, It Doesn't Matter</u>
<u>What Culture you Claim</u>
<u>Cause He's passing out Gifts</u>
<u>For All to Gain</u>
So, go with the flow
And get your passport in order
So, you can travel
From border to border
<u>So, come on now Church</u>
It's time to get ready
Cause God's Word says
He's Doing A New Thing!
<u>And He'll Do It Through You!</u>
(The Bottom Line)

END WORD

COLOSSIANS 2:8 (AMP)

See to it that no one takes you captive through philosophy and empty deception [pseudo-intellectual babble] according to, the tradition [and musings] of mere men, following the elementary principles of this world, rather than following [the truth – the teachings of] Christ.

NEWSPAPER ARTICLES, COMMENTS, PHOTOGRAPHS

Maulana Karenga and Hakim Jamal. Early US literature designated Jamal as the group's founder and Karenga as its chairman. Jamal was a close friend of Malcolm X. He left the US Organization in early 1966 apparently as the group became steeped in Chairman Karenga's own ideology rather than Malcolm X's. (Courtesy of the Harry Adams Collection, Center for Photojournalism & Visual History, Journalism Department, California State University, Northridge)

Early US circle meeting with Maulana Karenga. To the left of Karenga: Tommy Jacquette-Halifu, Ken Msemaji, Ngao Damu, Thomas Henson-Hakika, and Karl Key-Hekima. (Courtesy of Terry Damu)

Brenda Haiba Karenga, Maulana Karenga's first wife and founding member of US, teaches children at the Aquarian Center, US's initial meeting place. (Courtesy of Terry Damu)

Amiri Baraka, Maulana Karenga (left, below), Ken Msemaji (left, standing),
H. Rap Brown, presently named Jamil Amin (right, sitting), Imamu Halisi
(right standing), and Floyd McKissick (far right, sitting) at the 1967 Black
Power Conference. The conference took place in the wake of a massive urban
uprising in Newark, New Jersey. Baraka was still wearing head bandages from
wounds sustained by a police beating. At that point Baraka was in the process of
developing a close alliance with the US Organization. Later on in the early
1970s, Baraka's Congress of African People and Committee for a Unified
Newark eclipsed US as the foremost cultural nationalist force in the Black
Power movement. (Courtesy of C. R. D. Halisi)

Black Nationalist Leader Stirs Watts Teen-Agers

By THOMAS A. JOHNSON
Special to The New York Times

LOS ANGELES, May 26—Ron Karenga, the leading Black Nationalist figure in the Watts District of Los Angeles, told an enthusiastic Negro teen-age audience last night they should prepare to defend themselves—if need be—from whites.

Addressing a weekly discussion series at a community center in the basement of the United Christian Church, Mr. Karenga said that if the Negro community was ready and fully capable of defending itself, this show of force would discourage any group that might want to attack it.

His talk followed other weekly discussions that had been concerned with the war in Vietnam, narcotics and sex.

Mr. Karenga did not openly advocate fighting policemen although he and his audience accused the police of brutality toward the Negro community. Police officials claim little knowledge of Mr. Karenga and they estimate his following to be very small. Mr. Karenga's Neo-Black Nationalist organization is known by the pronoun 'Us.'"

Quotes Malcolm X

"We are free men," he told his audience of 60 youths in describing "Us." "We have our own language. We are making our own customs and we name ourselves. Only slaves and dogs are named by their masters."

Members of "Us" adopt African names, complaining that American Negroes have been given European names. "You are not Europeans," Mr. Karenga said. "You are Afro-Americans. Have you ever seen a Chinese named Jones or a Japanese named Whitfield?"

The audience laughed. "Talk that talk!" one youngster shouted, "I dig on this stuff," said another.

A short, stocky man, whose voice sometimes becomes strident, Mr. Karenga often refers to the preaching of the late Black Nationalist, Malcolm X, in much the same way Malcolm X had quoted the Black Muslim leader, Elijah Muhammad, years ago.

Mr. Karenga is 24 years old and of a light brown complexion. His head is clean-shaven and he has a long, Mandarin-type of mustache. He wears a dark green "buba," a loose, short toga-like garment. Some of the audience last night asked one another if he was Chinese.

Mr. Karenga, whose name once was Everett, explained that the group's purpose is to "make new names was to "make our own customs."

He denied that the group sought to present a mystical appearance and he said that they chose instead a Machiavellian approach. "We will do whatever works," he said. He said that "love, prayer and picketing have not worked" for the Negro and said that it would probably be necessary to defend Negro communities with "force, intelligence and deception."

He denied that his group had engaged in riot activity to date but he said that only his group had enough influence in the Negro community to stop riots.

Four Were Arrested

Four members of the Us organization were arrested Tuesday night and three are being held in $15,000 bail each on charges that include the carrying of a concealed and loaded .22-caliber pistol, resisting arrest, assault on a policeman and taking a prisoner from the police.

Two of those held wore the usual Us T-shirt with a picture of the late Malcolm X on the front. The police have reported persons wearing such shirts figured in racial violence last March, when two men were killed in Watts.

The arrests Tuesday were followed by rock-throwing incidents in which two white motorists driving through Watts were injured when their cars were struck.

The eight-month-old organization's membership is never disclosed. Mr. Karenga said the group followed a "traditionalist," self-created African religion that "is more functional than spiritual in working for the day-to-day good of black people."

The members study Swahili, an African language that they have adopted, and teach it to their children, Mr. Karenga said.

Mr. Karenga also teaches Swahili to adults at a local high school.

Graduate of U. C. L. A.

An articulate man, whose evangelist's zeal is reminiscent of the late Malcolm X, Mr. Karenga has an M.A. degree from the University of California, Los Angeles, in political science and is a candidate there for a Ph.D. in linguistics. He specializes in African languages.

The Us organization goes in for military - like formations similar to those employed by the Black Muslim's Fruit of Islam. Often, when Mr. Karenga walks along the Watts' streets, he is up of Us members.

When the wife of the late Malcolm X, Mrs. Betty Shabazz, spoke here recently to mark her late husband's birthday, she was flanked by Mr. Karenga and by an aide who stood with arms folded to guard her.

Mr. Karenga said he was a great admirer of the Black Muslims' "good sense of organization and of discipline."

The teen-age audience at the community center last night seemed impressed. Several of the Us organization headquarters.

Many professional Negroes here discount the importance of the organization. A school teacher called the group "amusing." But a Negro City Hall aide said: "Karenga will gather a following, just like Malcolm X did, because conditions are so bad and because the city will do nothing big enough and fast enough to make conditions any better for the Watts."

Comments On:
Black Nationalist Leader Stirs Watts
Teen-Agers Newspaper Article - 1965

At this juncture, let's take a closer look at the second column, fourth paragraph, and line 6. Start reading where it says, He said that, "love ..."

He said that, "love, prayer, and picketing have not worked for the Negro, and said that, it would probably be necessary to defend Negro communities with **"Force, Intelligence, and Deception."**

Karenga Has Accomplished His Goals
According To The Following:

1. FORCE:
- Murdered Black Panther Members\US Organization
- Sexual Assault on One (1) Black Woman
- Ordered Assault & Battery on One (1) Black Woman
- Ordered Assault & Battery on One (1) Black Man
- Torturing & Assaulting Two (2) Black Women
- Kidnapping Two Black Women
- Locking-Up His Wife In A Tiger Cage Housed In His Garage
- Domestic Violence
- Mentally Abusive

2. INTELLIGENCE:
- BA Degree
- MA Degree
- Ph.D. Degree
- Ph.D. Degree
- Educated Fool

3. DECEPTION:

- Kwanzaa African Religion\Cult
- Kawaida African Religious Values
- FBI Rat\Stooge\Informant\Agent\Snitch
- CIA Rat\Stooge\Informant\Agent\Snitch
- Counterfeit: Organization Us\US Organization
- Lied To Innocent Children, Youth, & Black Families
- Lied To The President of The United States of America
- Lied To The Department of Education, Colleges & Universities
- Lied To The USA Postal Service

UCLA STUDENT

Brothers Surrender In Panther Killings

LOS ANGELES (UPI) — The second of two brothers sought for the slaying of two Black Panther Party members at UCLA voluntarily surrendered to police early today and was booked on suspicion of murder.

Larry Joseph Stiner, 21, a UCLA student, surrendered to police at the airport in San Diego, Calif., after arrangements were made by his attorney, Frank Evans.

His brother, George Phillip Stiner, 22, turned himself in to West Los Angeles detectives in a similar arrangement through Evans Monday.

Police said Larry had a bullet in his right shoulder but officers did not know how he was shot. The wound was estimated to be three days old. He was reported in good condition in the prison ward at Los Angeles County-USC Medical Center.

Detectives here said the suspect made no statements about the slayings or why he was in San Diego. Police intended to seek a grand jury indictment charging the brothers with the murders later today.

Both suspects were free on $31,250 bail each pending trial Feb. 10 on charges in Orange County of armed robbery, attempted murder, assault with a deadly weapon and kidnaping.

The brothers were identified by witnesses to the UCLA shootings as members of US, a militant Negro organization founded by former UCLA student Ron Karenga.

The Stiner brothers were linked to the slayings by witnesses at the meeting of about 150 Negro students on the university's proposed Afro-American Studies Center.

The meeting had been called to resolve a reported conflict between the Panthers, US and the Black Students Union over who was to be appointed director of the center.

Killed in the shooting were two Panther officials, John Jerome Huggins, 23, and Alprentice "Bunchy" Carter, 26.

At news conferences Monday here and in San Francisco, the Panthers charged the slayings were "political assassination by pork chop nationalists."

Sherman Banks, Black Panther deputy chairman for Southern California, called Karenga "a spokesman for the pig power structure to divide the people." He said the US group was one of several "pork chop nationalists" because it seeks federal funds.

"EVERYTHING FOR T

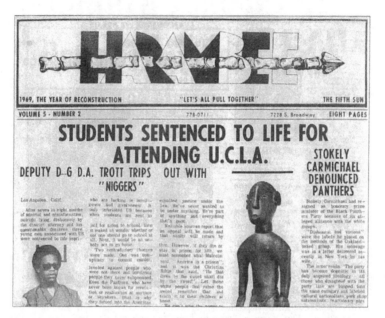

Front page of *Harambee* with the headline "Students Sentenced to Life for Attending UCLA." US's newspaper was reacting to the conviction of Larry Watani-Stiner, George Ali-Stiner, and Donald Hawkins-Stodi for the killing of Black Panther Party leaders Alprentice "Bunchy" Carter and John Huggins at UCLA in January 1969. The tragic events marked the beginning of the end of US's tenure as a premier Black Power organization. Throughout 1969 and 1970 US was plagued by the violent feud with the Black Panther Party, alienation from the Black communities of Southern California, internal factionalization and violent in-fighting among its own ranks, and eventually a leadership breakdown.

Comments: Harambee - US
Newspaper Article - 1969

At this juncture, let's take a closer look at The Harambee Newspaper Article.

THE LIE:

STUDENTS SENTENCED FOR LIFE FOR ATTENDING U.C.L.A.

Notice the word **Murdering** has been replaced by the word **Attending.**

THE TRUTH:

TWO US MEMBERS SENTENCED FOR LIFE FOR MURDERING TWO BLACK PANTHER PARTY MEMBERS AT U.C.L.A.

This article is an example of Karenga not being a truthful person. He continues to avoid telling the truth.

Gail Idili-Davis recounted a horrific ordeal of torture and confinement that occurred in the spring of 1970. She was one of the two women that Karenga and three other US members were convicted of assaulting with intent to do great bodily injury. (Courtesy of Gail Idili-Davis)

Black Militant Karenga Held In Torture Case

LOS ANGELES (UPI)—Black militant Ron Karenga was arrested with three of his followers Tuesday on charges he tortured two young women with a soldering iron and a vise.

Karenga, 29, founder and head of "US," a society to promote black culture, was charged with conspiracy and assault in the secret grand jury indictments returned last week and made public Tuesday.

District attorney's investigators said the alleged torture incidents occurred last May. Karenga was said to believe the women, former members of US, tried to poison him, and he subjected them to torture in an attempt to extract "confessions."

Beaten, Tortured

Investigators said the women were held at gunpoint, forced to disrobe and were beaten. At one point, it was charged, Karenga forced a hot soldering iron inside the mouth of one of the victims, while the other woman's toe was squeezed in a vise.

Karenga was quoted as saying to the women, "Vietnamese torture is nothing compared to what I know."

The victims were identified as Deborah Jones and Gail Davis, both 20, who were living at Karenga's home in suburban Inglewood at the time.

Karenga and Fred A. Glover, 19, Louis "Sedu" Smith, 19, and Luz Maria Tamayo, 23, all were arrested when they appeared at the Inglewood County Courthouse as defendants in a traffic case.

were held at gunpoint, forced to disrobe and were beaten. At one point, it was charged, Karenga forced a hot soldering iron inside the mouth of one of the victims, while the other woman's toe was squeezed in a vise.

Karenga was quoted as saying to the women, "Vietnamese torture is nothing compared to what I know."

The victims were identified as Deborah Jones and Gail Davis, both 20, who were living at Karenga's home in suburban Inglewood at the time.

Karenga and Fred A. Glover, 19, Louis "Sedu" Smith, 19, and Luz Maria Tamayo, 23, all were arrested when they appeared at the Inglewood County Courthouse as defendants in a traffic case.

Karenga was said to fear that the two women tried to poison him by placing "some sort of crystals" in his food and water and on his clothes.

It also was charged that a caustic liquid was poured into the mouths of the women and they were forced to put detergent in their mouths.

The women protested their innocence during the two torture sessions on May 9 and 10 in Karenga's garage. They were ultimately freed and went to live with friends. Their present addresses were not made public.

Karenga Arrested on Coast After Missing Arraignment

LOS ANGELES, Oct. 7 (UPI) —Ron Karenga, the black nationalist leader charged with torturing two young women followers, was jailed today after he failed to appear for arraignment.

A bench warrant was issued for his arrest, and less than three hours later he was found in a bail bondsman's office directly across the street from a police station.

A police sergeant saw him go into the office and Mr. Karenga was arrested. The bondsman Celes King, insisted the whole thing was a mistake, that Mr. Karenga did not realize he was supposed to appear in court today.

Black militant sentenced

LOS ANGELES (UPI)— Black militant Ron Karenga, who once allegedly boasted of knowing worse torture techniques than in Vietnam, was given a one-to-10 year prison sentence Friday for commanding the torture of a young woman follower.

Earlier this year Krenga, chieftain of the black nationalist group US, was convicted on two counts of felonious assault and false imprisonment in the two-day, 1970 torture of Deborah Jones, 20.

"Vietnamese torture is nothing compared to what I know," Karenga is alleged to have said to Miss Jones and her girlfriend, both of whom he suspected of harboring plans to poison him.

Testimony showed that the instruments of torture included Karenga thrusting a scalding soldering iron into the mouth of one girl, while a vise squeezed a toe of the other girl.

Karenga allegedly ordered his followers to torture Miss Jones and her friend, Gail Davis, also 20. Three of Karenga's followers were ultimately convicted in the case and sentenced to county jail terms and probation.

Above: Karenga along with Wesely Kabaila (left) and attorney Richard Walton (right) leave the courtroom after the assault conviction in May 1971. (Courtesy UCLA Library, Department of Special Collections)

Left: Maulana Karenga at the Men's Colony at San Luis Obispo where he served four years, from 1971 through 1975. Imamu Clyde Halisi chaired the US Organization throughout the period in which Karenga was incarcerated. (Courtesy UCLA Library, Department of Special Collections)

Tikisa, the First Runner-up for the "Campus Sweetheart" Contest, at Los Angeles Southwest Community College, in 1970.

Tikisa, The Coordinator, of The Watts Summer Festival Afro-American Fashion Show, "The Versatility of Blackness," held at Markham Edwin Jr. High School, Los Angeles, CA. on August 21, 1971.

MODELS

BIBLIOGRAPHY: (LISTED BY DATES)

ARTICLES, BOOKS\E-BOOKS, ESSAYS, INTERVIEWS, NEWSPAPER ARTICLES, OPEN LETTERS & WEBSITE BLOGS

1965 – Present: The Official Kwanzaa Web Site, Kwanzaa: Roots and Branches, www.officialkwanzaawebsite.org

09/02/1968 — Militant Negro Leader, Ron Ndabezitha Everett-Karenga, Philadelphia, New York Times.

10/2/1968 —— Nationalists Slowly Gaining Ground, The Bridgeport Post.

1977 — Karenga, Maulana, Kwanzaa: Origin, Concepts, Practice. Inglewood, CA.: Kawaida Publications.

1/21/1969 — UCLA Murders, Tucson Daily Citizen.

2\14\69 — Why I don't Do Kwanzaa, By Bruce A. Dixon, Black Agenda Report.

3/20/1970 — US Supported By Churches, Van Nuys Valley News.

9/18/1971 — Karenga's Trial, Daily Review.

9/21/1971 — Karenga Sentenced, The Dubois Courier – Express.

5/2/1973 — Karenga's Parole Denied, San Mateo Times.

1980 — Karenga, Maulana. Kawaida Theory, Inglewood, CA. University of Sankore Press.

1989 — Karenga, Maulana. The African American Holiday of Kwanzaa. Los Angeles, CA: The University of Sankore Press.

12/20/1990 — www.nytimes.com/1990/12/20/garden/in-blacks-homes-the-christmas-and-kwanzaa.

1993 — The Original African Heritage Study Bible, KJV, General Editor, The Reverend Cain Hope Felder, Ph.D., Professor of New Testament Languages and Literature, Howard University, Washington, D.C.

1997 — Maulana Karenga, Kwanzaa: A Celebration of Family, Community and Culture Los Angeles, CA.: University of Sankore Press.

12/20/1999 — The True Spirit of Kwanzaa By William Norman Grigg, The New American, www.thenewamerican.com.

12/24/1999 — http://www.discoverthenetworks.org/individualProfile.asp?indid=2222.

12/31/1999 — The TRUTH About Kwanzaa - By Tony Snow, Detroit News, http://www.martinlutherking.org/kwanzaa.html.

01/02/1999 — Ron Karenga Interview with PBS Frontline.

2000 — The Long March Through The Institutions By Tightrope, www.tightrope.com

12/21/01 — The Rotten Roots of Kwanzaa – By Thomas Clough, www.weirdrepublic.com

12/27/2001 —http://www.nytimes.com/2001/12/27/opinion/1-celebrating-kwanzaa-7283990.html.

12/28/2001 — The Assignment: The Dream & The Destiny, Volume 1, By Mike Murdock, www.WisdomOnline.com.

01/10/2002 — Did You Have A Happy Kwanzaa? By Joseph Farah, Commentator, WND.com

12/24/2002 — http://www.tysknews.com/Depts/OurCulture/kwanzaa_fbi.htm.

2002 — The Many Falsehoods of Kwanzaa, By Steven Hutson, Grace Centered Online Christian Magazine.

12/24/2002 — Kwanzaa: A Holiday From The FBI, By Ann Coulter, A New York Times Best Selling Author.

12/26/2002 — Happy Kwanzaa By Paul Mulshine, www.frontpagemag.com

2003 — Coaching 101 By Robert E. Logan and Sherilyn Carlton, Church Smart Resources.

12/26/2003 — http://www.nytimes.com/2003/12/26/opinion/a-case-of-the-kwanzaa-blues.blues.html.

12/06/2004 – Kwanzaa Is An Absolute Fraud – By Rev. Pat Robertson, The Christian Broadcasting Network, The 700 Club, www.cbn.org

12/21/2004 –Black Minister: Say 'No' To Kwanzaa By Rev. Jesse Lee Peterson, Founder and President of BOND www.bond@bondinfo.org. Rebuilding The Family By Rebuilding The Man, www.rebuildingtheman.com - TheFallenState.TV – JLPTalk.com Newsmaxtv.com – WND.com.

2004 — Maulana Karenga, Maat, The Moral Ideal In Ancient Egypt – NY, New York.

12/24/2005 — Kwanzaa: The Holiday From The FBI, By Ann Coulter, Best Selling Author.

12/29/2005 — Fighting For US – Maulana Karenga, The US

Organization, And Black Cultural Nationalism By Scot Brown, Associate Professor of History, University of California. (Paperback Book)

11/21/2006 — The Monster Who Made Up Kwanzaa By Thomas Clough, weirdpublic.com.

2006 — Kwanzaa By La Shawn Barber, Christian Research Institute. Article ID: JA075 – Volume 29, Number 6, http://www.equip.org

2008 — Coaching Questions; A Coach's Guide To Powerful Asking Skills, By Tony Stoltzfus – www.Coach22.com

2009 — Maulana Karenga An Intellectual Portrait - By Molefi Kete Asante, Polity.

07/09/2010 – On Dr. Maulana Karenga: An Open Letter By Wesley Kabaila. www.simbamaat.blogspot.com

08/2010 — Kwanzaa Invented by American Gang Member/FBI Informant, USA Seekfind.net.

12/10/2010 — The 'Real' Truth About Kwanzaa - By Carlotta Morrow, Christocentric Press, (Kindle E-Book) – www.christocentric.com/ Kwanzaa/religion.htm

2011 — CIA Informant: Ron Karenga (RAT 416 – NZA) & Kwanzaa Exposed By Agent Filez.com.

8/25/2011 — Kwanzaa Is Wack: There, I Said It! By Roland Martin,www. NewsOne.com

12/26/2011 — http://www.chicagonow.com/publius-forum/2011/12/ the-kwanzaa-con-created-by-arapistandtorturer.

01/02/2012 — Maulana Karenga's Haunting Ghost – Essay Online by Mukasa Afrika Ma'at. www.http://afrikan-resistance/blogspot.com/ maulana-karenga-haunting-ghost-by.html

12/13/2012 — https://www.washingtonpost.com/blogs/therootdc/post/confessions-of-a-kwanzaadropout.

12/26/2012 — The Holiday Brought To You By The FBI, By Ann Coulter, New York Times Best-Selling Author, In Trump We Trust.

12/26/20012 — Unhappy Kwanzaa – The Media Are Still Falling For That Fake Holiday Created By A Felon, By Paul Mulshine, The Star Ledger.

01/03/2013 — State Senator, Glenn Grothman, Declares War on Kwanzaa, By Adam W. McCoy, patch.com

02/01/2013 http://www.Blackhistoryheroes.com/.

02/2013 — 42-laws-of-maat-under-kemet-law-html.

12/26/2013 — Kwanzaa: The Holiday Brought To You By The FBI, By Ann Coulter, New York Times Best Selling Author

2013 — On The First Day of Kwanzaa… It's Time For The Lazy Journalist To Finally Start Doing Their Research: By Paul Mulshine, The Star-Ledger.com.

2013 — The Kwanzaa Con: A Fake Holiday Created By A Rapist And Torturer – By Warner Todd Huston, www.PubliusForum.com

02/03/14 — http://www.usorganization.org/30th/ppp.12/25/2014 — Celebrating Kwanzaa: Practicing Principles and Creating Good In The World, Los Angeles Watts Times.

12/27/2014 — Kwanzaa – A Made-Up Holiday, By Warren Beatty, AmericanThinker.com.

12/12/2014 — The Kwanzaa Hoax By William J. Bennett, thetextbookleague.org.

12/18/2015 — Perspective: Why I Quit Kwanzaa By Robbyn Mitchell, Tampabay.com.

12/23/2015 — Happy Kwanzaa! The Holiday Brought To You By The FBI, By Ann Coulter, Author, Townhall.com.

12/26/2015 — Nobody Celebrates Kwanzaa By History Buff, Crispus Knight.

12/26/2015 — Happy Kwanzaa! By Patrick S. Poole, tysknews.com.

12/27/2015 — Why I Don't Celebrate Kwanzaa By Judge Joe Brown Interview, http://www.judgejoebrown4da.com - www.webenews.org.

08/2016 — The Culture War, www.culture-war.info

9/25/2016 — Kwanzaa Born of Separatism, Radicalism, By Mona Charen.

8/22/2016 — The Long March Through The Institutions Is The Culture Way, By Lee Congdon, Ph.D., Professor Emeritus of History, James Madison University.

9/25/2016 — MacArthur, The Study Bible, Grace To You, gty.org.

10/17/2016 — Definition For Forgiveness, www.allaboutgod.com.

11/06/2017 — The Science Agenda To Exterminate Blacks, By Mike Adams, NaturalNews. www.NaturalNews.com.

11/06/2017 — There Is A Concerted Effort To Exterminate Blacks, By Mike Adams, NaturalNews. www.NaturalNews.com.

AUTHOR BIOGRAPHY

Barbara A. De Loach is the Mother of three wonderful adult Sons. She is blessed with six wonderful Grandchildren, and seven wonderful Great Grandchildren. She is a licensed and ordained Youth Minister. She is also a Life Coach and Consultant; professionally trained by America's #1 Success Coach, Jack Canfield, Cocreator of <u>Chicken Soup for The Soul Series</u>.

She was honored in 1999, with the "Woman of Distinction in Business Award," from Quinn A.M.E. Church, Moreno Valley, California. Barbara is an award-winning, published Poet. She has a published poem entitled: "When Will Judgment End And Acceptance Begin?" in the <u>Literary Magazine, Phineas 2002</u> of San Bernardino Valley College, English Department.

Barbara has three poems, published in <u>Deep River Rhythms, A Tribute to Our Ancestors: Past, Present, and Future</u>, October 2002 entitled: Looking For Peace In All The Wrong Places! - The Call of Wisdom, and Are You Ready To Meet Your Maker? She is the Inventor/Designer of The Game of Revelations, Christian Family Board Game, which sold nationally. Barbara is the "First Black American Woman" to Invent/Design a Christian Family Board Game in The United States of America. She is also the Inventor/Designer of Build Me Up! The Self-Esteem Board Game, which also sold nationally.

Build Me Up! The Self-Esteem Board Game, was evaluated

and approved by The Curriculum Frameworks and Instructional Resources Office of The California Department of Education for its Social Content; that can be used, in all the schools, in the State of California. The Honorable, Mayor of San Francisco, Willie L. Brown, Jr., endorsed Build Me Up! The Self-Esteem Game for children, youth, and their families.

Her passion is to fulfill her God-given Assignment on Earth. God's Word Says It Best: "For once you were darkness, but now you are Light in the Lord. Walk as children of Light [live as those who are native-born to the Light] (for the fruit [the effect, the result] of the Light consists in all goodness and righteousness and truth) trying to learn [by experience] what is pleasing to the Lord [and letting your lifestyles be examples of what is most acceptable to Him – your behavior expressing gratitude to God for your salvation.] Do not participate in the worthless and unproductive deeds of darkness, but instead expose them [by exemplifying personal integrity, moral courage, and godly character.] (Ephesians 5:8-11) AMP.

A WORD TO:

ALL GANG MEMBERS

WORLDWIDE AND ESPECIALLY IN CHICAGO!

My Dear Brothers and Sisters,

If you are a **Gang Member** please ask yourself this Question: How Much Is Your Life Worth? **Wait!** Before answering this Question: **FIRST COUNT THE COST!**

For instance, God has put inside of you some Gifts & Skills. **Some Awesome Gifts & Skills!** But, if you never give <u>Yourself</u> the chance of finding out what the Gifts & Skills are; then you are **SHORT CHANGING YOURSELF! – BIG TIME!**

No man on Earth: {Red, Yellow, Brown, White, or Black} can stop you, **if you make-up your own mind to do the right things with your life**; instead of doing the wrong things with your life. It's just that simple.

{**Listen to me. Don't you allow: Another Gang Member, Father, Mother, Brother, Sister, Uncle, Aunt, Cousin, Friend, Neighbor, Co-Worker, Enemy, Whoever or Whatever**} <u>**STOP YOU FROM**</u>**:** FULFILLING YOUR GOD GIVEN ASSIGNMENT ON EARTH! YOU GO FOR IT! YOU CAN DO IT! WHATEVER

IT IS THAT GOD REVEALS TO YOU – YOU CAN DO ALL THINGS THROUGH JESUS CHRIST WHO WILL GIVE YOU THE STRENTH AND THE COURAGE TO REACH YOUR GOD GIVEN DESTINY!

THE HOLY SPIRIT WILL HELP YOU! YOU WILL NEVER BE ALONE AGAIN! JESUS SAID, "I WILL NEVER LEAVE YOU NOR FORSAKE YOU! HE LOVES YOU JUST LIKE YOU ARE! COME TO HIM AND HE WILL TURN YOUR LIFE AROUND FOR YOU! YOU CAN'T TURN IT AROUND WITHOUT HIM! PLEASE BE TRUE TO YOURSELF – GIVE GOD A CHANCE TO REVEAL TO YOU WHO HE CREATED YOU TO BE AND YOUR PURPOSE IN LIFE!

When I joined US Organization, I didn't think of it as a gang. I truly was deceived; by the fact that, when I was growing up, gangs didn't have weekly meetings; in an office building; and meetings for the public to attend. I thought that, I was joining a **Cause**. I thought that, I was joining a **Movement,** to help my people; and especially the children.

As I shared with you in the Introduction, I was raised in South Central L.A./Watts; where gangs were made up of the children who lived in your neighborhood. I was a gang member because, of my two older Sisters; both had a boyfriend in a gang, and I had to go wherever they went, because I was the youngest.

Back in the day, gangs were more like clubs. We mostly had a lot of parties. We went horseback riding, had picnics at the local parks, where we would go swimming. We had wholesome things to do. For some of us, the Gangs served as a substitute for the Family. The Gang Members made you feel like you BELONGED somewhere. But, in reality, you didn't BELONG with the wrong people.

Yes, sometimes there were fights between the gang members; but they didn't kill each other! They fought fists to fists, not with guns! And, after the fight, was over, they were still friends. Another thing that happened to the Black Family, besides Gangs, was the <u>Great</u>

<u>Exodus of Fathers</u> leaving their families! As I shared with you, in the Introduction; my Father was involved in a car accident at the young age of twenty-one. What I didn't share was, his destination, when the car accident happened.

Well, my Mother was three months pregnant with me. My oldest Sister was five years old, and my other Sister, was two years old, when Daddy left my Mother for another woman. My Father and his girlfriend, had just arrived in Los Angeles, California, when the car accident happened. My Mother was notified by the Hospital that her husband, was involved in a terrible car accident and reported his condition as critical, and that he was in the Intensive Care Unit.

My Mother contacted Daddy's Father and Mother to tell them the bad news. Then my Mother, left Louisiana right away, to go see about Daddy in Los Angeles. At that time my Mother didn't know that my Father had left her for another woman. She did not find out, until she arrived at the hospital; and met the other woman visiting with Daddy in the hospital room. I often wondered, how did my Mother handle all that **drama**; and especially since, she was **three months pregnant with me!**

Every time my Sisters and I asked questions about their relationship, before he became a paraplegic; my Mother would start cursing and become very angry. After a while we stopped asking questions about their marriage. And, no one in our extended family ever talked about my Father and Mother's relationship. In those days, it was considered, taboo, to get a divorce; have a child out of wedlock; or a Father leaving his Family for another woman! So, after that happened, our family moved to Los Angeles, California.

And, when we visited with our Father and Big Mama, he would only talk about the times when he was a teenager, and how he and his friends would shoot his gun at other boys in the forest, just to have fun! I was horrified! I vowed to myself, that I would not be like my Father when I grew-up! I couldn't understand why he thought that shooting at boys, was fun; when the boys could have been killed!

I couldn't get that picture out of my mind. So, I actually felt that I could do without a Father in my life. I didn't know what I was missing! I always knew something was wrong with my life, but I never thought it was because, I did not have a Father in my home; to show me how Special I was!

Therefore, when I became older, I didn't realize, that my **Anger** toward my Father, had turned into **Resentment** because of leaving me, when I was only three months in my Mother's womb! And, as a result, **I always felt abandoned and unwanted.** I also became **Angry with my Mother**, for taking it out on me, what my Father did to her, and our family. I felt her **Anger** toward me; until she died.

However, the Good Thing was; I did make my **PEACE** with my Mother before she went home to be with the Lord. I took care of my Mother, for the last three months of her life. She had developed Alzheimer's, and I had Hospice Care, for her at my home. While she was at my home, **The Holy Spirit**, led me to tell her some of the things that she did to me growing up; and that I forgave her for everything.

I told her how she turned her **Anger for Daddy, toward me!** I told her that I understood, that she was three months pregnant with me when he left her; and she had to raise three children alone. My Mother was at the stage of Alzheimer's, that she couldn't walk, talk, or do anything for herself anymore; but God! **While, I was talking with her; TEARS STARTED RUNNING DOWN HER FACE!! SHE UNDERSTOOD WHAT I WAS SAYING TO HER!! GLORY TO GOD!!**

After becoming a Born Again Christian, and being ordained, and licensed into the Ministry of Jesus Christ; I still did not know anything about, "Returning To The Father." **Now listen carefully**; for this is one of the most important things that has ever happened, to me in my life! And, it could happen to you too! While, I was doing my research for this book; I found an article that, Rev. Jesse Lee

Peterson had written about Kwanzaa. Then I went to his YouTube Channel, and watched his Church service; live on YouTube.

The name of his Ministry is: **BOND**: (The Brotherhood Organization of a New Destiny). His organization is, "Rebuilding The Family By Rebuilding The Man." www.rebuildingtheman.com. At first, I was **just watching**, instead of listening. Then The Holy Spirit told me to **start listening, and I did!** Rev. Jesse Lee Peterson, was sharing that we needed to forgive our Father, for not being in our lives, for whatever reason; and especially forgive our Mother; for messing up our life; because she did not know how to raise children, and especially boys, without a Husband and Father in the home.

Rev. Peterson shared, "That we needed to forgive our Parents, so that Jesus Christ could forgive us for our sins." He also, talked about how God took away the **Anger** he had toward his Father for leaving him, and especially for his Mother; because she tried to keep him from knowing his real Father. After forgiving my Father and Mother; I started praying Rev. Peterson's "Silent Prayer" called, "Be Still And Know." (a free download on his website) **My entire life changed for the Better!** And, I know the same thing will happen to **YOU!** Therefore, I urge you to check out, Rev. Jesse Lee Peterson's Radio Talk Show on YouTube, NewsMax Television Channel; and his TV Talk Show on YouTube, (The Fallen State). Believe me, if you do; you will never be the same again; **YOUR LIFE WILL CHANGE FOR THE BETTER!**

Last, but not least, I must tell you that, **SATAN IS LAUGHING AT ALL GANG MEMBERS WORLDWIDE AND ESPECIALLY IN CHICAGO!!!** SATAN WANTS YOU TO CONTINUE TO RUIN YOUR PRECIOUS LIVES BY BEING A GANG MEMBER!!! Why is Satan Laughing? Glad you asked. Because, you are doing his **KILLING** for him! God's Word Says It Best: "The thief comes only to steal, and **kill**, and destroy; I came that they may have life and have it abundantly." **(John 10:10) NASB**. You are **killing** each other, so Satan doesn't have to do it!!! Satan doesn't want you to know who you {really} are, and how **Special You Are To God!** Satan wants you to continue to be **ANGRY, so you will continue to be BLIND, SO YOU CAN NOT SEE HIM WORKING EVIL THROUGH YOU!!!**

I believe that it's time for **YOU** to **WAKE-UP!** And, find out who you were {really} meant to be! And remember: <u>The only Power that Satan has, is the Power that **YOU** give him. Satan doesn't have any Power of his **OWN** because Jesus Christ took it back at **THE CROSS!**</u> Therefore, I Would Like To Leave You With A Challenge: **I DARE YOU TO BE GREAT! I LOVE YOU!**

UNBELIEVERS

My Dear Brothers and Sisters,

I remember being just like you, many years ago; I had no peace in my life. I feared death; because I didn't know what would happen to me after death. I heard several points of view; but, I didn't know for sure. I wandered around in the wilderness of life, for seven more years, after ending my membership in US Organization. Then one day, a dear friend of mine, came to work at the same place I was working; The Department of Public Social Services.

We had not seen one another for a long time. While we were talking, she said, "Barbara, I have been saved." I said, saved from what? She said, "Saved from going to Hell!" I said, there is no such place! She said, "Oh, yes there is!" We talked at lunch time, and she invited me to attend her Church, at Crenshaw Christian Center; where the Apostle, Dr. Frederick K.C. Price, Sr., was the Senior Pastor.

So, I went to Church and heard the Word of God; and I could relate to what I heard Apostle Price teaching out of the Holy Bible. Hearing the Word of God became real to me, and I believed it! When Apostle Price, gave the invitation to receive Jesus Christ, as your personal Lord and Savior; I almost knocked people down, in my row of seats, trying to get to the Altar!

Afterward, my friend shared with me a lot of things. For example, I didn't know that, there are only two families in the World! Either one is in the family of Jesus Christ, or one is in the family of Satan. I didn't know that God's Word, made life simple to understand, so that even, a naïve person, like I was; could understand the Bible for my own life.

I didn't know that what happened, in the Garden of Eden, affected everyone's life on planet earth! When Adam disobeyed God, Satan took Adam's Authority and Power of being the God of this World; and Adam's Inheritance of Owning Everything, In The World! For example, it's like a natural family operates; the Father tells the child, not to do something, and the child disobeys the Father; and the child gets into trouble. However, our Elder Brother, Jesus Christ agreed with our Heavenly Father that He would leave Heaven and come down to Earth to **SAVE US** from going to Hell with Satan; **And To Return Us Back To Our Father Forever!**

Before I became a Believer, I couldn't visualize the Spiritual World, because Satan blinded my eyes; so that I couldn't see him in the World. God's Word Says It Best: "In whom the god of this world hath blinded the minds of them which believe not, lest the light of the glorious gospel of Christ, who is the image of God, should shine unto them. (2 Corinthians 4:4) KJV.

Then, after asking Jesus Christ to come into my heart and becoming Born Again; the scales fell from my eyes, as it were, and I could see the Spiritual World! I then understood what life was all about; Jesus Christ and Him Crucified, for our sake. I went from being Spiritually Dead to being Spiritually Alive; in a second!

Instantly, I experienced **Peace in My Heart!** It was amazing! Before asking Jesus Christ to come into my heart, I felt so unworthy, because of my lifestyle I had been living. **After asking Jesus Christ, to come into my heart, I found out how Special I {really} Am! – Because, I Am My Father's Daughter!** I also learned, that after one dies, their spirit goes to Heaven, to be with Jesus Christ. God's Word Says It Best: "And we are not afraid but are quite content to die, for then we will be at home with the Lord." (2 Corinthians 5:8) TLB.

Another reason, I was without Peace, in my heart, was because of all the Lies, that I heard about Christianity from Karenga. Karenga taught me how to **HATE** White people, and Jesus Christ taught me how to **LOVE** White people. What Karenga cannot understand, is that **Christianity is not a Religion; it is a Relationship with Jesus Christ**. <u>God's Word Says It Best</u>: "But a natural man does not accept the things of the Spirit of God, for they are foolishness to him; and he cannot understand them, because they are spiritually appraised." (1 Corinthians 2:14) NAS.

Another thing that I learned, was the fact that, we are a spirit, on the inside of our bodies, and our spirits have no color; therefore, we are like God on the inside! <u>God's Word Says It Best</u>: "And God said, let us make man in our image, after our likeness: and let them have dominion over the fish of the sea, and over the fowl of the air, and over the cattle, and over all the earth, and over every creeping thing that creepeth upon the earth." (Genesis 1:26) KJV.

He meant, Spiritually! <u>God's Word Says It Best</u>: "God is a Spirit: and they that worship him must worship Him in spirit and in truth." (John 4:24) KJV. We live inside our bodies like we live inside of a house. Our houses are just, different colors, on the outside; and that is because of God, being so Creative! He didn't want, to make all of us the same color or the same temperament, or the same type of persons. That is why he made us all different from one another; because He is so Awesome and Amazing!

But, don't forget we have an enemy called the Devil. <u>God's Word Says It Best</u>: "Be sober, be vigilant; because your adversary the devil, as a roaring lion, walketh about, seeking whom he may devour." (I Peter 5:8) KJV. The Devil wants to prevent us from coming together against him. Satan, uses the color of our skin (our houses) to Divide and Conquer the Races.

Therefore, I Am Asking YOU To Consider The Following:

At this juncture, I would like to take a close look at the two words: Righteousness vs. Lawlessness according, to the Word of God.

Righteousness: Is the condition characteristic of faith, which is believing before you see it come to pass. Righteousness both declared and bestowed by God on believers, creates the possibilities of obedience and holiness.

Lawlessness: Is the condition characteristic of unbelief, which is iniquity. They are deeds that manifest rebellion against God. To be "full of lawlessness" is to lead a life characterized by wrongdoing; for example, being a gang member. Sin, therefore, is an act of rebellion against God; and cannot be thought of as harmless, neutral, or imaginary.

As the contrast continues, it becomes clear that the two categories have nothing in common: they are as different as light and darkness. Moreover, <u>God's Word Says It Best:</u> "We who have run for our very lives to God have every reason to grab the promised hope with both hands and never let go. It's an unbreakable spiritual lifeline, reaching past all appearance right to the very presence of God where Jesus, running on ahead of us, has taken up his permanent post as high priest for us, in the order of Melchizedek." (Hebrews 6:19) MSG. The Son distinguishes himself in manifesting the attitude of God toward these two states: **God hates Lawlessness but loves Righteousness**. Finally, it is clear that one has a conscious choice to make: to live in the condition of Lawlessness and do its deeds, or to serve Righteousness and do its deeds.

So, you see, it is up to **YOU** to decide; what kind of life **YOU** desire to live? That Is The Question! Thus, my dear Brother or Sister; here's the Deal:

Whose Side Do You Choose To Be On?
You Can Only Choose <u>ONE</u>! God's Family or Satan's Family?

Do You Choose To Go To Heaven & Live With Jesus Christ Forever?
Tip: <u>You Do</u> Have To Make A Choice To Qualify To Enter Heaven.

OR

Do You Choose To Go To Hell & Live With Satan Forever?
Tip: <u>You Do Not</u> Have To Make A Choice To Qualify To Enter Hell.

If I must beg and plead for your soul; I will! I just want you to come to Jesus Christ and let Him show you how much He loves you! **HE WILL BLOW YOUR MIND WITH HOW POWERFUL HIS LOVE IS FOR YOU!** He died so that you could be free while you are here on Planet Earth; and to live with Him and our Father in Heaven! I know that you can clearly see how Jesus Christ changed my life from being a gang member to becoming an Ambassador for Christ in The Kingdom of God; and He will do the same thing for **YOU! He Will Turn Your Life Around And Make Your Life Profound!** I also discovered that, **Jesus Christ Loves Everyone The Same!** <u>God's Word Says It Best</u>: "For God treats everyone the same." (Romans 2:11) TLB. I hope you decide to {Come Back Home Where You Spiritually Belong!} **Yes Right Now!** Join The Family of God By <u>Believing and Praying</u> the following:

Prayer of Salvation

Heavenly Father, I come to You, in the name of Your Son, Jesus Christ. You said in Your Word that "Whosoever shall call upon the name of the Lord shall be saved." Father, I am calling on Jesus, right now. I believe He died on the Cross for my sins, and He was raised from the dead on the third day, and He's alive right now in Heaven.

Lord Jesus, I am asking you to, come into my heart and live Your life in me and through me. I repent of my sins and surrender myself totally to You. Heavenly Father, by faith I now confess Jesus Christ as my Lord and Savior. From this day forward, I dedicate my life to serving You. Amen

Salvation Scriptures

Romans 10:9 = "That if thou shalt confess with thy mouth the Lord Jesus and shalt believe in thine heart that God hath raised Him from the dead, thou shalt be saved."
Romans 10:10 = "For with the heart man believeth unto righteousness, and with the mouth, confession is made unto salvation."

By Faith: Welcome Into The Family Of God!

Barbara A. Nairn at the Self-Esteem Facilitating Training Graduation
Banquet held at the Westin Hotel, Costa Mesa, CA on July 29, 1995.

Barbara A. Nairn is a Certified Self-Esteem Facilitator and Consultant.
Barbara was professionally trained by one of the world's foremost authorities
on self-esteem training, Jack Canfield, President of Self-Esteem Seminars, and
Author of <u>Chicken Soup For The Soul.</u>

(Pictured above from left is Barbara Nairn and Jack Canfield at the Self-Esteem
Facilitating Training Graduation Banquet held at The Westin Hotel in Costa Mesa,
California on July 29, 1995)

"Build Me Up!"® - The Self-Esteem Game made it's National Television Debut on the Mark Walberg Show (Fox Network) in New York as one of the "Hottest New Toys" at The American International Toy Fair '96!
(Pictured from left is Prince Nairn, Mark Walberg, and Barbara Nairn)

At The American International Toy Fair '96, Toy Buyers had fun playing "Build Me Up!"® - The Self-Esteem Game!
(Pictured from left are Toy Buyers and Barbara Nairn demonstrating game)

The Late Rev. Jerry P. Louder, President of The United States
Pastor's Association, African American Clergy, and The
Honorable Willie L. Brown, Jr., Mayor of San Francisco - 1996

The Mayor of San Francisco, CA, Willie L. Brown, Jr. endorses Way-Kool Toys, Inc.'s
Build Me Up!® - The Self-Esteem Game for Children, Youth and Their Families.
(Pictured from left is Barbara A. Nairn, President/CEO, Mayor Willie L. Brown, Jr. and
Prince E. Nairn, President/CFO).

Barbara A. Nairn, The Late Rev. Dr. Jerry P. and Philia Louder, Pastor's
At New Jerusalem Church, Riverside, CA. Barbara is presenting to the
Late Rev. Dr. Jerry and Philia Louder with a Marriage Anniversary Poem
And a Stock Certificate in Way Kool Toys in 1996.

Way-Kool Toys, Inc. was invited by Mayor Willie L. Brown, Jr. to participate in the "First" San Francisco Children and Youth Summit in The City's history on October 4 -6, 1996.
(Pictured from left is Prince E. Nairn, President/CFO, Danny Glover, Actor, and Barbara A. Nairn, President/CEO).

OFFICE OF THE MAYOR
WILLIE LEWIS BROWN, Jr.

401 Van Ness Avenue, Room 336
San Francisco, California 94102

October 24, 1996

Ms. Barbara A. Nairn, President/CEO
Way-Kool Toys
1904 East Riverview Drive, Suite 105
San Bernardino, CA 92408-3036

Dear Ms. Nairn:

Thank you for your generous support to the San Francisco Children and Youth Summit. With your help, we were able to bring together more than 500 San Franciscans for an unprecedented two-day discussion about the priorities for the children and youth of this city.

By all accounts, the Summit was immensely successful. The vision that emerged, through both the seven Community Summits and during the course of the weekend, is one that will transform the current service delivery system as we know it. We are now prepared to embark on a journey to create a five year blueprint that will guide us beyond the turn of the century.

Your partnership uniquely distinguishes this endeavor from all others, past and present. For the first time in The City's history, all sectors have joined hands to affirm a shared vision for San Francisco's young people.

Again, thank you for supporting this extraordinary effort. I hope we can continue to work together in partnership during the coming years.

Very truly yours,
WILLIE L. BROWN, JR.
Mayor
City & County of San Francisco

Coach Barbara with the Self-Esteem Workshop Participants at
The Youth Intervention Program, Los Angeles, California.

Barbara A. De Loach, President   April 25, 1997
Self-Esteem Empowerment (SEE) Workshops
1904 East Riverview Drive, Suite 105
San Bernardino, CA 92408-3036

Dear Ms. De Loach,

It is with immense pleasure that I write this letter of recognition for the workshop you conducted here at the Youth Intervention Program. YIP is a community-based organization committed to the elevation of at risk youth and their families. Our on-site Alternative Education Work Center provides educational services to students who have been failed by the public school system.

The student population consists of gang members, teen parents, juvenile offenders, foster care recipients, and group home residents. These adolescents and teens suffer from low self-esteem, depression, negative self-image and stress.

As Educational Director for the program, I have been charged with the difficult task of motivation and empowering these students to become positive members of society. They seldom come into contact with people who have the necessary skills and drive to impact their lives; Ms. De Loach, you have made a definite impact.

Your workshop, "Loving and Understanding Self," was not only inspirational, but utilitarian. The students left charged with the knowledge that change is possible and armed with the tools to love and encourage themselves.

Your capacity to facilitate and lead such a diverse population demonstrates organization, competency, genuine empathy, and acumen to communicate complex ideas with surprising clarity. These gifts are essential when working with people from various socio-economic and ethnic backgrounds.

Ms. De Loach, you are professional, articulate, and genuinely committed to underserved populations. I have the opportunity to regularly witness the good work of many dedicated individuals. Rarely do I get the opportunity to write a letter of gratitude and support for someone I can endorse unequivocally. I have no doubt that your work will continue to affect and improve the quality of life for many people.

Sincerely,

Kimberly A. White

Director, Education and Training

Operation Hope, The New Leaders "Youth Workshop."

Operation Hope, Inc., The New Leaders "Youth Committee."

Los Angeles, CA. in 1996.

The President/CEO of Operation HOPE, Inc., John Bryant, presented Way-Kool Toys with a distinguished Certificate of Appreciation at The Banking On The Future's 1st Annual Appreciation & Awards Dinner for 1996 held at the Biltmore Hotel in Los Angeles, CA. (Pictured from left is Prince Nairn, John Bryant, and Barbara Nairn).

THE BANKING ON THE FUTURE

Certificate of Appreciation

is presented to

Way Kool Toys

1st ANNUAL APPRECIATION & AWARDS DINNER

*

One Hundred Years from Now...

*

it will not matter what your bank account was,
the sort of neighborhood you lived in,
or the kind of car you drove.
but it will matter that you "invested" time
in the lives of our youth...today.

★ Banking on the Future

a project of Operation HOPE

for the year of 1996

_____
John Bryant
President & Chief Executive Officer
Operation HOPE, Inc.

_____
Jodi Brockington
Program Director
Banking on the Future

Coach Barbara and Participants at The Riverside

Community College Tiger Camp.

Coach Barbara with the Self-Esteem Workshop Participants at The Riverside Community College's Tiger Camp. Riverside, CA.

Coach Barbara and Participants at The Riverside

Community College Tiger Camp.

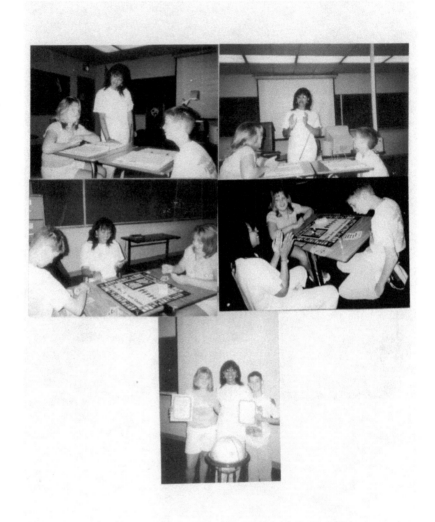

Coach Barbara and Participants at The Real World

Workshop at The Riverside Community College For Kids.

Coach Barbara and Participants at The Real World Workshop at The Riverside Community College For Kids. Build Me Up! Game Demonstrated on Weekend Gallery, Channel 5 in Los Angeles, California.

RIVERSIDE COMMUNITY COLLEGE

4800 Magnolia Avenue
Riverside, CA 92506-1299

April 20, 2001

To Whom It May Concern: This letter recommends to you Barbara A. De Loach, or Coach Barbara, as the students she has taught at Riverside Community College affectionately know her.

Barbara came to visit me in Spring, 2000 about presenting classes through RCC's Community Education Program. It was love at first sight! Barbara's "Build Me Up!" Self-Esteem Program was a perfect fit for our College for Kids offerings, and Barbara herself is a perfect fit for our vision of a Riverside Community College Educational Instructor.

Barbara is knowledgeable and passionate about what she teaches, and she is a woman who "walks the walk" in her dealings with students and with this college. During the Summer of 2000, she was a key to the success of our first Tiger Camp, a two-week long, 8am-5pm camp for the children of the community. Coach Barbara taught them how to raise their own self-esteem levels every day. The magical thing was this – the kids loved it! The kids got the concept and immediately put it into effect in their interactions with one another! And they came back enthusiastically for more every day!

Barbara also teaches adults these same self-esteem skills to be used in their own lives or the lives of others on a professional or personal level. She has re-invented this program for Riverside Community College as an online class now being offered to many colleges nationally via the Internet.

As you can see, Barbara is a versatile, multi-talented woman always growing and looking for new ways to share her skills and knowledge with more and more people. She is an asset to my program and I'm looking forward too many years of partnership with Barbara.

Sincerely,
Cyndi Pardee,
Community Education Supervisor

NEW JERUSALEM

6476 Streeter Avenue
Riverside, CA 92504
Dr. Jerry & Phalia Louder, Pastors

April 8, 2001

Barbara A. De Loach, President
Self-Esteem Empowerment (SEE) Workshops
1904 East Riverview Drive, Suite 105
San Bernardino, CA 92408-3036

Dear Barbara:

Grace be unto you from God the Father and our Lord Jesus Christ. We would like to express our appreciation to you for presenting to the youth your Self-Esteem Empowerment (SEE) Workshop.

It was a tremendous blessing to the youth. They were even telling the absent youth that they missed a "Very Good Workshop." Once again, we thank you and look forward to working with you more in the future.

In His Service,
Rev. Anthony & Carol McComb
Associate Pastors

SAN BERNARDINO VALLEY COLLEGE

701 S. Mount Vernon Avenue
San Bernardino, CA 92410

May 31, 2001

To Whom It May Concern,

Dear Sir or Madam:

I am penning a letter of recommendation for Barbara A. De Loach who is an employee for me during the evening hours at San Bernardino Valley College. I have known Barbara for approximately six months and she has been an excellent employee to our District as well as to me personally. I am very proud of the many successes that she has to offer; especially to the educational system. Barbara is business-minded and is part of our Future Teachers of America Chapter. She enjoys working with young minds and has developed and marketed educational game materials that help to improve student self-esteem as early as preschool to adult years. As Director of the Transfer Center, it is always a pleasure to see employees continue their educational pursuits in life. Ms. De Loach is on the career path to becoming a Curriculum Specialist. What an enhancement she will be to our community. Barbara has a son who performs professionally, and I had the opportunity to view his creativity on "Sesame Street." This speaks for itself. She was an outstanding role model for the community as well as her family. She has set an example to her

262 | Barbara A. De Loach

children to further their education and would be an asset to your school. This is the kind of person we enjoy telling others about. Barbara is loyal, dedicated, motivated and inspirational. My whole staff enjoys being around her and I highly recommend her to work with students as an Instructional Aide because she will be an asset to our future students and to the educational institution overall.

If you have any additional questions, please feel free to contact me at (909) 888-6511 extension 1669.

Sincerely,

Pamela E. Slade-Pryor

Director, Transfer Center/Associate Professor

RIALTO POLICE DEPARTMENT

128 North Willow Avenue
Rialto, CA 92376-5894

February 2, 1999

To Whom It May Concern,

Barbara A. De Loach, was employed by the Rialto Police Department from August 10, 1998 to February 5, 1999. Ms. De Loach was a very productive employee during her time with the Rialto Police Department. I found Ms. De Loach to pick up very quickly on new procedures. Ms. De Loach was able to work independently in a very short time. Her professionalism and job skills were an asset to our Records Unit. Ms. De Loach has a pleasant personality, very friendly, cheerful, and helpful to all. It has been a pleasure to work with Ms. De Loach for the last 6 months, and to have her as a part of our Records team.

During Ms. De Loach's time with our department, she has had the following training:

Super Names
California Law Enforcement Telecommunications System
National Crime Information Center

Central Name Index Training
Traffic Management Sub System

Please feel free to contact me for further information at 909-820-2575.

Sincerely,
Debra J. Carpenter
Records Supervisor

CALIFORNIA STATE UNIVERSITY,

LOS ANGELES
5151 State University Drive
Los Angeles, California 90032

February 10, 1993

Barbara A. De Loach, President
Way Kool Toys, Inc.
1904 East Riverview Drive, Suite 105
San Bernardino, CA 92408-3036

Dear Barbara,

What a fantastic game! "Build Me Up!" is by far one of the most innovative and rewarding games on the market today.

It's such a pleasure to see a game inspire children to think positively about themselves and others. You've done a terrific job; keep up the good work!

Sincerely,
Marcy Porter,
Reading Instructor

CALIFORNIA STATE UNIVERSITY,

LOS ANGELES
5151 State University Drive
Los Angeles, California 90032

Barbara A. De Loach, President
Way Kool Toys, Inc.
1904 East Riverview Drive, Suite 105
San Bernardino, CA 92408-3036

February 2, 1993

To Whom It May Concern:

I am writing in support of "Build Me Up!" The Self-Esteem Game, manufactured by Barbara A. De Loach.

The Self-Esteem Game is an excellent learning tool for all people of different ages. The game is especially suitable for school age students who are coming to know themselves.

It can also be used in a variety of educational, social and religious settings. It is a benefit and an asset to anyone's personal development.

"Build Me Up!" teaches priniciples that enlighten and assist with increasing self-esteem. I highly recommend this game to anyone who can read, and who are teachable.

It is a creative and meaningful piece of art, designed to implement change of attitude, behavior and feelings about life and self. I enjoyed it and intend to share it.

Sincerely,
T.J. Walton,
Assistant Director
Admissions and University Outreach

January 26, 1993

Barbara A. De Loach, President
Way Kool Toys, Inc.
1904 East Riverview Drive, Suite 105
San Bernardino, CA 92408-3036

Dear Barbara,

Build Me Up! helps families do what so often seems undoable – let each other hear what others like about them. Sitting together watching a movie won't do that. Playing video games won'tdo it. But this Game is a fun way to let them know not just that you care, but why you care.

Parents so often get stuck talking about the negative – it's nice to have an entertaining tool focusing on the positive.

Sincerely,
Steve Teixiera
Coordinator
Learning Resource Center

BRET HARTE PREPARATORY
INTERMEDIATE SCHOOL

9301 South Hoover Street
Los Angeles, California 9004

July 11, 1992

Ms. Barbara A. De Loach, President
Way-Koo Toys, Inc.
1904 East Riverview Drive, Suite 105
San Bernardino, CA 92408-3036

Dear Ms. Barbara A. De Loach:

Thank you so very much for your generous contributions in time spent with four of Bret Harte's classes and the donation of two of your Self-Esteem Games. All of the teachers were excited about the game and the potential for helping more of our students improve their self-esteem. I am delighted that Mrs. Rivers invited you to make a presentation for her summer school program. As you are acutely aware, our students are in dire need of enhancing their feelings of self-worth if we and they are going to have hope for a brighter, more productive future.

It was evident that the students enjoyed the game as well as being videotaped for future use. Please be assured that these students and teachers will serve as resources in sharing the benefits of the game with their peers and colleagues. I do anticipate purchasing additional games to provide access to more teachers and students. Thanks again for sharing your time, talents and game with us. May God bless you with great success and prosperity as you give back to the community in a time of need.

Respectfully Yours,
Catherine Sumpter,
Principal

Office of Tom Bradley, Mayor
Small Business Assistance
City Hall – Room 1400
Los Angeles, CA 90012

Mr. Fred Snowden, Vice-President   September 16, 1991
Quality Foods International, Inc.
5531 Monte Vista Street
Highland Park, CA 90042

Dear Fred:

I am transmitting this letter to express my support of Ms. Barbara
A. De Loach of Way-Kool Toys, in her efforts to demonstrate
the uniqueness of a learning tool that may be of interest to your
organization. "Build Me Up!" The Self-Esteem Board Game, is a new
challenging and inspiring game that promotes a positive attitude
and helps enhance the self-esteem of individual players. Because the
players are using words to play "Build Me Up!" Game; it will enhance
the players' communication skills and build their vocabulary.

I have worked closely with Ms. Barbara A. De Loach, for the
past several months to help her build her enterprise. We, here in this
office are impressed with Ms. Barbara A. De Loach's qualifications

and desire to expand her business activity. Please be assured that my office will assist her in any way possible. We would appreciate it if you would afford Ms. De Loach an opportunity to meet and discuss with you her product. Within the next several days, she will contact you and arrange for an appointment. If you have any questions, please feel free to contact me at (213) 485-6142.

Sincerely,

Bill Raphiel, Deputy Director

Coach Barbara with Self-Esteem Workshop Participants
At John C. Fremont High School, L.A. CA

Coach Barbara with Self-Esteem Workshop Participants
At The University of California, Riverside

Two Brothers playing "Build Me Up!" The Self-Esteem
Board Game at The Orlando Florida Convention Center.

Hot! to Watch!

Building Self Esteem!
God's Way

Build Me Up!, a revolutionary board game, has been predicted to break racial barriers and bridge communication gaps between youth and adults.

Created by game inventor, **Barbara Nairn**, of *Love Creations Games & Toys*, "Build Me Up!" has been designed to have a powerful impact upon society by incorporating the basic concept of positive thinking into the ABC's of everyday life! Barbara states that the game not only builds self-esteem, but deals with high finance like monopoly, and also deals with one being one's self instead of role playing like Dungeons and Dragons.

This action-packed and fun "BUILD ME UP!" game is for ages 10 to adult and can be played with 2 to any number of teams.

For more information, call 1 (800) 743-7456 or write to: P.O. Box 889, San Bernardino, CA 92402-0889.

ALBUM

I AM PERSUADED
Fred Hammond
Benson Music Group

'I am Persuaded' that Fred Hammond is one man that will 'Wake Up' the nation to 'That Rugged Cross' with 'Grace'...His rare poetic vocal mastery and powerful contemporary music will keep you in love with Jesus...Praise be to God 'I'm Not Afraid to 'Keep On Lovin You'.

Sylvia Bronson

BOOK

WOMEN WHO CHANGED THEIR WORLD
by Jill Briscoe
Victor Books

Author Jill Briscoe does her usual fine job in this her latest work, spotlighting 8 worlds and how they were affected by women whose actions sometimes externally didn't always appear Holy or Honorable and yet GOD allowed it and yet GOD loved them. Could it be that He's not nearly as interested in a flawless walk as He is a clean heart.

This book can help you think clearer about which of the two ways you're changing yours.

Paperback available through bookstores.

Loeta Z. Shavers

BUSINESS

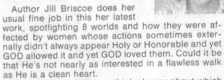

Kevin Burroughs Neeley
MORE THAN A MUSICIAN

When you need the ultimate in sound management, coupled with experience, love and dependability, Kevin Burroughs Neeley should receive your call.

Not only does this ministry offer the finest in musical technology for your next affair, but the brother can sing! So, the next time you need microphone or speaker set-up, or a minister of music, regardless of the size of the event, call Kevin Burroughs Neeley. (213) 298-0980.

A Prophetic Word Given To
Barbara Ann De Loach
Regarding All Christian Men {Global}

June 23, 1997

The Holy Spirit showed me that there is a heavy covering — a blanket like covering over the Men in the Body of Christ and especially the Men in the World — a blanket of laziness preventing them from being as sensitive as they should be to receive Spiritual Revelations and Ideas that would manifest as Material Wealth in the natural realm!

The Church must pray and fast for that covering to be lifted from our Men and to bring forth a great bursting of Wealth – Spiritually, Mentally and Emotionally within them! For that is one of the sins that came upon Adam in the Garden of Eden — the hindering of Man's Spiritual Antennas; his Mental Ability to be quick to receive many thoughts and ideas from Me and the Emotional Expression and Sensitivity that he had before the Fall. Pray for Restoration and Resurrection and Re-Positioning of Men in the World but especially for those Men of The Household of Faith!

For then they shall rise to the level of the Dimension and the Anointing that is needed to usher in the coming of Jesus Christ — To such an awesome degree that the Youth will run to the Church from all directions — all over the World — just to be around the

Anointing — just to become like what they see with their own eyes – Supernatural Men of God!

My children — not until then will you witness the Great Revival in The Body of Christ that all have been praying, hoping and looking for! As a natural body operates — so does a Spiritual Body — My Body — it begins with the Head! — The Head tells the rest of the body what it wants it to do in other words it Leads the other parts of the body – so it is also Church with — The Body of Christ — The Head Will Lead and I have made the Man to be the Head of My Body!

The Heat is on! — I have turned up the fires inside the Women of God for such a time as this! It is I that have caused the Women in My Body to become more visible — to go ahead as I sent John the Baptist ahead of Jesus to prepare the way for Him — Yes! — Women of God have been preparing the way for the Men of God to come forth in these End Times – like never before! You will soon witness a Great Re-Positioning of Men that will shake the World! — Turning things upside down and all around – But after the shaking is over – Then things will be set in Order — Set in Right Order by and through the Men of God for the Whole World to see and Marvel!

And – Oh such Peace and Rest will come to the Women and Children of God! Because you All will then take your True and Divine positions in life as My Family - My Body – My Church - My Bride! And then The End will come!

Thus Saith The Lord

SPEAKING OF

THE END

COMING

WE HAVE NOW

COME TO

THE END

OF

OUR JOURNEY

THROUGH

MEMORY LANE

IN

THE BLACK POWER MOVEMENT

OF THE

1960s & 1970s

THANK
YOU
FOR
WALKING
WITH
ME!

To The Five-Fold Ministry And Leaders: God Is Doing A New Thing!

The Lord asked me to share with, The Five-Fold Ministry, and Leaders what has been in my heart, for quite some time. As you well know, the state of the **CHURCH** is in a **CRISIS!** The Body of Christ is **SILENT!** Jesus Christ told me to tell you to: **"Wake-Up! Stand-Up! And Fight The Good Fight of Faith! For The Kingdom of God Is At Hand!**

Too many Christians, have left God's House of Prayer. What is going on in the Church in America? Maybe not enough. I would like to suggest, from the perspective of a Christian Life Coach; to add a New Format to the Church. The Format of Love Workshops. I have long ago, thought that the local Church does not have enough to offer the members for their support of the Ministry. Members and visitors give their tithes and offerings faithfully every week. It is time that they received more for their money, time, and loyalty. In other words, they need to receive, more benefits as members; without having to pay for everything, all the time. The members are making an investment in their Church; now it is time for their Church to make an investment into their lives; on a Personal Level. However, I do understand that it is the Pastor's decision to make; if there will be a need, for a free-will offering, for the workshop.

People are coming to Church Services and Bible Studies, and not getting their needs totally met. Please, let me make myself real clear. Of course, I am not saying, that Pastors are not fulfilling their call to Shepherd God's Lambs; quite the contrary. I am simply saying, that I believe, that it might be time to Do A New Thing! <u>God's Word Says It Best</u>: "Remember ye not the former things, neither consider the things of old. Behold, I will do a new thing; now it shall spring forth; shall ye not know it? I will even make a way in the wilderness, and rivers in the desert." (Isaiah 43:18-19) KJV.

I also believe that this New Format will be a 'key' factor in 'Rebuilding God's Church.' Therefore, Pastors do not need to feel intimidated, about adding a New Format, along with the Sunday Services and Bible Studies during the week, etc. The Love Workshops, can assist the Five-Fold Ministry and Leaders, to fulfill your Assignment in The Kingdom of God; to take care of the needs of God's people in a 'Godly Environment.' I believe that the, Love Workshops, are a part of the Helps Ministry in The Body of Christ.

Another reason the Christian Group Life Coaching Workshops, would be a Great Blessing to the members, is because, a lot of members are not financially able to hire a Christian Life Coach, to help them work through, some of their challenges at home, work, and school, etc. By conducting Love Workshops, gives people a 'Special Place' to have good wholesome FUN while they are building-up their most Holy Faith!

The Church could have, weekly, bi-weekly, or monthly workshops, depending on the size of the Congregation, and how often you want to have FUN getting to know yourselves, and your Sisters and Brothers in the family of God; the larger the Congregation, the more Love Workshops, you can have during the month. This way, we can Heal some things in our lives in a Godly Way. For example, the Pastor could choose Ministers and Leaders in the Church, to be professionally trained, to conduct Love Workshops; or the Church could hire a Professional Christian Group Life Coach/s to facilitate The Love Workshops.

Love Workshops is the name that, the Lord gave to me. You do not have to call your workshop, The Love Workshop. I am simply sharing what our Lord shared with me. I liked the name because God is Love. And, we will know each other by His Love. How cool is that? Also, I am NOT talking about Therapy or Counseling. I am talking about Christian Group Life Coaching.

Week, after week, the Congregation sits, facing the Pastor, and we are preached to; without the opportunity to ask questions. And, not only ask questions; but just to talk, with one another, on a consistent basis; so that we can get, to know each other, including the Pastor/s. God's Word Says It Best: "Wherefore comfort yourselves together, and edify one another, even as also ye do. And, we beseech you, brethren, to know them which labor among you, and are over you in the Lord, and admonish you." (I Thessalonians 5:10-12) KJV.

I don't have to remind you about the Society, in which we are living in now. You know that it has Changed - Big Time! That is one of the reasons, that the Church needs to Change, with these Changing End-Times. Why? Because our needs, are different than they used to be. For instance, people do not visit one another's homes, like we used to. Therefore, it is more difficult to meet people, to build good relationships, and have good Fellowship, amongst their Brothers and Sisters in their own Church Home; on a regular basis.

More and more people are lonely, depressed, cost-of-living increases, living alone, single parenting, and need help with everyday issues of life; especially senior citizens, adults, children and the youth. Hey, that includes everybody! Also, people whatever their age; need to communicate with other Brothers and Sisters in Christ, with the same precious Faith. God's Word Says It Best: "Iron sharpeneth iron; so, a man sharpeneth the countenance of his friend." (Proverbs 27:17) KJV.

Christian Group Life Coaching:

- A partner in achieving personal and business goals.
- A teacher in life and communication skills.
- A sounding board when exploring choices.
- A motivational mentor.
- One who gives unconditional support.
- A beacon during stormy times.

The Benefits of Christian Group Life Coaching As An Essential Part of The Edifying of The Members and Community Outreach

Christian Group Life Coaching Makes A Difference When Two Factors Are Present:

1) The Participants are willing to change and grow.
2) There is a gap between where the Participants are now and where he or she wants to be. Period. The gap can be many things: Their personal life, love life, work life, boundary issues, fears, etc.

With Christian Group Life Coaching The Participants Will:

Have a more balanced life because they designed it. Without a balanced life, people don't have a solid base, to begin to make changes in their life. The Christian Group Life Coaching helps them determine what it means to balance your life.

Christian Group Life Coaching works Miracles in people's lives. They will feel more like they BELONG to the Church where they attend each week. One reason they will feel more like they belong is that they will be talking with one another, about 'The Issues of Life' in a 'Safe Environment,' with their Brothers and Sisters in Christ; the members will feel closer to one another as they BOND together.

The Church will begin to come together, more in the **'Unity of the Faith.'** <u>God's Word Says It Best</u>: "Till we all come in the unity of the faith, and of the knowledge of the Son of God, unto a perfect man, unto the measure of the stature of the fullness of Christ:" (Ephesians 4:13) KJV.

People need to share their challenges, health problems, work-related issues, family, and other relationships, on a Personal Level; other than just saying to the Congregation, "Tell your neighbor ..." or "Tell three people that you ..." In a word, that is not enough. We Need To Talk And Fellowship With One Another On A More Personal Level.

Make Better Choices And Be In Action Because You Set The Goals You Really Want

The Christian Group Life Coach will nudge them out of their comfort zones. The Christian Group Life Coach will make them reach more and more without them being consumed by the process.
Help them to make better decisions because their focus is much clearer and defined.

Have a lot more energy because they will be happier and more productive.
Improve their relationships with others.
Having a happier, more trusting connections with family and friends.

Help clear-up unresolved issues.
Find closure with issues that seem to keep re-surfacing.

Get their needs met.
Learn to ask for what they want from their selves and others.

Strengthen their support system.
When you have a strong support system such as Family, Church family, significant other, and friends; they can do anything.

Simplify their life.
By eliminating "should" and people pleasing, and streamlining some of their daily tasks, their life will be more serene.
Have healthier boundaries.
By establishing and enforcing boundaries, they can learn how to say "no" without feeling guilty.

Eliminate major stressors.
By identifying and toning down, unnecessary stress in their life.

In conclusion, please talk with The Holy Spirit regarding implementing, The Love Workshops In These End Times. Thank you.

Respectfully Submitted,
Your Sister In Christ

THE SCIENCE AGENDA

TO EXTERMINATE BLACKS ...

Bombshell Health Ranger
Lecture Documents
Race-Based Crimes
Against Humanity
By Mike Adams - 2017

(**Natural News**) As promised, I've now released a one-hour science lecture video that documents the multiple vectors through which people of African descent are being targeted for depopulation, covert infertility, and extermination by "science" and "medicine." Watch the full video lecture at: www.NaturalNews.com.

This video lecture documents the pattern of heavy metals poisoning, medical experimentation, organ harvesting, covert fertility task forces and other tactics that seek to eliminate blacks from our planet. It uses, with credit, video footage from the shocking documentary film Maafa21, available at www.Maafa21.com. (not affiliated with this site, but it's filled with shocking information on many fronts).

You can hear more news from watching, Counter Think with Mike Adams on www.InfoWars.com.

And, to view NaturalNews's Videos, go to: https://vimeo.com/healthranger//videos.

These genocidal tactics are carried out in the name of science and medicine via the following vectors:

- Food supply (laced with infertility chemicals, confirmed by the New York Times quoting a U.S. President's science advisor).
- Water supply (heavy metals poisoning, as we recently witnessed in Flint, Michigan).
- Medical experimentation (Tuskegee, Guatemalan prisoner experiments funded by the U.S. Government, etc.).
- Immunization campaign (covert sterilization of young women in Africa)
- **Cancer (disproportionately affects people of darker skin color due to vitamin D deficiency).**
- Abortion activities that target blacks in order to harvest baby organ tissue for use in vaccines – medical cannibalism.

THERE IS A CONCERTED EFFORT TO

EXTERMINATE BLACKS IN THE NAME OF "SCIENCE" AND "MEDICINE"

By Mike Adams 2017

I am the only predominantly Caucasian scientist in the world who dares to tell the truth about the science agenda to exterminate blacks. The reason I can do this is because my science laboratory receives no funding from any government or university. I have zero financial ties to the medical establishment that's systematically exterminating blacks; thus they cannot threaten me by attempting to withhold funds from my scientific research.

The real America is not simply carried out by a small number of people in white pointy hats. The real, deep racism is carried out by men in lab coats who are systematically pursuing an agenda to exterminate blacks through food, water, medicine, biological weapons and more.

Today, Maafa 21 is exposing the hidden and bitter realities of Black Genocide in modern America. But the mainstream media –

and the multi-national corporations who control our nation's film distribution system – will not help us deliver this message to the people. And the simple fact is, this holocaust won't end as long as the public doesn't even know it exists.

MY QUESTION TO THE FIVE-FOLD MINISTRY (THE SHEP-HERDS) IN THE BODY OF CHRIST: WHAT NOW? WHAT SAY YOU ABOUT THIS CRISIS? WHAT IS GOD'S CHURCH GOING TO DO ABOUT THE WOLVES IN **(WHITE LAB COATS)** SHEEP'S CLOTHING AND, ESPECIALLY YOU MEGA CHURCHES. MEGA PEOPLE HAVE MEGA POWER! WHY DO YOU THINK GOD CREATED MEGA CHURCHES? FOR SUCH A TIME AS THIS! TO PROTECT GOD'S PRECIOUS LAMBS FROM EXTERMINATION! AND IF WE PERISH – WE PERISH! WE HAVE BEEN CALLED TO FIGHT THE GOOD FIGHT OF FAITH FOR THE KINGDOM OF GOD!

MY QUESTION TO GOD'S PEOPLE: ARE YOU NOT YOUR BROTHER'S KEEPER? AND, IS THERE NOT A CAUSE? IT LOOKS LIKE HISTORY IS TRYING TO REPEAT ITSELF. REMEMBER, HITLER TRYING TO EXTERMINATE JEWISH PEOPLE FROM PLANET EARTH? SO, THIS LOOKS LIKE A GOOD TIME FOR THE CHURCH **(DAVID)** TO PICK-UP A ROCK & YOUR SWORD! GOLIATH **(SATAN)** IS APPROACH-ING! I HOPE EVERY BORN AGAIN CHRISTIAN ON PLANET EARTH IS FEELING **RIGHTEOUS INDIGNATION** IN YOUR SPIRIT ABOUT THIS HORRIFIC SATANIC ATTACK AGAINST BLACK PEOPLE AND ESPECIALLY **GOD'S BLACK PEOPLE** ON PLANET EARTH!

THE NATIONAL CLERGY NETWORK

Scripture tells us that a good man leaves an inheritance to his children's children.

(Proverbs 13:22a)

We have a plan. **CURE's National Clergy Network** seeks to educate our pastors to understand the damage of current policy related to poverty, family, and religious freedom issues. If clergy are concerned, knowledgeable, and engaged in these topics, then they can more easily help the real congregations and communities who are struggling every day. **CURE** seeks to equip pastors and their congregations with principles of faith, freedom and personal responsibility so that all can give input and voice to the critical issues we face together.

The **National Clergy Network** will have collaborative power and influence as we grow with like-minded team members. Too often we have seen examples of clergy engaged on important issues and then disengaged when they pass. Our times demand more consistency, as these issues are not going away. The sustaining leadership of the NCN will allow for **CURE** to remain in this space and build up for future generations. Cohesion is a challenge in this day and age, but yet we know that more than 1/3 of the population thinks similarly. It is time for a united organization to arise and make an impact.

Indeed, there is currently no organization like **CURE** whose direct mission is to be in our nation's Capital and advocate for the issues and people we hold dear. From our book club program, our policy summit, and our regular clergy briefings, **CURE** travels the country every year counseling, listening and education pastors on solutions to the issues facing their communities.

The Voice of Clergy is crucial as we seek to renew the forgotten conscience within our culture. Your participation in the growth of our network will advance **CURE's** voice in the halls of government and provide a practical way for pastors to actively engage in this movement from a broken society to a stronger world. Knowing that you are making a difference will build pride not only in self but in our cooperation with others to accomplish real change." (Taken From CURE's Website).

I highly recommend, to **All Black Pastors in America**; please contact Star Parker, President, and Founder of **CURE**, which is located in Washington, D.C. The Center for Urban Renewal and Education is a 501 (c) 3 non-profit think-and-do tank. www.urbancure.org.

CURE has a solid track record; and would make an excellent, resource to **HELP** deal with this **CRISIS TOWARD BLACK HUMANITY!**

Also, please **HELP** by getting the word out that, Scientist Mike Adams, has revealed on NaturalNews.com; by causing the information to go **VIRAL ON SOCIAL MEDIA!** Thank you!

RACISM AND THE SPIRIT OF DEATH

BY THE ORIGINAL AFRICAN HERITAGE STUDY BIBLE – 1993

General Editor

The Reverend Cain Hope Felder, Ph.D.

Professor of New Testament Languages and Literature

Howard University, Washington, D.C.

"Racism releases the spirit of death from one culture onto another. In the face of this satanic world ruler, God is opening the floodgates of His River of Life; He shall bring healing to the nations. Indeed, even now, in the House of the Lord the phrase 'white church, black church' is being banished forever."

You cannot pick up a news magazine without finding an article on racism. The need for reconciliation and healing between races surfaces in nearly every form of media. It cries for attention and healing. Racism is a complex and sensitive issue. Yet, the healing of our cities will not occur until the church is delivered of cultural pride and insolence and has, itself, become a source of healing.

Therefore, regardless of your ethnic background, we entreat you to stay soft and open toward God. It is likely that old wounds shall resurface, and yesterday's fears and opinions rekindle. However, as the Lord is granting us grace, let us walk forward together toward Christ's healing.

TO THE WHITE CHURCH

Much of the violence we are reaping in our cities today was sown during the era when the Blacks were enslaved. To understand racism and its effect upon our society, therefore, we must step back into the days when slavery was an American way of life. Let us also note that racism is to modern times what slavery was to our forefathers; racism is the spirit behind slavery. As you read, we would encourage you to put yourself in the place of the one enslaved.

When a people were subjugated, not only did they lose their national and cultural identities but, also, all they had amassed and attained was stripped from them as well. The family unit itself was frequently disintegrated; preteens and teenagers were often separated from parents and then auctioned while their grieving parents watched. Wives were abducted from their husbands and frequently subjected to sexual abuse from their white masters. In general, the black male was reduced to a position in American society just slightly more respected than livestock.

The enslaved soul travelled a torturous road. All the landmarks in the individual's soul were shattered, devasted beyond our present faculties to understand, and broken beyond human abilities to repair. Having been robbed of their freedom, most slaves finally accepted their fate; and as they did, oppression and death soaked into their spirits.

There were, of course, a few Blacks who overcame extreme difficulties and were esteemed and respected by many whites. But they were the rare exceptions. For typically, whenever a people were taken captive, they faced death in one of two ways: they physically died due to hardships, or they experienced death through the psychological bondage of slavery itself. You see, The spirit which manifests through the victors upon the vanquished is the spirit of death. Thus, slavery exacted a quantitative and qualitative loss of life upon the Blacks. It immersed their culture in a flood of death.

TODAY'S CITIES AND YESTERDAY'S SINS

Although slavery was legally abolished in the eighteen-hundreds, racism continued. Its wound remains today in the soul of many Blacks, propelling a growing percentage of young black men toward violence. These men neither understand their actions nor can they find a way out from the shroud of death which broods over their neighborhoods.

The fact is, much of the violence in our cities today is the bitter fruit of a tree the white race cultivated in the soil of racism and slavery. In America today one in our black males over twenty-one is in some form of incarceration. And the highest cause of death among black men under twenty-five is homicide. It is only by the grace of God, Who became the strength of the black man early in his struggle, that the remaining majority found creative and productive ways to apply their lives.

The indignation in the soul of the black man can be traced to the unresolved conflict between their wounds and the ancestral sins of the white who caused them. After studying what was done to the Blacks, it is amazing that anyone should be puzzled by the deterioration of society in the black community. They were humiliated, separated from their homeland and families, treated as property, often subjected to great cruelty and violence, and still we ponder: How did the black districts come to such decline? It came through the hands of the white race. But together, through Jesus' shed blood, both Blacks and Whites, as well as all races, are being called to reconciliation in the body of Christ, a first-fruits of the healing of all nations.

RACISM AND THE JUDGMENTS OF GOD

It was as we wept before God, crying out to Him for the soul of our cities, that the Lord began to reveal to us the consequences of racism. He said that it was not just a regional principality; its influence was global. It is a world ruler. Racism releases the curse of death indiscriminately from one race upon another. The Lord said that it is the spirit of death which is destroying our cities, and it has for its entry point the stronghold of racism and cultural contempt in the people.

As we sought the Lord, He brought us to the Civil Rights Movement. There were two things that emerged from this campaign. First, it broke the legal impasse in America as it dealt a powerful blow against the strongholds of prejudice in our land. The Lord used this movement. Indeed, I would remind the reader it was largely the black church that spearheaded this assault against racism. In spite of the oppression set against it, the black Christians had grown sizable and strong. Like all other believers, they were imperfect; yet Jesus Himself was their captain.

Since then, the black race has won limited victories in nearly every forum, from sports and entertainment to housing, education, and employment. As a result, a number of better educated Blacks began to move upstream toward greater opportunity.

But another change occurred among young black males, and this was not good. This change was the result of the nearly three hundred years of racist oppression: The pent-up anger, which had been latent in the heart of the black man, surfaced in the form of violence.

Consequently, during these past thirty years we have seen a tremendous increase of lawlessness and suffering in our cities. There are other sources of this breakdown in our cities. However, a significant part of the social collapse today is directly related to racism.

Although we point to drug abuse and gang violence as some of the strongholds in our society, in most cases these were but symptoms of the greater problem of racism. In the genealogy of our cities' violence, cultural pride and envy begot racism, racism begot oppression, oppression begot fear, futility, and hatred; these have produced the current chaos in our cities.

The fact is, our cities are under the judgment of God. The Lord set a standard and put it in the spirit of America. Our founding fathers believed, and were willing to die for the truth, that "all men are created equal." They understood that every individual was "endowed by their Creator with certain unalienable rights life, liberty, and the pursuit of happiness." God has taken our own words and is using them to judge us. For we fought a war to secure freedom and then denied it to the Blacks.

We should also understand that God's judgment is not always in the form of hailstones and earthquakes. Often He simply allows us to experience the consequences of the sins we have demanded. Author C.S. Lewis has said that in the end, there are only two types of people. Those who say to God, "Thy will be done" and they reap hell.

What we are experiencing in our cities is our will being done, and we are reaping hell. Yet, there is still time. If we choose to step away from racist attitudes and, working first in the church, bring healing, we can ultimately see heaven prevail in our cities. If we fail to obey God, our cities will continue to bear an increasing likeness to hell.

THE ANSWER: THE HOUSE OF THE LORD

I know large numbers of you are totally free from racism. Although Daniel was innocent of the sins of his ancestors, he prayed as though he were guilty, saying, "Lord we have sinned." We should know that it is the nature of Christ to number Himself with the transgressors. As believing white Christians, we share the responsibility for the sins of our race. We must therefore take the initiative in repentance.

I believe as races are healed and united in the love of Christ, the contrast between God's life in the church and the death in the cities will draw multitudes into the Father's house. Yes, "Darkness will cover the earth, and deep darkness the peoples." But the promise to the people of God is that, through them, God shall raise up a standard of both deliverance and glory. In the midst of great darkness. He promises that He Himself "will rise upon you, and His glory will appear upon you. And nations will come to your light" (Isaiah 60:2).

What does it mean, that the Lord will rise upon us, except that there shall be a new race of people to whom Christ is all and in all-a people whose love and faith for one another demonstrates the power of eternal life.

THE CRY FOR RECONCILATION

In his guild, the white man has thrown literally trillions of tax dollars toward the inner-city problems, yet the situation is only worsening. Why? Our problems are not rooted in economics, but sin.

Originally, the average black man was simply saying, "I want acceptance. I want you to admit what you did was wrong, so I can forgive you and put to rest the unresolved conflict in my soul." Today, however, increasing numbers of Blacks are becoming more bitter toward Whites. The fear and death in our cities is escalating.

I do not expect the world to heed this message, but the church must. It was primarily the work of the white church that saw slavery abolished in the 1860's. It was predominately the black church which spearheaded the Civil Rights Movement in the 1950's and 1960's. As we come to the end of a millennium, I believe God's anointing is again upon the church today. Now, however, He is seeking us to carry the mantle of healing beyond the passing of laws into modeling the life of Christ with His healing power of love. Out of this release of love between races, there will come a great harvest.

"And there will be very many fish, for these waters go there, and the others will be healed; so everything will live where the river goes" (Ezekiel 47:10 lit). Wherever the River of Life flows, it will gather "very many fish" as it flows toward healing the nations.

I would remind you that in Ezekiel's vision, the River of Life flowed out from the House of the Lord. Its flow originated from the place of unity and love in the church, were the stronghold of cultural pride was demolished.

Of course, all white men and black men are not going to be reconciled before Jesus returns. However, in the House of the Lord there will be healing, for this great end-time harvest will be from "every nation and all tribes and peoples and tongues" (Revelation 7-9).

There will not be segregation, racism, "white churches" and "black churches" in the Kingdom of God. There will be one people, one body, one flock and one Shepherd Who unites us all in one flow of His forgiving, overcoming love. Even now, the true House of the Lord is becoming a colony of Heaven, picture of God's eternal life on earth.

Remember also that , while the church was instrumental in bringing healing, it shall be the false church which shall fight the healing of races. Therefore, I entreat you by the mercies of God to hear Jesus' heart in this matter. Indeed, the soul of your city hangs in the balance. We must choose God's side.

Therefore, in obedience to Jesus, we are calling for white believers to repent, as individuals and congregations, of the sins of their forefathers. We must also renounce any lingering racist attitudes we may still harbor. We are not saying you must be reconciled with every Black, whether they want to be united with you or not. Rather, in the context of the body of Christ there must be functional love and healing. The comparison of the glory of the Lord rising upon us in the midst of ever-deepening darkness in the world shall bring not only cities, but "nations ... to your light" (Isaiah 60:3).

Thus, we would entreat church leaders to call for a citywide day of fasting and prayer, the humbling of the church and the confession of sin, Among the black and white churches in the city, a new beginning must be launched, christened with forgiveness, set to run a course where the love of God among all men grows brighter and brighter unto the full day.

As a member of the white church, I ask you to join with me in prayer, Lord Jesus, by sinning against Your brethren, I have sinned against YOU. Forgive me for the sins of my forefathers in the area of racism. I confess, as a white person, that all my righteousness is as filthy rags. I have been born into a legacy of contempt for other races. Deliver me, O God, from this delusion! Wash me in Your blood, lead me deeper into the River of life, until my life flows with healing to nations. Amen.

TO THE BLACK CHURCH

People often ask me what my ethnic background is. I tell them, "I used to be Italian." We laugh, but I am very serious. While my old nature is, of course, still Italian, in my spirit I am a new creature in God, a living member of His new creation.

In Jesus Christ, God brought forth a second genesis. The Father's purpose was to complete His original mandate, which was to make man in the image of God. When you were born-again, you too entered that new creation. You have a new Father, a new nature, a new heart, and a new spirit. As I "used to be" Italian, so you also are no longer limited by the confinements of your natural heritage.

Not only did I, as a son of God, surrender my restricted identity as an Italian, but I found my true identity in Christ. As a member of the black race, you have been on a quest to find your true identity as well. As you sought to regain what the white man took, your identity has subtly changed from being a colored person to a Negro, then a Black and now an African American. Now that you have found it, Jesus says you must lose it again to Him. As Christians, we have new "roots:" our life is planted in Christ. Together, we all are "firmly rooted and now being built up in Christ" (Col. 2:7).

Additionally, as a new creation, my old nature lost all its rights. The one right I retain is the right to become a son of God. As it is written, "But as many as received Him, to them He gave the right to become children of God, even to those who believe in His name" (John 1:12).

This means we do not have a right to be bitter, unforgiving or unbelieving. Our "one right" is this that in every dimension of life, whether pleasant or unpleasant, just or unjust, we have a right to expect that God will use all things to transform us into the likeness of Christ. It is our right, as we go through life's adversities, to emerge with greater love and stronger faith. When we are tempted, it is our heritage as sons and daughters of God that we will become pure, not impure.

From now on, you must not let self-pity or any excuse, however legitimate, trap you in a fleshly reaction to racism. You must not absorb rejection into your soul, no matter what another person does to you. God has sent you to bring Jesus into the church and the city; this present trouble is your opportunity to do so.

Even though I still look Italian, my spirit is filled with Jesus and I am a new creation. Likewise, because your skin is still black, you can reach with understanding to those who have been hurt by racism. Yet, because you have Christ, you can bring God's Answer to the wound of their soul.

It is vital for you, the Black church, to forgive the Whites for their ignorance and rejection. You must learn to love like Christ, forgive like Christ, see mankind like Christ. Simply to survive, you must see society around you through Christ's redemptive purpose.

And you must see that your real enemy is spiritual – not natural. Colossians 2:13-15 tells us that Jesus disarmed the principalities and powers by forgiving us all our transgressions. He disarmed them by forgiving us. These spiritual rulers of darkness are your enemies. Even as Christ disarmed them through forgiveness, so also shall the enemies' weapons be rendered powerless as you repeat Christ's prayer "Father, forgive them."

Therefore, we are going to deal with any bitterness you may have toward the white church. You may have done this a hundred times already, and you may have to do it many times again, but we must disarm this principality of racism. By forgiving, you are going to take the weapon out of Satan's hand and release grace to your white brethren in Christ.

The promise of the Holy Spirit is this: even as Satan has sought to destroy the black man, so God in this hour is seeking to manifest Himself in glory through the black race, and especially through young black women and men. For where sin abounds, the grace of God abounds all the more. The Lord has promised a generation of Blacks who shall persevere in Christ until they are walking blamelessly. They shall be examples of Jesus, armed with His truth and anointed to bring healing to their generation.

This is your right, your inheritance in Christ. While civil rights shall still be a focus of prayer, the most compelling issue of your life will be the divine right you have to become a son of God who reveals the character and power of the Lord Jesus.

Heavenly Father, I thank You for the River of Life that brings healing. Thank You, Lord, for making me a new creation and for the blood of Christ which delivers me from every curse of death.

Now Father, I forgive the sins of the whites where they have hurt me, tried to oppress me, or were racist. I submit to the love of Christ. I submit to Your plan for Your church and this city. In Jesus' Name I disarm and take out of the hand of the enemy these weapons that could be used against the body of Christ. I forgive my white brothers and sisters. For Jesus' sake, Amen.